COLLECTIVE CONSCIOUSNESS

Art Performances in the Seventies

Edited by Jean Dupuy

Performing Arts Journal Publications
New York

First Edition

Library of Congress Cataloging in Publication Data
Collective Consciousness
Library of Congress Catalog Card No.: 80-83856
ISBN: 0-933826-26-5
ISBN: 0-933826-27-3 (pbk)

Design: Gautam Dasgupta
Printed in the United States of America

**Publication of this book has been made possible in part by a grant
from the National Endowment for the Arts, Washington, D.C., a
federal agency, and public funds received from the New York State
Council on the Arts**

à Jeanine et Louis Dupuy

Contents

INTRODUCTORY ESSAYS	4
SOUP AND TART	18
3 EVENINGS ON A REVOLVING STAGE	30
ONE SUNDAY AFTERNOON ON A REVOLVING STAGE	40
GROMMETS #3	46
GROMMETS #4	56
CHANT A CAPPELLA	62
A TOWER AT P.S. 1	72
MUSEE DU LOUVRE	82
ABOUT 405 EAST 13TH STREET (#1)	98
ABOUT 405 EAST 13TH STREET (#2)	112
ABOUT 405 EAST 13TH STREET (#3)	126
SCALE 1/1	133
13 x 33	138
FRONT/BACK	150
ARTISTS' STATEMENTS	152
INDEX	242

Introductory Essays →

JEAN DUPUY TALKS
WITH JOHN HOWELL

Tell me about your first collective show.
The first one was *About 405 East 13th St.*
That's where you lived.
Yes. It is a building which belongs to Larry Rivers and Claes Oldenburg, and to the cleaner downstairs who owned two floors. Also, it is a building that is very separated from art activity in Soho, an out of the way place, but not unknown to artists in New York.
Did Oldenburg actually live there?
No, but Rivers, yes. It's a building some two hundred feet long which goes through from Fourteenth St. to Thirteenth St. My loft was one hundred and fifty feet long, so it was quite a big room and easy to divide with canvas to make a public part.
Why did you want the public in your loft?
At this time, I had a leftist attitude toward classical art structures. In other words, I was part of the structure when I was at Sonnabend, and when we separated after 1972, I stayed isolated for two years outside gallery activities. This building, this loft I was living in, was very strange, very mysterious to me, so I became interested in it. It was like a very long corridor with eighteen windows. I had these windows which gave on the brick walls of a church about three feet away. This shaft between the buildings was so close that I would open the window and look in a mirror which I had put out there at a forty-five degree angle to see the sky. Then I did the same thing with the chimney. I put a mirror on the floor so you could see the sky some sixty feet up. That just happened because this place was an inspiration in many ways. For example, the other side of the sheet rock wall was a beauty parlor, and I put in some microphones which amplified the sound of that shop. I thought, why not show these places? Then I thought, why not invite other people to do the same? why not do something which will bring more discoveries to this place? That's what I did. I invited people living in the building, Atkinson, Edwards, Rivers, Patty Oldenburg, Craven and artists of my generation like Nam June Paik, Claes Oldenburg, Tony Smith and also people I didn't know who were recommended by other artists. In a sense, I met a new generation of artists like that. Also, it was practical. I went to Soho often, but I liked this Lower East Side District and the space where I was living, so it happened there.
When was the first Thirteenth Street show?
In May, 1973. It was ten days of show. There was thirty-five artists, each showing a piece, so that was a lot of publicity by itself. That first show was really astonishing, a public success. The show was most interesting because a lot of the pieces were invisible. The artists had to really show their own pieces. Each day there were artists giving guided tours.
I had just moved and lived down the street from you, and although I knew many of the artists in the show, I came often so that I could feel like I was even able to see their work.
Even at the entrance, Lizbeth Marano put a life-size photograph of the door glued to my door, so it was really invisible.
Particularly if one hadn't seen your door before.
And even if you had, it was still an invisible work. That show was about something between architecture and art. My windows were very dirty where they opened onto a courtyard which was very gray and a little frightening. So what Gordon Matta did was to just clean one window, that was his piece. Was it about invisiblity or visibility?
An invisible visibility I would say, like other works. I remember thinking it strange that none of them were marked or signed.
It was an anonymous show although everyone knew who was in it. It was really about a certain place.
And you had performances as well.
The first performance was by Charlotte Moorman during the show. She came and played her cello while wearing a mask of Pablo Casals' face. She pretended to play

but sat on this tape recorder, the sound was really taped. But that was her piece. Not until the second year did I start to ask people to do performances. At this second *About 13th St.*, I made my first performance.

Why did you want performance?
My friend Brendan Atkinson, an Englishman who lived upstairs, did a performance I thought was quite nice, and he was really the one who opened my eyes about performance. He showed a new thing to me. I was very interested that he was performing as an artist and directly about performing, not like Klein making a painting in front of the public. So, I performed the first time myself. I rigged a revolving stage to show something in public that I had been showing behind a translucent screen.
You mean, of course, the shaving of your mustache.
Yes.
And why did you revolve on a stage?
I wanted to shave in shadow, but to show the end by making half a turn. To do that, I decided I had to be on a stage that turned. So I built the stage which another person had to manipulate by turning a handle on a wooden wheel. I built this lazy susan piece myself with the help of Murphy. And on the same evening, Philip Glass played some solo music on his organ and electric piano. I thought it was a nice evening. Then, performances were in my head. After the second *13th St.* show, I made a piece using a videotape, and The Kitchen asked me to make a video installation. I thought about it, and proposed to have a dinner at The Kitchen.
So a performance space called The Kitchen sometimes gets a cook when it asks for a show.
Sure.
When did you decide to ask other people to take part?
I like to walk couple of hours a day, and things come to me from the street. I met people walking around, and since the people I know in New York are artists, I asked them to entertain at this dinner party. A long time ago, we had lunch parties on the day of St. Jean at my grandfather's house in the country. Jean is the name of both my grandfather and myself, and every twenty-fourth of June, we had such a lunch with champagne and everything. At the end, the children were invited to do something. We were all a little drunk and excited, and performed for our large family.
What was your particular talent?
I sang. My sister used to recite poems, and others gave Latin recitations. It was nice—real happiness.
Did *Soup and Tart* at The Kitchen match that feeling?
Sure. There was a kind of excitement in all the surprises. It was one of those evenings where the public becomes as good as any artist.
And everyone got tarts as well.
Technically, the cooking was the hardest thing to do. We had to play because there were only two ovens in the kitchen of The Kitchen, so we brought some trays specifically for having the maximum of tarts cooking at the same time. But that was a terrible mistake, because when an oven is full like that, it takes two or three times longer than ordinary to cook anything. I didn't think about it, so we had a bad surprise because we couldn't give out many tarts until the end. But we were also fortunate because the weather was cold enough so that we could put thirty bowls of dough in a little room there with the windows open.
So *Soup and Tart* was your first group performance show?
Yes. Well, not exactly the first. In 1970, I was invited by the city of Bordeaux to organize a show of performances with twelve people from my class. We filled up three floors of a museum with a show called something like *Art and Technologie*.
But you must have known from the big response to *Soup and Tart* that you were on to something unique?
I was surprised by the fact that when I invited artists like Richard Serra, Yvonne Rainer and Philip Glass, they said yes. In fact, Serra said "Sure, I'll be your material." For Yvonne Rainer, I think, that was one of her few recent, public performances. And to hear things like the music of Philip Glass which is based most of the time on duration for only two minutes was very interesting. So *Soup and Tart* became like the *About 13th St.* shows, a salad of generations.
And The Kitchen was happy with what you did?
We got four hundred people together, and had to refuse at least two hundred reser-

vations. It was crazy and popular, I don't know why. I called it *Soup and Tart* because of the food and perhaps the food attracted as many people as did the names of the artists.

Dinner and a floor show for four dollars is a good deal.

What's amazing about this show is that someone like Jana Haimsohn became famous after having danced three minutes in *Soup and Tart*. That was the only limitation, one of time, and in fact, I said two minutes originally. In a sense, the limitation is similar to what I am doing with my art pieces which use lenses.

You mean a short look?

Exactly.

So after *Soup and Tart*, you did another *13th St.* show?

Yeah, the last one. I had decided not to do another one, but I don't know why I was tempted to do it. So I called it *About 405 E. 13th St.: A Contradiction* because I had decided not to do it and I did, and not only that but I had another place in Soho at which to put it on, at James Yu's Gallery. First he gave his two big rooms to eleven artists to make a show called *Scale: 1 to 1*. I invited ten sculptors to make a drawing show with me, again about the space. So James Yu said "Okay, after that I will take the *About 405 E. 13th St. Show*." Then, three days before the opening, he tells me he needs the other room, but will give me the front room. I said, "No, I don't want any other show with this show, it's confusing for me." So I cancelled everything. Then coming back to Thirteenth Street, I met Jayne Bliss, my neighbor upstairs, and I talked to her about it and she said, "Why don't you take my loft?" I thought that was a good idea, the same building but another floor.

Which made for an even bigger contradiction.

Absolutely. The show was not the best show I would say, the idea was already routine, but it was okay.

So *Revolving Stage* came next?

I don't know how that happened. One day I just thought to use a real revolving stage. I went to see some at a midtown theatre property place. There I saw this tiny stage, a beauty in black steel, which was two feet in diameter and yet could carry eight hundred pounds as it turned at two and a half revolutions per minute. I wanted to put that in a big space and I thought about Judson Church. In 1968 I organized a show there so I already knew the church. I was cooking at an uptown place for a party for Al Carmines, the minister of Judson whom I had known since 1968. I told him the idea for this revolving stage in the middle of the sanctuary, and he said "Good." This time I invited fifteen artists to use more time but the space was limited to the stage, and of course there was the slow motion movement too. It was a big surprise for each of us when we saw this little object in the middle of the church for the first time. It looked so small but it was strong, when you stepped on it, there you went.

And you put on this show three times?

Yes, it was called *Three Evenings on a Revolving Stage*. It was so popular I thought we could take a theatre and do it for a month.

You could turn on a Broadway size stage for the big bucks.

We made money you know, I paid each artist seventy-five dollars.

That came from the gate?

Yes. The church charged us only a little money. Howard Wise gave me a grant through NEA and he made a videotape of the show for cable television. That was terrible because I had to deal with videotape technicians and suddenly I realized he wanted to give priority to the videotape and not to the performances. So I had to argue with Wise.

So you went on to other troubles at the Whitney Museum. How did that happen?

Because Marcia Tucker heard about these art performances, I don't think she saw them, and she invited me to do a similar thing at the Whitney. I titled it *A Sunday Afternoon on a Revolving Stage*. We had this terrible problem with the Whitney because Marcia was really having trouble with the sponsors. To have avant-garde artists at the museum is not pleasing for the sponsors I think, especially performance artists. She did a good job to invite us because we were doing all these performances in lofts or places like The Kitchen, Judson Church or Artist Space, where I rarely saw any art critics. Robert Pincus-Witten came to the first evening at Judson, but I think it was the only time he saw such a thing. He wrote me a note saying he liked it, but he never came back to see others. Perhaps he saw some shows I put together, but not performances. And Max Kozloff, who was editor of *Artforum* then, I never saw him at any of these evenings.

So you thought being at the Whitney would attract the attention of art critics?
At this time, the Whitney had a problem because of the Rockefeller collection of art they were showing for the Bicentennial. To show such a collection, made by a Rockefeller and only of white male artists, was bad taste. Some artists picketed the museum and Michael Krugman made a film of that. But some of the people I invited for this Sunday afternoon refused to do it because of the Rockefeller show. Also, the museum decided not to pay us. Then after they decided to pay us, it was seven dollars for each performer. So when I said all that as a protest to start the show, Marcia answered, "Well, that's two hundred and ten dollars per hour I'm giving you." I think she was a little afraid of what was going to happen. We just showed the film and then everyone performed. But the worst was that I asked for twenty-four hours of rehearsal time, and they managed to give us two hours just before show time. We were treated like students and Marcia Tucker was like a school mistress. Ridiculous. She didn't want Maciunas to make a sign saying something about his pole. He was going to fix a pole to the revolving stage at the level of the stage so that people would have to lie flat when it passed over. A quiet piece but very dynamic indeed. And he was writing a sign saying that the poles were electrified. So Marcia said that was impossible, that he couldn't say that even if it wasn't true. She was saying you have to do a piece like this and not like that. Six artists refused to perform, but I decided I would be in the place and would do it as a protest. So it was like having a little political activity.

Didn't she leave the musuem not long after that?
Yes, just some months later. I don't know the reasons, but she was in a bad situation between sponsors and artists, I should say, she chose the bad side. She didn't choose the artists' side.

Too bad, but it makes a good story. Next you did *Grommet*, is that right?
Yes. I was invited by P.S. 1 to make a collective show. I invited ten people to make performances behind a translucent screen and this screen was behind canvas as a door with grommets put into the canvas as the initials of the name of each artist.

Where did you get the idea to use grommets?
It came from an installation I made for *Soup and Tart*. It was a videotape placed in the lower right hand corner of a screen on which was projected a slide taken from the videotape every two seconds. You would see these two things through a grommet because the tape itself was long and boring, just sex activity of these two parts, male and female going together for an hour.

So the grommet was kind of a voyeur's eyepiece.
It allowed me to have a door for a screen with grommets in the initials "I" and "J", for the male and female names. Those peepholes allowed several people to look at the same time.

I've never seen Duchamp's piece in Philadelphia, the one where you peep through a door to see the spread nude inside.
Oh you must see it, it's very nice. I don't remember when I saw it. I don't think I can say I was directly influenced by Duchamp. I have used lenses for a long time. Anyway, this video installation was quite practical and surprising too, very shocking. So the P.S. 1 show was a double perspective like that first through grommet holes, then Chinese shadows behind the translucent screen. Some of the performers were nude. Jana Haimsohn was massaging a paralytic man on a chair, then on the floor, and he was nude. I was typewriting a description of all this, although I wasn't typing in the nude. Olga Adorno was modeling nude. Everybody was lit from behind by a projector which made very precise forms appear as shadows.

And that gave you the idea to do a big grommet show in your new place?
Yes. I had moved from 405 E. 13th St. to Broadway where I organized a grommet show. I used the mezzanine by putting up six ladders so I could invite more people. But I invited too many, although some didn't perform but only made installations. It was very uncomfortable. There were twenty artists, each in their little room behind canvas walls and on two floors, so the public had to wait on line too long. And it was difficult for the artists to stay in their rooms for two hours not knowing what was going on outside. And it was spring and very warm which made it more uncomfortable.

Everyone was performing at once, so you had a lot of noise.

Right. The biggest problem was that people couldn't see everything even in two hours. So that was a very uncomfortable show for everyone. What was interesting was the feeling created by all the simultaneous performances.

It was like a carnival.

I did that show twice here. The next time, I did it with fewer artists.

Did you have any grants to produce these?

No. The first time we had to buy so much heavy canvas, which was very expensive, that I had to ask each artist for twenty dollars. I had sent to Oldenburg and Rauschenberg a letter with a "grommet" in it saying that we were twenty artists who were going to make a show and could they help sponsor the show. I asked each one for five hundred dollars. Then we could have split the gate money among the artists.

And what happened?

They didn't answer. Later, I met Claes and he said he couldn't do it. And Rauschenberg didn't answer either, he probably didn't see the letter. So I had to ask each artist for money, and we split the gate, half for the artists and half for me because of expenses.

What did the artists think of that arrangement?

I just proposed it and everybody seemed happy with it. For the second grommet show here, with sixteen artists, I would say ten of them called me up to ask if they could be in the show because they heard about it. So I invited ten artists and I didn't know what they were doing. I did that on purpose to try something different. After those ten, I wanted to show some artists I knew, so I asked six more.

Did you ever refuse anyone because you didn't like what they did?

No, I only said no when there were too many performers. I try not to have a judgement about their work. I think the limitations take care of that problem. For me, the limitations are giving a good situation for each one to think about, a good structure.

Which creates a certain atmosphere in which those who don't feel comfortable probably don't want to perform.

Right. I think the only person scheduled to perform who couldn't was Vito Acconci at Judson Church. He went over there several times and he tried to do something, but he couldn't. That was interesting as a problem that you can resolve or not. Sometimes, I invite people who refuse to do anything for different reasons.

Let's talk about *Chant A Cappella*.

That show was also at Judson Church. I had been at a party and invited Julia Heyward to chant in this show; she was the first one I asked. She was very pleased and immediately said yes. She is someone who always used this chant method. Several other artists used voice like that as well. It was "a cappella" for a practical reason, because I had no grant and no money to rent equipment. Also, I wanted to use the natural acoustics of the sanctuary. Gregorian music is one of my favorite musical styles and I was thinking of it. So I invited a group of people, fifteen I think. I had some trouble with the church because I was not dealing with Al Carmines, he was sick.

What kind of trouble?

They charged too much at the door. We had a good audience, but it was not as successful as the *Revolving Stage* show. But I enjoyed the three *Chant A Cappella* evenings.

After all this activity, what do you think about the situation of performance now?

Now I'm writing a book, which is looking back isn't it? Some would say it's already a history about a certain area of art in the seventies. Looking back, it is interesting that while some of the artists were visual artists, other were mixed-media artists and still another group were performing artists like musicians and dancers. It is amazing how all those artists did a piece in a visual art context. That's an interesting point, because few people in the art world saw these performances, I don't know why. Perhaps it was because these mixed-media and performing artists were not part of the gallery-museum structure. And, of course, performance doesn't make any business because there are no objects to sell. The structure of gallery, dealer, and collector is big business.

Some galleries have sponsored performances.

But only some, and with a great deal of trouble, and only to be *au courant*. There is a circuit of performance spaces now, but that makes for a very small audience and a very specific one. The real avant-garde of the seventies was not followed by art critics, museums, and art dealers at all. Therefore, as artists we must have a job to survive. Through these performances, sometimes you can see the jobs of the artist. So mixed-media and performance artists are very close to everyday reality and reflect something very real, the world where he or she is living and working. It is not an ivory tower kind of art. And mixed-media and performace make it possible for the artist to use anything. In art terms, it's probably a consequence of the Marcel Duchamp revolution. Part of that is escaping the structure too. This mixed-media and performance define seventies art to me. Happenings also dealt with objects, but most of the artists were already established visual artists, therefore the museum and gallery structures were interested in these activities.

But you were invited to the Whitney even if it didn't work out so well. Do you think performance should stick to its own small territory?
The idea I have of an artist is to have to constantly think and go ahead and change and stay aware of all aspects of life. There are several books about performance to come out this season and I would say that if we write them it's because performance is partly finished.

P.S.

This book is the first of my collective pieces to be fixed in time. The only limit is the definition of each artist's work in one or two photographs and a short text.

Some artists are not mentioned, either because I couldn't get in touch with them, or because they didn't answer my request for material. Fortunately, these omissions are few. Also, some pieces are imcompletely documented; either photo or text are not available. I have printed all texts received. Nothing is shown about Grommet #1 (at P.S. 1 in September, 1976) as no photographs were available.

Several of these works and shows resulted in collective videotapes: *Artists Propaganda #1* and *#2*, and *Artists Shorts* (by Kit Fitzgerald and John Sanborn), *Artists Propaganda #3* (realized at the Beaubourg Centre), and *Chant A Cappella* (by Davidson Gigliotti).

I should like to mention and give credit to some other collective art activities, especially those of Stefan Eins and Robin Winters, and to **Art-Rite** magazine's Edit Deak and Mike Robinson, who were the first to recognize these activities in print. Also, I would not have become a performer myself without the example of Olga Adorno. By nature she is a performer (I am not), and she must take credit for stimulating me to perform and to organize these shows.

Also, "un salut" to Charlotte Moorman.

J. D. TALKS WITH PETER FRANK

I want to talk about Fluxus. I met George Maciunas in 1976. We became very close. I was attracted by this man's work, and I invited him to participate in each performance I put on after meeting him.
Starting with the revolving stage?
Right, George and I maintained a very interesting relationship and I understood Fluxus through George. I know Ben Vautier, and Robert Filliou very well—he is a very old friend of mine. I don't know George Brecht, but I know Jackson MacLow, I know Dick Higgins, Alison Knowles. But Fluxus for me is really focused on George Maciunas. I would say that, as George has died, Fluxus is dead too. But then movements have to die. When Larry Miller invited me to be part of the Fluxus performance at The Kitchen recently I said I didn't want to. I thought that a Fluxus concert now . . . .
Well, the intention of this concert is to realize performances of Fluxus pieces conceived during George's lifetime. The only new piece is Alison's non-Fluxus work that begins the evening. Everything else is billed as a "classic" piece.
Well, I wasn't part of it at all . . .
Yes, but you were quite friendly with George during the last two years of his life . . .
I don't say I'm not sympathethic to Fluxus. I just don't feel myself to be a Fluxus member. That is what I don't like about Fluxus, that one is or is not a member of the

Fluxus "family." One aspect of Fluxus is the realizing of art for everyone, communciation with and by everybody through crazy, absurd, infantilist activity. Each time I was invited to make an activity with Fluxus, and each time I did it, I was astonished that it was not presented publicly. George was not concerned with the public, but only with his little circle, the little family of Fluxus friends. Basically I agree with the Fluxus philosophy of opening art to a larger public, but . . .

Is that the philosophy, though, or is it just to make available an artistic circumstance to anyone? To propose a gesture, an activity that anyone can do? I think it's the proposal rather than the activity itself that draws people together. Maybe that's why George felt justified in having these very intimate gatherings for the performances rather than making them public, because the ideas that were being realized as activities at these intimate gatherings could still go on independent of their realizations at these gatherings, to be realized by other people at other gatherings, or public situations . . .

But it's too bad it has to be private at all. Why do we have to be timid like that? Why not perform publicly?

There have been public performances.

Not in the last three years.

The harpsicord concert at the Anthology Film Archives was, I think, early 1976 or 1977.

1976 or even '75. I missed it. I met George after that. Therefore I don't remember seeing George do something publicly under the name Fluxus. He participated several times in my collective performances. Do you remember the piece he did on the *Revolving Stage* at the Whitney Museum?

Yes, it was a very effective piece, I thought. As I recall, he constructed some sort of horizontal barricade on the stage that extended about 10 or 20 feet into the audience.

Oh, it crossed the room, it almost touched the walls. It was a pole measured to the distance of the walls.

It sought, then, in a very formal way—in the kind of way people nowadays realize—to define the space, to define the physical attributes of the space. But of course George was most interested in having this movement interact with the audience sitting around the stage. I remember the audience ducking and running out of the way, the kids having a great time . . .

That was in February of 1976, just after the *Revolving Stage* evenings at the Judson Church. I met George after the three evenings in January, and invited him only then to participate in the Whitney presentation. So he had 3 weeks to figure out and construct a piece. We met very late, but I did know something about his activity. He never knew anything about mine until he met me, but I knew of his. I saw him in Paris in a performance in 1962 or '63. I didn't talk to him then, though. It was a wonderful performance. He was dressed in a tux, and tails, just as he was in the *Chant a Cappella* evening. His fiancee, later wife, Billie was dressed in a long white dress. George asked a volunteer from the audience to sit on a chair on stage. A woman sat on the chair, and George and Billie took long cardboard tubes, each 6 feet long, and made sounds through the tubes into the ears of the woman. The audience was not able to hear anything.

But the audience was able to figure out what was going on, the idea . . .

Did you see the piece he did in the second *Grommet* presentation? He had a grommet situated in the corner, on the upper level and was squirting water on the people, squirting shaving cream . . .

And also sticking a long stick through the grommet . . .

A long wire, 100 feet long, a wire with no end. The public was constantly being attacked.

I remember being annoyed at first because I was getting wet, but then when I realized it was George, and saw other things come through the hole, I realized that George was one of the few people in the Grommet Theatre using the grommet not just as peephole, but as an actual physical aperture between 2 spaces that were otherwise closed to each other. He was interjecting material from his space into ours. Like his piece for the revolving stage, it was of a spatial nature.

He was making spatial trouble.

George told me once about studing architecture at Carnegie Tech in Pittsburgh. This

story is an excellent example of both his sense of the gag and his sense of working with space. The working with space is not something that he talked about with regard to Fluxus, but it is there. Anyway, George was studying architecture and living with other architecture students, and they were all kicked out by the landlord. They didn't like the landlord to begin with, so they were happy to screw him on this last occasion. The last thing they did before leaving was to construct a solid concrete block or table in the dining room, tremendously heavy and occupying almost the whole of that room. It sounds like a minimalist sculpture, but George did it, as a vengeful gag, back in the 50's. As I recall the story, the concrete object was George's idea and he got everybody to build it. I wouldn't be surprised if that were the way Fluxus itself came about.

You say that you have had problems with George's autocratic style. You told me of this argument you had with him when you let 10 people you didn't know into the *Grommets* show and he argued with you that you were being too democratic and reducing the quality of the presentation. And you called him fascistic for that, and he stormed out. It was an argument just like he had with almost every one of his friends. But even though he was like that, still his organizational capabilities were very important.

He was a master of organization. I may have had some reservations, but I admire the man for that!

The Fluxus movement was different from the Dada or Surrealist movement. It was different from the Dada movement in that it had a single person who was responsible for coordinating its activities and it was different from the Surrealist movement in that everybody who worked with that single person did plenty of things independent of him, too. He was as you say, a general, but he wasn't the pope Breton was.

I also admired George's practicality in "marshaling" artist-performers. I had a crowd of performers at Judson Church, and in *Soup and Tart*. I saw having a large group of performers as a practical measure. I didn't have to make a mailing or do advertising or anything, just make a poster, and depend on word of mouth. Collective art is very practical that way.

Isn't there something autocratic about requiring as you do that people work with a very limited physical framework?

Yes, perhaps, but that's the challenge of it, that limitation. I talked about it with George. It's like using lenses in a telescope or periscope. In a sense a 2 feet diameter revolving stage is like lens. You saw it from a distance, a very small circular space.

Or the *Grommets*.

Or the *Grommets*. It's really very close to the objects I'm building. There is also a limitation in time. But in the *Grommets*, the public was invited to see one room after another. It was very uncomfortable.

Well, at the same time, I found that the *Grommet* format was the most satisfying of all your presentations, because it presented kinetic performance—things that changed, things that were engaging because they changed, unlike the static installations (except for a couple of projected pieces at 405 East 13th). But unlike the stage performances, one could move towards them and from them, go to them and leave them at one's own speed, rather than sit there like an audience for a play.

But it was uncomfortable because the audience had to wait in line for a long time, like two hours.

Yes, but still it was fun.

I don't think it was fun for the artists. Each artist had to work two hours in his little booth. I saw Laurie Anderson playing her violin. It was a beautiful piece, but to do that for two hours! For five nights! Even an afternoon on Sunday!

Well, maybe there was another restriction besides working for a grommet-type peephole situation that people didn't take into consideration: that they would have to present something that was primarily visual. They could do action but they couldn't exhaust themselves. I remember Jana Haimsohn doing this extremely active piece where she ran at the grommet. The artist also had to be able to address the looker; she ran at the grommet every time someone looked through. She had to be aware of when they were looking through.

Most of the time the artists didn't really know what was going on outside, except by the sound. We knew that there were people outside of the curtains, but we didn't know who or when they appeared.

These group shows are very much like the Fluxus performances, many of them, anyway, in which the nature of the space in which they are being presented—or, say, a concern with a specific instrument, like the Fluxus harpsichord concert at the Anthology Film Archives in early 1975 or '76—acts as a kind of leitmotif, tying everybody together.

The difference is in the spirit of each thing. Fluxus has to do with a steady flavor of derision, absurdity, infantilism. In the groups I organize, I don't know what is going to happen each time. It's a surprise to me, We never had anything like group rehearsals.

What is the aspect of derision you see in Fluxus? The infantilism I can see (although I think there could be a better word), and certainly the absurdity, but. . .

I met George and got together with him very often, got to know him very well. He had this sense of derision, this way of manipulating the derisive aspect. . .

Who or what was he deriding?

I don't know; it was more an attitude, not so much aimed at a target. . .

I know he had very little respect for governments or bureaucracies of any kind, and certain of those pieces did mock the pretensions of those who wield power—which, in a funny way, was self-mocking.

But I would say that it tied in with George's love for comedy. That's what I'm trying to do, too, to create comedy situations. That was probably the basis of the relationship between us, the desire to engage in hilarious activity.

Were you involved in a performance done in the basement of James Yu's old gallery on Prince Street—a sequence of performances that had not a common device, but a common theme, that is, the comet Kohoutek?

No I wasn't, but I did see it. It was very pleasant. It was one of the first art performances I saw in New York. When was it, do you remember?

I think Fall of 1973. . .

Yes, September, October, something like that. Brendan Atkinson performed in that. . .

There were several early post-Fluxus performances artists involved in that, such as Ralston Farina.

Now I think art performance has reached an end. It's like Fluxus, you know? We have to change. It's very important to change. This May I'm organizing a show called Large Objects. Last year I organized a show of Small Objects, at 3 Mercer Street. I don't think I'll be doing art performances anymore. I've affected and interacted with so many artists, so many people, it's enough.

Well, art performance can be considered a medium, an available format, and if you ever want to return to it, it's there, and if other people want to pick it up in the meantime, it's there for them. It seems to me that Fluxus is an attitude that also is available to anybody who wants to avail themselves of it. It's sort of an attitude that has always been available, just that George and the people he worked with isolated it as something that hadn't been paid attention to in an isolated fashion before, and brought it to people's attention, and made people aware of this kind of thing, of an emphasis on humor, on the gestural stance. . .

The situation I proposed made people like doing comedy and use humor most of the time, because the situation sometimes was a challenge to be funny, and sometimes made it easy to be funny. But my groups link up with Fluxus in that they bring together artists involved with mixed media. This is the definition of the '70s for me. If we look at the work of Dick Higgins, in connection to George, and in connection to other things in the '60s, we see things in that decade happening in waves. In the '70s I think the avant-garde has focused on performances.

I disagree. On a general level I feel it's been a question in this decade of media. It's a question that was raised in the '60s. . .

The mixed media artist is the characteristic artist of the '70s. . .

Working with time and space. . .

Mixed media artist make performances. They do other things, too, but performances define their nature as mixed media artists.

Well, they also make books, they also make conceptual proposals, they also make installations. . .I guess all these could also be considered performances, couldn't they? A book is a performance of a type, or at least activates a performance situation

of a type.

I don't know about that. If your intention is to make a book performance, it's a performance. If you want to make a performance, I don't see why you would make a book. Except for this collective book: I am trying to make this book as much a result of collective effort as possible. I refuse to make any introduction myself. I'm making a collective piece out of the introduction you are going to edit of our conversation, John Howell is going to edit my conversation with him, Edit DeAk will edit my conversation with her—in otherwords, I don't do anything myself.

Just as you did not edit the contributions by the artists. Well, in a sense, you *did* edit them, by presenting every participant with whatever proscription happened to pertain. They had to work with a revolving stage; they had to work with their voice; they had to work with dance. Your movement away from art performance, I was going to mention, was reflected in last week's group performance at The Kitchen because all the performers were dancers. In otherwords, you seem to be saying that *this* is the kind of performance that continues to go on.

Two years ago I did something with the voice—*Chant a Cappella*. This year it was dance, But it was not really premeditated. It just happened like that. Each time I am surprised by what happens, by what ideas come from just pulling together these things.

Is it fair to consider you a curator of these group shows?

I don't think of myself as a curator, because I participate in every show.

Then is it fair to consider these group shows artworks of yours?

Well, when I asked Richard Serra to participate in *Soup and Tart,* he said yes, "I will be your material." He pointed out something. Are artists my material? Can I consider these relationships between people in terms of matter? I can be their material, my ideas can be there for them to use as material. . .

What you're doing in a funny way is one thing George was doing, breaking down the definition between the organizer of a collaborative art effort and those just participating. There needs to be someone galvanizing the activity, but he or she is not responsible beyond a certain point for the content.

Well, the organizer is responsible for a certain idea and script.

Right.

I'm more and more interested in reaching a large audience. In the '80s I'm going to try to reach a larger audience, like that for television. That's why I'm doing an accumulation of pieces on color video. TV art?

You've already produced three. . .what were they called again?

I did several hours of taped works called *Artists' Propaganda* here and in Paris. I've worked with Davidson Gigliotti on *Chant a Cappella,* on the consequences of what I did at Judson Church. Then, after that, I worked with Kit Fitzgerald and John Sanborn on a production we call *Defess.* And we've just produced the last one, called *Artists' Shorts.* I'm really very attracted by that idea of communication, of showing *Artists' Shorts* or *Chant a Cappella* to several million people. I think an artist having to make a piece for television has to know he or she will face an audience of several million people. I think this is a new challenge for most artists.

It's not a matter of getting your work out in front of all these people, but getting a lot of people's work out there, so that instead of a point to point communication, or a point to many-points communication, it's a many-points-to-many-points communication.

Again, it's practical. I couldn't do that by myself. I couldn't accumulate hours and hours of material by myself. Also, I sometimes talk about "lazy art." Several of my own pieces are "lazy art," letting other people do the work. One piece has other people make prints on paper by putting their faces and noses on the paper when they look through a lens. This is "lazy art" because I don't do the art myself, I have other people make it. At the same time I offer something to the viewer for his work.

You activate the viewer to make the art.

In a sense collective art can also be lazy art. But lazy art is a lot of work.

Yes, as George Maciunas demonstrated, you have to work even harder to get other people to do work than you do to get yourself to do work.

Right. In a sense he was a tragic figure, you know. He was very frail. He was very careful, very exacting, I found this very attractive. He did his job perfectly all the time. His nature was perfectionist. He trusted himself, and only himself. I stayed at his place, at his country house, and I wasn't allowed to make my own bed! He said, "You don't know how to make a bed!" and he did my bed.

Is that a model for your organizing?
No, I don't do the same thing. I'm more invisible.

George tried to be invisible too, but he was too much of a perfectionist.
That's right. And I'm probably much lazier than he was.

Both perfectionism and laziness have positive effects.
Absolutely.

J. D. TALKS WITH STEPHEN PAUL MILLER

I've done two interviews already, one with Howell, one with Frank. The idea is to have the interviewer edit the tape. This is close to my idea about a lazy art. It depends on the situation, but even in the appreciation of art, laziness can be a virtue. For instance, the "Printing Table" I did. People had to look—in a table in a lens in the middle of a drawing paper—and to look in it, each viewer had to put his/her forehead and nose on the paper. After 4 or 5 thousand people (that's what happened in a museum) a print is produced since the traces of forehead and nose become very oiled on the drawing paper. This is lazy art because the print is made by itself, it takes awhile of course.

Collective Art, if it is lazy art, is a lot of work. Art Performance came for me in 1973, in my loft at 405 East 13th St. where I started organizing collective art shows. I started art as a painter and that probably explains my attraction to canvas. For "Grommets" I use canvas. In "Grommets" the viewer was alone; one to one or one to whatever the number of performers in the room. You had 16 rooms separated by canvas. Most of the rooms contained one performer who had to perform one hour and a half in front of a little hole, the Grommet. The performer was totally isolated from the audience. He/she didn't know what was going on past the grommet and the viewer was in a hurry to see what was going on inside since there was a line of people waiting at his/her back. Choosing the size of the grommet (the hole) in *Grommets* was an important decision because it reduces or blows-up the viewers perspective—"the view of the field." Perspective has concerned me: The collective performances focus on limitations of time and space, creating a situation which is for me a sort of vanishing point...I organize collective performance pieces in which artists are completely free within limitations they've accepted. Grommets came to me when I showed a video tape at the Kitchen of a couple fucking, a point of view that was boring...Name June Paik said something like: "Art has to be boring because the television is entertaining..." That sounds funny because Nam June is, sometimes, one of the most entertaining artist... I believe in the eighties we are going to see entertaining art...TV art on broadcast television! Anyway in this first *Grommets* installation I made the viewers "voyeurs." The effect was shocking. I often use the effect of surprise.

By TIM MAUL

Writing about Jean Dupuy's group activities is difficult for me. They function on so many levels it's dizzying, yet they remain a rich area yet untapped by N.Y.'s art criticism establishment. The most provocative of Jean's activities basically extended the premise of a group show by imposing limited conditions on what was to be presented; a problem for the artist to solve which was adhered to by the participants in varying degrees, some did, some didn't. Unlike just a lot of artworks in a room or performances in an evening, a unique kind of growth of ten resulted. Because of Jean's limitations (diabolically French, I think) a situation was provided where a young artist could show a work with established artists without feeling that anyone had the upper hand. A mutual curiosity in seeing what someone else could come up with often pervaded. Despite the community feel to many of Jean's activities, they clearly seemed to function outside the grant-hungry downtown alternative gallery scene. Jean shouldered the burden of endless organization and one-man advertising campaigns with one eye on the box—office dollars that were equally shared with all the participants. Jean also avoided a lot of the alternate scene clubbishness by his mysterious method of choosing participants, mixing local stars, friends, not-so-friends, and people solely on the basis of a good recommendation. To Jean's delight, the end results were sometimes incredibly logical. Some shows were more of a Dupuy than others. I can't resist the comparison of Jean using artists like Arman uses objects, in just the accumulative sense, cramming video works, objects, and even performances into all kinds of physical spaces and time spans—The time element reoccurring as Jean's toughest restriction and perhaps favorite material. The exchange between Jean and the artists working with him was mutually beneficial in a rare way. Many artists first came to public attention through Jean's activities, while others maybe returned to their own work feeling stretched in some way, a benefit which remains unique to participation in Jean Dupuy's activities which grows more conspicuous in their absence.

DAYTIME EXHIBITIONS: (TUESDAY-SATURDAY 1-6 PM)

JUAN DOWNEY «CHILE» NOVEMBER 19-23
AT 484 BROOME STREET

JEAN DUPUY «⋮ & ⋰» NOVEMBER 30-DECEMBER 14
AT 59 WOOSTER STREET

JOAN JONAS «TWO WOMEN» DECEMBER 17-21
AT 484 BROOME STREET

PERFORMANCES: (ADMISSION $2 UNLESS OTHERWISE NOTED)

JEAN DUPUY «SOUP & TART» SATURDAY, NOV 30 8:30 PM
A DINNER AND THIRTY-EIGHT TWO MINUTE PERFORMANCES $4.00
MENU OF EVENTS:

JOANNE AKALAITIS	TINA GIROUARD	RICHARD LANDRY	KATE PARKER
LAURIE ANDERSON	PHILIP GLASS	GIANFRANCO MANTEGNA	YVONNE RAINER
BRENDAN ATKINSON	DEEDEE HALLECK	LISBETH MARANO	CAROLEE SCHNEEMAN
CHARLES ATLAS	SUZANNE HARRIS	GORDON MATTA-CLARK	JOAN SCHWARTZ
SCOTT BILLINGSLY	GEOFF HENDRICKS	ANTHONY McCALL	RICHARD SERRA
BRAYNE BLISS	GENE HIGHSTEIN	DONALD MONROE	ANNE TARDOS
ROBERT BREER	JOAN JONAS	TONY MOSCATELLO	NANCY TOPF
DEIGO CORTEZ	OLGA KLUVER	NAM JUNE PAIK	DAVID WARRILOW
JEAN DUPUY	SHIGEKO KUBOTA	CHARLEMAGNE PALESTINE	HANNAH WILKE
JON GIBSON			SYLVIA WHITMAN

RESERVATIONS ARE NECESSARY: CALL 925-3615 (TUESDAY-SATURDAY 1-6 PM)

THE KITCHEN
59 WOOSTER STREET
NEW YORK CITY
(212) 925-3615
CENTER FOR VIDEO AND MUSIC

THE KITCHEN IS OPERATED UNDER THE AUSPICES OF HALEAKALA, INC. WITH PARTIAL SUPPORT FROM THE NYSCA.

Soup and Tart

SOUP & TART · JEAN DUPUY · THE KITCHEN · 59 WOOSTER · SATURDAY 30 OF NOVEMBER · CALL FOR RESERVATION · 925 3615 · 8:30 PM · SUPPORTED IN PART BY THE N.Y. STATE COUNCIL ON THE ARTS

By PETER FRANK

Now that artists' attention is concentrated more and more on performance, it seems as though these performaces should benefit from the same variety that group shows offer paintings, concerts offer musical compositions, and programs of shorts offer films. Jean Dupuy put together such a shuffled deck last Saturday, in a manifestation at the Kitchen entitled "Soup and Tart."

The title indicated the fact that soup—along with wine and bread—was served before the procession of events began, and that apple tarts were distributed by the panload during the intermissions and at the end of the evening. This gave a festive air to the proceedings (especially since the aforementioned fare was by all accounts mighty tasty).

The audience was merry and responsive, but not so rambunctious as to spoil the more introspective events in the show. In front of any large audience, however, the most effective pieces are the most extroverted, especially those which don't obnoxiously play to the galleries. In "Soup and Tart" these included the music of Jon Gibson and Dickie Landry, both of whom played solo saxophone pieces (Gibson's a lilting tune for soprano sax, Landry's a straight old-time rhythm and blues riff), Sylvia Whitman's group dancing after imbibing different quantities of tequila, a staged personal spat between Donald Munroe and Joan Schwartz, and, natch', Jean Dupuy's pixillated film showing how to make tarts at breakneck speed. Also a show-stopper was the soulful *decollete* of toga-(un) clad Hannah Wilke, the Narcissist With Flair.

Quieter events of substance did not get lost in the parade, either. Laurie Anderson's autobiographical account with music, all too fleeting, was yet affecting. A new Robert Breer film showed the great animator still going strong. Diego Cortez's botched magic trick had a macabre twist to it, catching everyone off guard. Tina Girouard's slides of four people in different costumes and postures had an attractive insouciance. Phil Glass's rhythmic vocal piece was a revealing sketch in modular music. Joan Jonas, speaking and giving off brief whistles underneath a green drape, played a reserved shaman. Tony Mascatello conjured up the '50s as he coated his hair in greasy kid stuff and combed it back into a d.a. Gordon Matta-Clark conjured up his house-halving piece of last spring as he sliced a gingerbread house into edible portions. Nam June Paik played the Moonlight Sonata in another room; ah, sweet mystery. Charlemagne Palestine sent a singing telegram. Arthur Russell sang an attractive song, accompanying himself on the cello. Richard Serra recounted one aspect of his relationship with his father, an aspect with peculiar relevance to his sculpture. David Warrilow nearly took his first drink since being cured of alcoholism, but someone from the audience, which at Joanne Akalaitis's behest was imploring Warrilow to stop, seized the drink from his hand. And wrapping up the Ted Mack Avant Garde Evening was Anthony Mc-Call who announced the duration of each of the previous pieces, charting them on a large wall graph.

These were only the best of thirty-seven different events, the rest of them less effective or downright wastes of time. When something worthwhile occurred right after something dumb-ass, the good piece would almost be lost in the bad aura left behind by its predecessor. In future such productions I would suggest slight pauses between events. This would necessitate shorter programs. In fact "Soup and Tart" was a bit long any way you look at it, running three hours plus the preceding hour of audience entering and eating soup. The grand scale of "Soup and Tart" seemed appealing in description, but in actuality worked against the program. Twenty pieces or less sounds about right. Anyway, it was great. But was it tart?

Soho Weekly News (Dec. 5, 1974), repr. by permission.

By EDIT DEAK

"*Bateau Lavoire*" was not some leaky laundromat, it was the name of Picasso's Paris studio. *The Kitchen* is not a restaurant, but an experimental multi-media showplace. No one in Paris was hilarious enough to make a point of doing watered-down artwork at "Bateau Lavoire;" but in NY a Frenchman (Jean Dupuy) was daringly literal-minded enough to conceive of a huge dinner in *The Kitchen*, which managed to turn the performances of some of NY's finest artists into afterdinner entertainment.

Some 300 people were wined and dined and then entertained by about 40 performers, with each "act" limited to 2 minutes. The meal, eaten crosslegged, was a delicious combination piquant and French: whiskey vegetable soup, bread and wine, followed by apple tarts.

The audience was active, receptive, and professional, while the performances were slapstick and lighthearted, giving the evening the feel of a neighborhood circus, or a court entertained by lively jesters. The entire operation was overseen by Dupuy, who faded into and out of the spotlight like an underground vaudeville director.

And as restaurants are rated importantly for "ambiance," running throughout the evening at *The Kitchen* was a peculiar atmospheric tension. It was a community evening, but SoHo is not truly a community. It is a neighborhood of homogenous professionals — reputations precede intimacy. But on this night the performers loosened up, and gave something different of themselves; usually it went over well. Richard Serra, the massive sculptor, played a taped story touching and telling about him as a boy and his father. It was a personal scene, not the tired canned art audience you find mostly. Though "Autobiographical Art" has produced little major work, it has sneaked into the artworld mentality and loosened up their self consciousness, making events like "Soup and Tart" more likely.

The short performances themselves were a succession of barely esthetic statements. They were good because they were casual, extremely non-arty without labored non-art gestures (you remember how seriously difficult it was to do non-art 10 years ago). The serious fine-artworld has stooped down and dropped their lofty guise for a series of short campfire skits and sight gags. The evening stands as a monument of concentrated non-art, and non-art of the highest quality.

Can art be so casual, so enjoyable, and still be respected? Can art be entertainment? Do we all labor under the Judeo-Christian ethic; are there no genuine hedonists here? Was the evening truly Dionysian, or was it a parody of a parody of the Greeks? We cannot shed the reserve generated by the non-serious, "minor" guise of each piece; this was a night to go down in the elevator (or was it history; I don't remember).

Art Rite (1975), repr. by permission.

THE FLOOR/TABLE

SOUP

IN THE KITCHEN OF THE KITCHEN

OLGA ADORNO

LAURIE ANDERSON

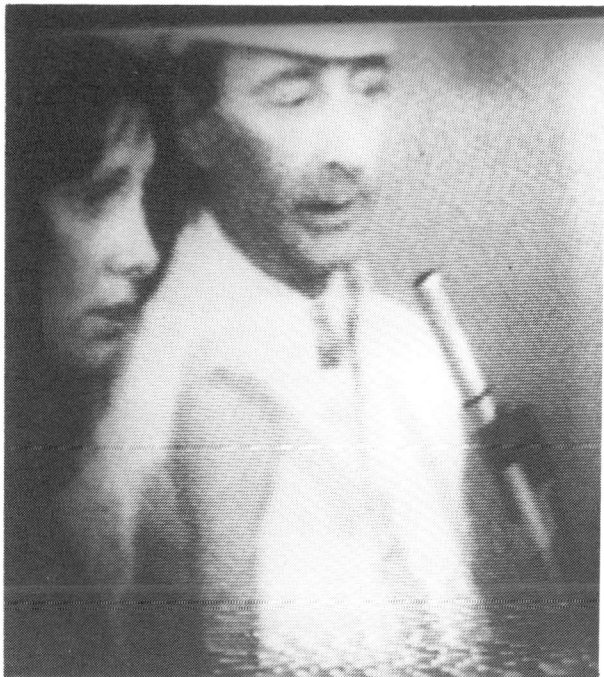

JOANNE AKALAITIS
DAVID WARRILOW

BRENDAN ATKINSON

ROBERT BREER

CHARLES ATLAS with KATE PARKER

RALSTON FARINA

DIEGO CORTEZ

JEAN DUPUY

TINA GIROUARD

PHIL GLASS/YVONNE RAINER

PHILIP GLASS

JON GIBSON

JANA HAIMSOHN

GIANFRANCO MANTEGNA

JOAN JONAS

GORDON MATTA CLARK

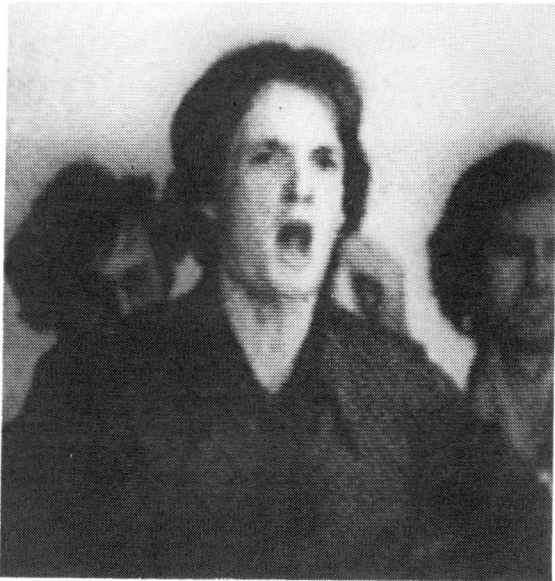

DICK LANDRY

Peter Grass

DONALD MUNROE

Peter Moore

TONY MASCATELLO

Peter Moore

JOAN SCHWARTZ

YVONNE RAINER

CAROLEE SCHNEEMANN

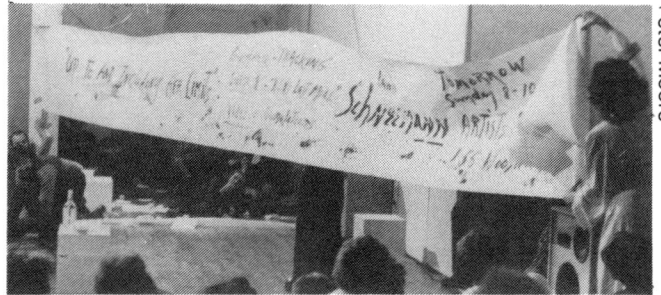

ANTHONY MCCALL

RICHARD SERRA

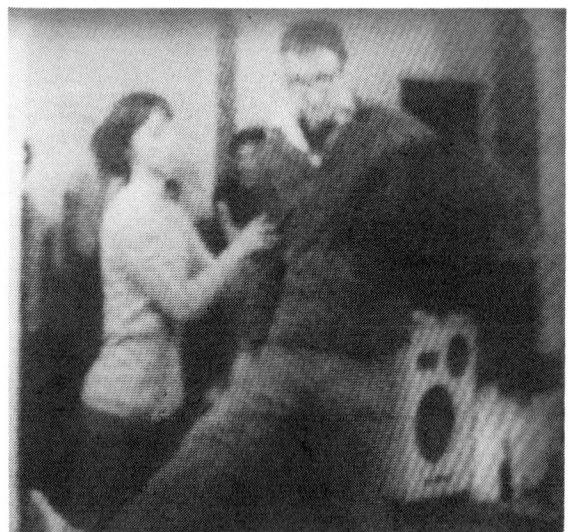

NANCY TOPF
with JON GIBSON

SYLVIA WHITMAN

Peter Grass

HANNAH WILKE

ARTHUR RUSSELL

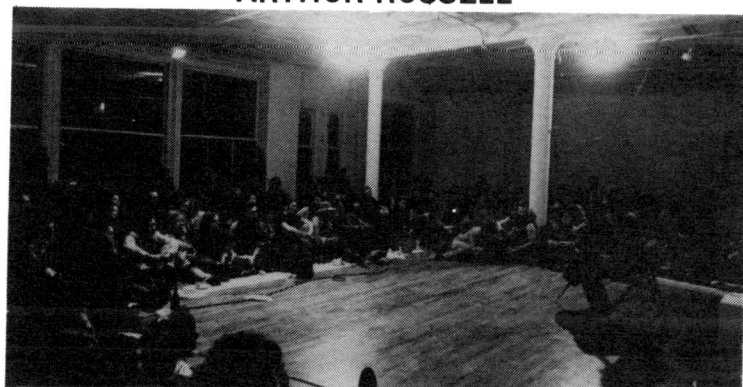

"3 EVENINGS ON A REVOLVING STAGE"

JUDSON CHURCH   JAN 8, 9 & 10, 1976

We hold these Truths

13

PRODUCER : JEAN DUPUY - PRODUCTION MANAGER : CHRIS MURPHY
Ass. PRODUCTION MANAGER : JOHN TRAYNA - STAGE MANAGER : REBECCA
LITMAN _ SOUND BY BERNARD GENETTE MOREL - LIGHTING : PASCAL
DE PINDRAY _ VIDEO PRODUCTION : ELECTRONIC ARTS INTERMIX _,
DIRECTOR : JOHN TRAYNA _, CAMERAS : BILL SCHAB, SAL YANOTTI,
HOLLY DUANE, KIT FITZGERALD _, TECHNICAL DIRECTOR : STEVE
MURATORE

VENERABLE SHERAB :" THE OFFERING OF WATER " _*OLGA ADORNO
& JEAN DUPUY :" THE YOLK & THE WHITE OF AN EGG " 1 Rt PART :
" MAONNAISE ", 2nd PART :" MERENGUE " _ PHIL GLASS - ANDY DEGROAT _
MICHAEL KRUGMAN :" ARTICULATIONS (RED THREAD)", AN EPISODE
FROM THE ABECEDARIAN HERESIES ", WITH RUTH RACHLIN, ASSISTANCE :
RICK LISS _ JANA HAIMSOHN _ NAM JUNE PAIK (SANS VIDEO) _
RICHARD SERRA & DEEDEE HALLECK :" BRONX , OUT TAKES " _ MABOU
MINES :" N.L.G. SJ AND ME " BY JOANNE AKALAITIS , RUTH
MALECZECH & DAVID HARDY _ PETER VAN RIPER :" HELLO , THANK
YOU ", CINEMATOGRAPHY BY MULTIPLEX . SAN FRANCISCO _
SIMONE FORTI : " ISAAC'S ANGEL ", HOLOGRAPHY BY MULTIPLEX _
NANCY LEWIS & RICHARD PECK :" DRAGON " _ JULIA HEYWARD :
" SHAKE , DADDY SHAKE " _ CHARLEMAGNE PALESTINE _ NANCY
TOPF GIBSON & JON GIBSON :" GATHERING " _ HISACHIKA . T :
" LUNA PARK "
* READING : KWAN LAU

MADE POSSIBLE BY A GRANT FROM NEA THROUGH ELECTRONIC
ARTS INTERMIX and THE JUDSON CHURCH .

3 Evenings on a Revolving Stage

3

EVENINGS ON
A REVOLVING STAGE

JAN. 8, 9 & 10   JUDSON CHURCH
8⁰⁰ P.M.   55 WASHINGTON SQ. S.

VITO ACCONCI   JANA HAIMSOHN   NAM JUNE PAIK
OLGA ADORNO   JULIA HEYWARD   RICHARD PECK
JEAN DUPUY HISACHIKA·T CHARLEMAGNE PALESTINE
SIMONE FORTI NANCY LEWIS   PETER VAN RIPER
PHIL GLASS MICHAEL KRUFMAN   RICHARD SERRA
JON GIBSON MABOU MINES VEN. SHERAB NANCY TOPF

MADE POSSIBLE BY A GRANT FROM THE NATIONAL ENDOWMENT FOR THE ARTS

THROUGH THE VANISHING POINT
By ROBB BAKER

Judson's football field bleachers were shoved back on either side of the room, leaving the whole area open. People were asked not to sit on the bleachers (though some did), but to occupy the floor and a limited number of chairs circling the room. In the middle of all this was a small black lazy-susan type circular platform of about three feet in diameter, spinning, mobilized by means of a long grey cord leading off to one side of the room.

This disc, the revolving stage of the title, was the one constant for Jean Dupuy's conceptual celebration, his wild and wonderful all-star collection of New York Avant Garde 1976; it was the center, the focus, of the evening's parade of talent and fun.

First out was the Venerable Sherab, as the program noted, who covered the little circle-stage with a maze mandala, placing a black Buddha on a silver base at the midpoint. Someone carried on a table with bowls, candles, water, incense, a flower. Ritual invocation. Worship as performance.

Michael Krugman's "Articulations (Red Thread)" was a dance, a play, a painting about turning string into crow's foot and jacob's ladder designs, then snipping the fragile constructions back into formlessness. Jana Haimsohn danced, too, in construction boots and a trackrunner outfit, walking, leaning, lassoing, jogging—a kind of mini-olympics. And Nam June Paik ("sans video." said the program) simply sat down and played 78 rpm records on a wind-up victrola, smashing the ones he didn't like on the floor. At one point he said. "I can play that," and went to the grand piano and did just that (and well). At another, he took a wad of Wrigley's doublemint gum out of his mouth and stuck it on one of the spinning records, while everyone strained to see what would happen when the gum hit the needle.

Richard Serra's and Deedee Halleck's video, "Bronx Out Takes." was about black-and-white baptism. Mabou Mines' "NLG, SJ, and Me" had its own revolving stage and was about being blindfolded and not being blindfolded, about throwing and getting hit with raw eggs and rotten tomatoes, about a woman with oval face looking at herself in an oval blue mirror ("the exercise is easier than working on the body or touching on the soul—the surface of the face only meets the surface of the mirror"), about hammering nails into shoes and being attacked by pigeons in the park and remembering a butterfly flying up your skirt when you were three.

Peter van Riper's "Hello, Thank You" ended up being a few moments of silence for Chou en Lai, but that may have been due to problems with a projector ("cinematography by . . ." the program said).

Simone Forti arrived with a suitcase and large box. The suitcase held three bricks and a candle; the box, a large translucent lampshade-like cylinder, which she placed on top of the upended bricks and around the candle (the whole arrangement resting on the revolving stage). The lights were lowered and the candle lit; Forti pronounced her mantra and stepped back to look at a tiny image of herself dancing down in the middle of the turning cylinder, some sort of strange miracle effected by holograph photography, the spinning images on the surface of the cylinder somehow being animated into three-dimensional, full-color substance by the single candlepower. It was the most magical moment of the evening.

Julia Heyward recited poetry into movement, talking about her father or someone having a kind of muscular (shaking) disorder while a film was projected of a smalltown 1950s protestant congregation coming out of a church and shaking, shaking, shaking the minister's hand. "Shake, Daddy, Shake."

Nancy Lewis, wearing belled soft-orange corduroy pants, danced a yawn, a squat, a pout, effecting a gentle sort of comic relief after the high-powered intensity of Andy de Groat's dervishlike whirling (pretzeling, corkscrewing, opening and closing his body, himself, to the parameters of the space, the universe) to the calm circling revolutions (expansion, release, expansion, release) of Phil Glass's live electric organ score.

Following Lewis, Richard Peck stepped to the grand piano and established a string of melodic runs, cut through with strange chords and minors, with everything twisted just out of shape from prettiness into beauty. Then almost imperceptibly he took the line out of the comfortable resonance of the piano chording into the single soaring one-note-at-a-time solo on the saxophone.

Nancy Topf Gibson came on in a long black satin skirt, full of kangaroo pockets that contained square sticks of variously colored chalk. She approached the black revolving stage and touched its outer rim with a piece of red chalk. Pushing in steadily, she spiralled inward until she found the center. That done, she mounted the stage itself and began to establish colored circles outward: Yellow, blue, orange, purple, green, black. Performance as rainbow.

The lights went up as if that were the end. Charlemagne Palestine hadn't appeared, and the program still listed one more person. "Hisachika T," who was to do something called "Luna Park." But with the light up full, people began to mill around and get ready to leave.

Then Hisachika appeared, carrying a yellow garbage bag and a silver suitcase. He set to work finding objects inside objects inside objects (performance as unpacking), with which he began to build a kind of doll-sized scene on the revolving stage: table, chairs, layers of table cloth. This was topped by regular sized glasses (of many shapes and descriptions) and a bottle of Piper Heidsick champagne. Balancing some of the champagne-filled glasses on their edges, he set the platform spinning again (he'd unplugged it momentarily at one point) and let it turn until the balances unbalanced and the glasses tipped and spilled.

For his (and the) finale, he headed offstage again and returned with more garbage bags (green this time) from which he removed dozens of empty tin cans, large silver aluminum-foil balls, and three little 42nd Street gadget store toys: an Uncle Sam bank, a bobbing-head gorilla, and a Mickey Mouse. He then threw all the silver balls at the audience and then invited them to destroy the spinning replica of tin-can Uncle Sam nodding-gorilla Mickey Mouse Americana, which the crowd did with great gusto. Hisachika rushed in at the last minute to save Mickey, but Uncle Sam's bank got smashed to smithereens.

While all this went down, people like photographer Peter Moore clicked away with still cameras, and several videopeople did the same with film that moved. The weekend was over, finished, but in another sense prolonged, preserved, captured albeit two-dimensionally and "differently"—reduced and confined, but expanded and extended. Dance critic Marcia B. Siegel has written about the fact that dance, like all performance art, exists precariously "at the vanishing point"—we lose it as soon as we experience it. But in a sense that's exactly the beauty of it, the magic, the transcendence. Alice through the mirror, darkly. Dissolving into becoming.

By JEAN DUPUY

The first stage I built for a performance which was given in May '74, at 405E 13th Street, and called "the shaving of my mustache" was circular 3 feet in diameter, moving mechanically on ball bearings; a translucid screen 7 feet high was attached to this lazy-susan turntable, behind which I stood for the duration of the performance, shaving my mustache while facing a mirror hung around my neck, showing a Chinese shadow image of my left profile, thrown by a light projector behind me.

When I had finished, I showed the public my freshly shaved face by turning very slowly on the mechanically activated stage (a 360° rotation).

This performance played on a small moving stage was followed on January 8, 9 and 10, '76, by 15 short performances, about 10 minutes each, called "3 evenings on a revolving stage" which took place at Judson Church. In order to do this show, I received a grant from the national endowment for the arts through electronic art intermix, with the purpose of video-taping the 3 evenings. It was difficult to deal with the lighting and sound technician to insure priority be given to the performances and not to the video-tape as he doggedly tried to do.

The stage was very small (2 feet in diameter rotating electrically at a speed of 2 and ½ revolutions per minute) and was placed in the center of the sanctuary, screwed to the floor, and able to carry 800 pounds. At first the performers were surprised and disconcerted by the very small size and the movement of the steel top platform placed in the middle of the large church hall.

In my choice of the artist I made one mistake: Bryan, the venerable Sherab as he called himself, dressed like a Tibetan monk, asked me for permission to participate in the 3 evenings, by giving a 1 minute prayer at the very beginning of each evening. It was clearly understood that he would stay on stage no more than 3 minutes for the 3 evenings; instead he stayed or rather he held the spot-light for a total of 34 minutes for the 3 evenings...in French we say "l'habit ne fait pas le moine" ("it's not the habit which makes the monk").

Olga and I performed a piece called: "the yolk and the white of an egg, Maonnaise and Merengue." At the beginning of "Maonnaise," I asked Kwan Lau to recite in Chinese excerpts from a speech of Chairman Mao Tse Tung related to art and literature (conference of Yenan, May 23, '42). At the time I didn't give the translation; here it is: "revolutionary in art should create a variety of characters out of real life and help the masses to propel history forward...writers and artists concentrate such everyday phenomenon, typify the contradictions and struggles withing them and produce works which awaken the masses, fire them with enthusiasm and impel them to unite the struggle to transform their environment... whether more advanced or elementary, all our literature and art are for the masses of the people, and in the first place for the workers, peasants and soldiers; they are created for the workers, peasants and soldiers and are for their use..."

Then I prepared the maonnaise—during this time I played a Chinese chorus sung by Chinese children. When I had finished I played: "the International" at the same time I raised my fist, covered with a little mountain of maonnaise, above my head. For the sound effect I used a Chinese tea box to mix the maonnaise—this type of box makes a quadrophonic sound because being in the form of a cube it made a sound each time the fork, which I worked with, struck one of its sides...for the same reason, I used a similar box to prepare the meringue, introducing at the same time Olga's Merengue dance.

During the time we spent in the Church, the people who run the church gave us their help; they showed great discretion. Unfortunately I cannot say the same about a similar situation, several weeks later when the Whitney Museum invited me to put the same revolving stage in the center of the room on the 4th floor. I invited, then, 19 artists to perform on 3 minutes each during an afternoon: "One sunday afternoon on a revolving stage" on Feb. 22: Olga Adorno, Charles Atlas, James Barth and Dale Scott, Steven Crawford, Diego Cortez, Jean Dupuy, Angela Frascone, Andrea Halpern, Dick Higgins, Pooh Kaye, Alison Knowles, Tony Mascatello and John Howell, George Maciunas, Dick Miller, Dale Scott, Hannah Wilke, Norman Carey.

Finally obliged to recognize art-performance as a major activity in the arts which has been going on for several years, in N.Y., the Whitney Museum decided to invite me to organize a performance of underground mixed media artists, who generally show in their lofts or in some large space like 112 Green Street, St. Mark's Church, Artists Space, the Kitchen...

The Whitney decided to give a very small fee to the artists invited to perform in this festival and consequently some of them declined the invitation...on the contrary I decided to perform to touch a different audience and also to denounce publicly the reactionary aspect of the museum, showing a film of the anti-Rockefeller pickets, revolving on Madison avenue in front of the museum door, several weeks ago.

But I have to say that it was very difficult to perform and the quality of the show suffered because the rehearsal time was cut from 18 hours promised by the curator to ONE, without any explanations and during this hour our activities were scrutinized by a museum guard and Marcia Tucker herself. Rebecca my stage manager told me M.T. was very anxious to know why I was carrying in the pocket of my jacket two long knives (actually they were in my pocket for a practical reason: because I was going to use them in my performance!). Angered by the school mistress attitude of M.T. and uncomfortable in this police station like atmosphere, I started the show by a short speech: "The 19 artists invited to perform on the revolving stage today, will receive each 7 dollars as a fee given by the Whitney Museum—Let us PROTEST for ONE MINUTE!"

The explanation of the low fee being that each artist, performing for 3 minutes only, was paid on a base of 210 dollars for one hour...

Olga and I came on the stage at the beginning of my piece, dressed as if we were standing outside (it was Feb. 22) in winter coats, hats and scarves to announce the title of the piece: "New York-Minneapolis-New York." Then we left the stage and went to the back room from where I announced again through a microphone: "Les voyageurs pour Chicago-Minneapolis-en voiture, s'il vous plait!" Then after a 3 minute delay, we came back inside a large box, tied with cord, carried by 4 people. They put the box on the stage and the box started to revolve. At this point, the sound of the train was supposed to be heard—but we didn't rehearse, as I said, and I was obliged to scream from the inside of the box "Sound, Please!", to the 2 confused sound men. When the sound went on, we started to cut with the 2 long knives 2 of the 4 walls of the box. We were packed inside like sardines—we had some problems manipulating the knives—but finally we appeared to the audience, from the box split in 2 parts like a trunk. Olga was wearing my coat, my hat and my scarf and I was wearing her coat, her scarf and her lipstick on my lips.

I got the idea of "New York- Minneapolis-New York" from 2 incidents: last year when I went with Olga on a train trip, to deliver to a museum of Minneapolis, 3 large boxes containing a piece of mine. During the time I was working on the Whitney show, I was in the process of moving, from 405E 13th Street to 537 B'way — like my Grandmother, Elisa, I rarely threw things away...so, for several weeks, I was packing my things in boxes.

OLGA ADORNO

JEAN DUPUY

ANDY DE GROAT

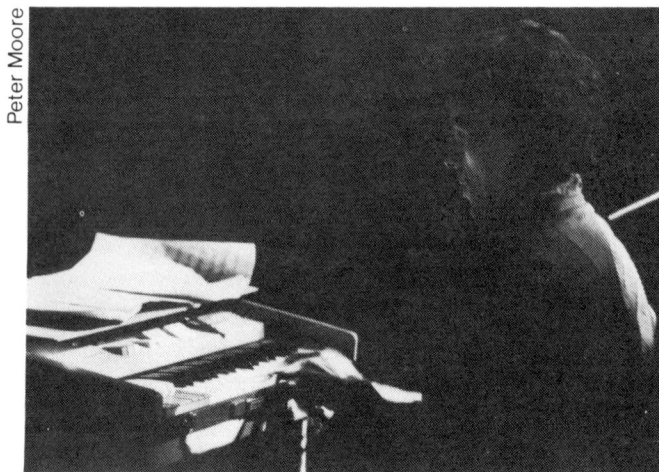

PHILIP GLASS

NANCY LEWIS

Charles Dreyfus

SIMONE FORTI

Peter Van Riper

Peter Moore

JANA HAIMSOHN

JULIA HEYWARD

HISACHIKA

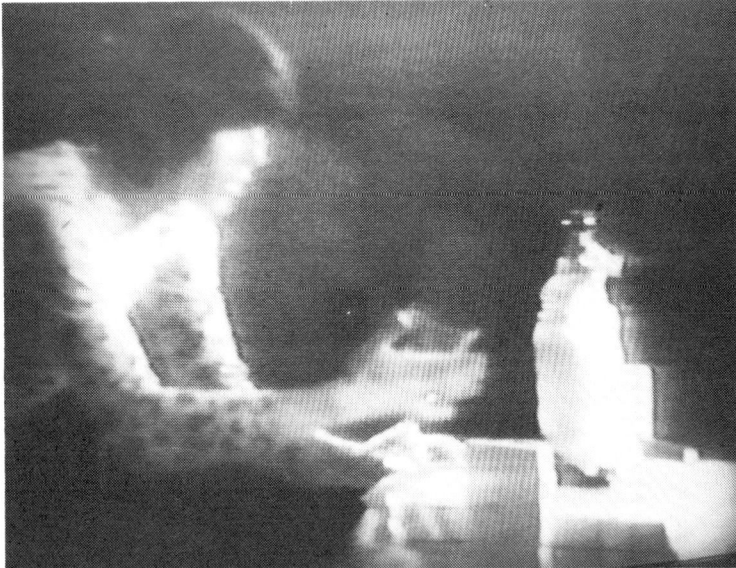

MICHAEL KRUGMAN with
RUTH RACHLIN

Peter Moore

Peter Moore

KWAN LAO

Peter Moore

MABOU MINES

NANCY TOPF

NAM JUNE PAIK

Peter Moore

Peter Moore

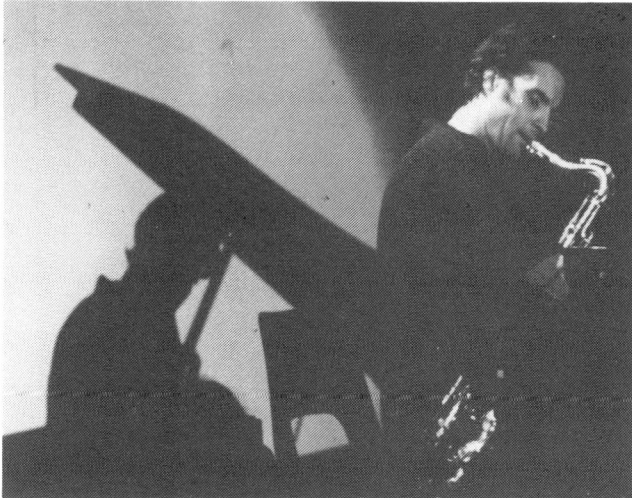

RICHARD PECK

Peter Van Riper

PETER VAN RIPER

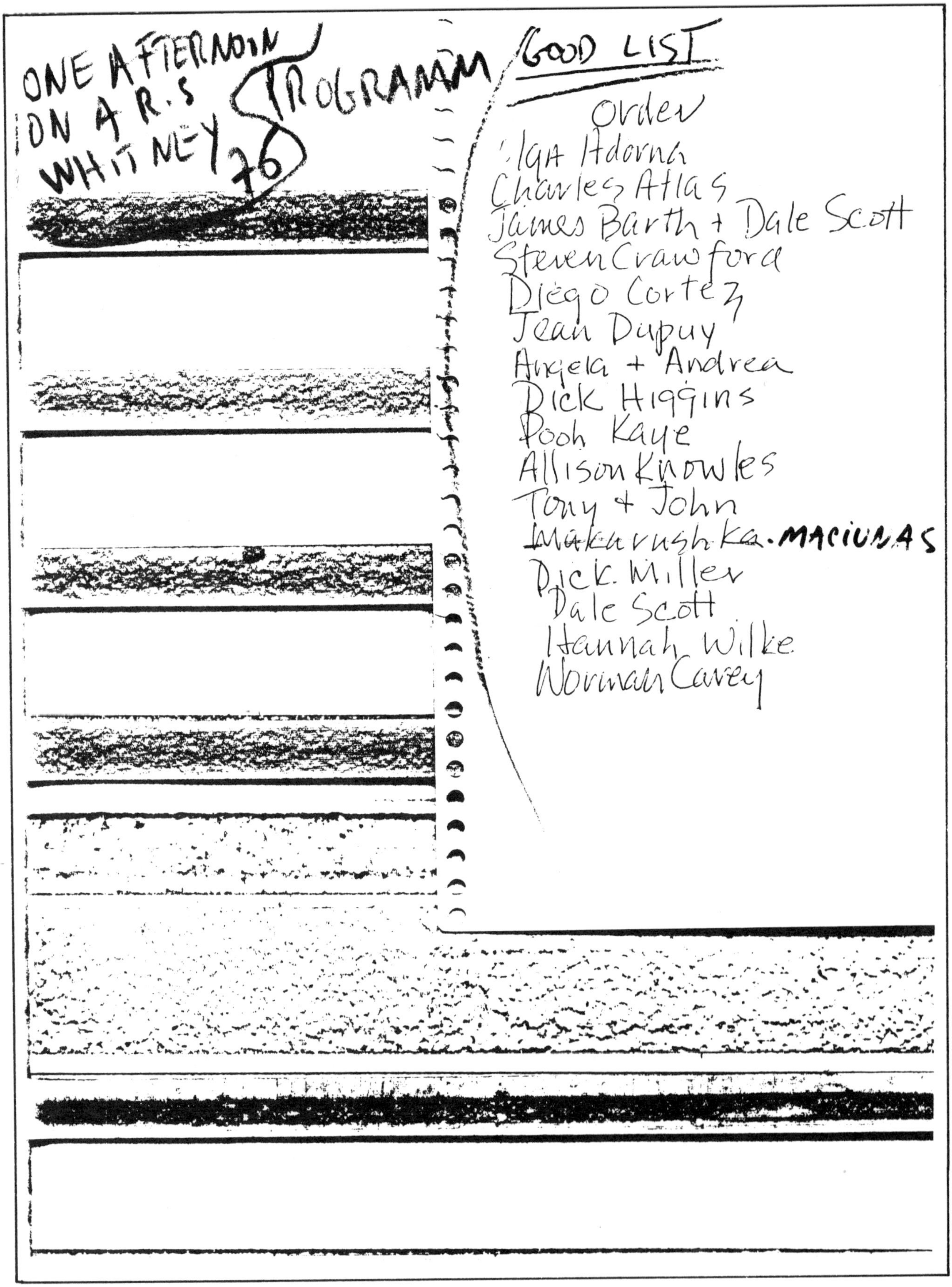

ONE AFTERNOON
ON A R.S
WHITNEY 76 **PROGRAMM**

GOOD LIST

Order
Olga Adorna
Charles Atlas
James Barth + Dale Scott
Steven Crawford
Diego Cortez
Jean Dupuy
Angela + Andrea
Dick Higgins
Pooh Kaye
Allison Knowles
Tony + John
~~Makarushka~~. **MACIUNAS**
Dick Miller
Dale Scott
Hannah Wilke
Norman Carey

One Sunday Afternoon on a Revolving Stage

PERFORMANCE DIARY

By PETER FRANK

Occupying the whole post-intermission part of the afternoon was Jean Dupuy's remake of the Revolving Stage revue he had organized at Judson Church in January. Not a restage, a remake—(almost) all-new cast! New faces of February! And, to add a twist political subversion: the group show began with Dupuy's protestation against the fee being paid each performer by the Whitney, and was followed by a film of the anti-Rockefeller pickets marching outside the museum. Not the height of politesse, but well-taken points (I understand the museum coughed up some more dough afterward); for their parts, the Whitney employees tried to interfere with the film (bad karma, bad public relations—benign neglect would have been the mose graceful way out), and attempted explanation of the low fees (a more rational tack). The realness of the brouhaha disrupted the controlled, comfortable feeling of here's-the-audience-there's-the-performer-it-s-only-a-stage. For a minute.

Like its Judson predecessor, the Revolving Stage revue was a smorgasbord of presentations, from the visual to the conceptual, from the crafted to the insouciant, from the sublime to the ridiculous. The revue as a whole was slow-moving, what with all the setting up before each piece (usually longer than the piece itself), but there were high points aplenty—perhaps more than at the Judson (or was it just more comfortable to sit in the Whitney?). Among these: Diego Cortez's odd, muffled tour of "New Vienna," led (or attended?) by some famous art historians; Jean Dupuy's skit, performed with Olga Adorno, about travelling from France to New York to Minneapolis—by crate; Dick Higgins's clean, bright little piece in which he stands, dressed in white with a huge white stove pipe hat, on the revolving stage and has a red ribbon wound about him; Pooh Kaye's frantic emulation of a wind-up jumping monkey's movements; Alison Knowles sitting on the stage, spilling beans all around her, and picking out names from the spill and reading them; the eerie storytelling-cum-magic trick of Dick Miller (done, of course, with mirrors); and, my favorite for its disruptive involvement of the audience (reawakening the excitement of the protest), the two ten-foot poles George Maciunas mounted horizontally across the stage, sweeping half the spectators away. (Maciunas had wanted to electrify the poles, but couldn't pull that off—or wasn't allowed to—or something.)

Soho Weekly News (Mar. 18, 1976), repr. by permission.

OLGA ADORNO

Peter Moore

JAMES BARTH with DALE SCOTT

Peter Moore

Peter Moore

DIEGO CORTEZ

Peter Moore

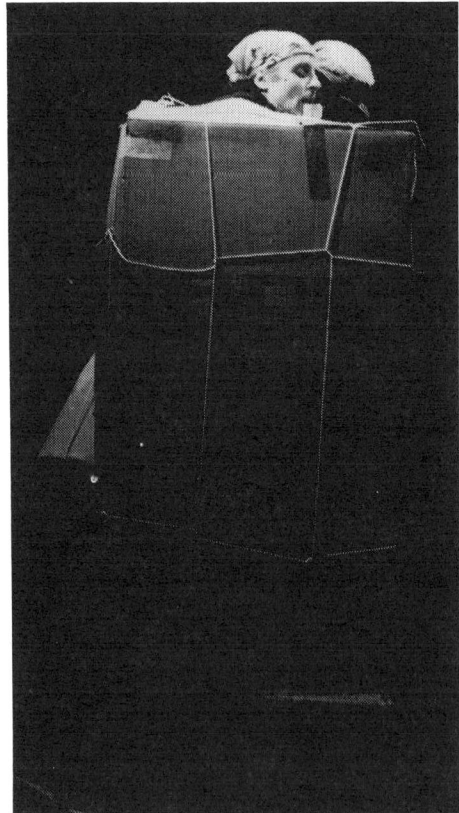

**JEAN DUPUY
with OLGA ADORNO**

ANGELA FRASCONE

ANDREA HALPERN

ALISON KNOWLES

DICK HIGGINS

GEORGE MACIUNAS

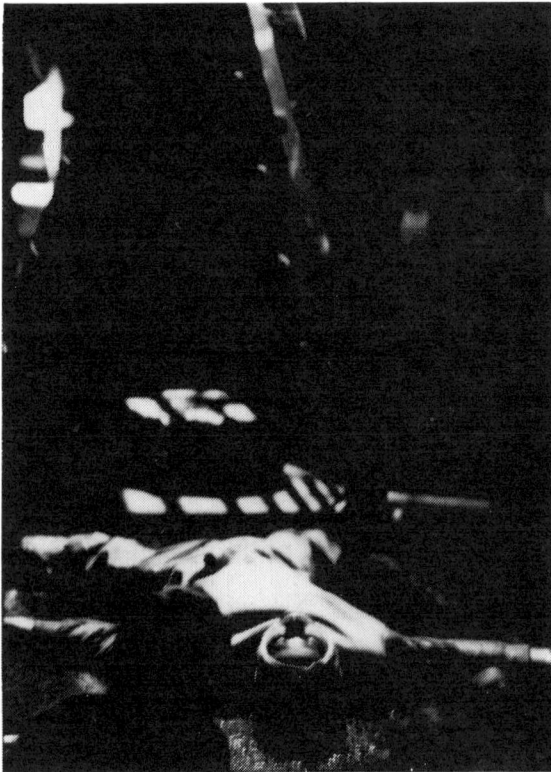

TONY MASCATELLO

DALE SCOTT

DICK MILLER

Teri Slotkin

HANNAH WILKE

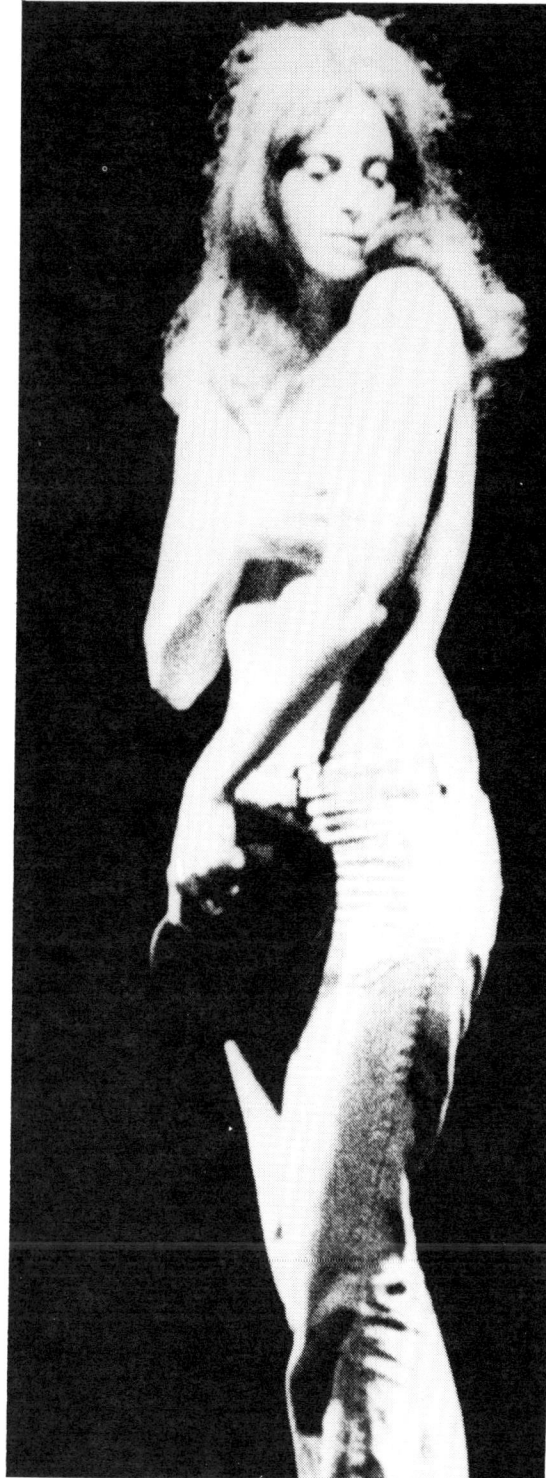

Walter Robinson

22 simultaneous ART PERFORMANCES

537 B'WAY (1 FLIGHT UP)

GROMMETS

DEC. 76

THURSDAY 2
FROM 8 pm to 9 pm

FRIDAY 3
FROM 8 pm to 9 pm

SATURDAY 4
FROM 9 pm to 9 pm

SUNDAY 5
FROM 2 pm to 3 pm
" 8 " to 9 "

CONTRIBUTION : $3

OLGA   ADORNO
LAURIE   ANDERSON
CARMEN   BEUCHAT
JAMES   BARTH
MAUREN   CONNOR
JAIME   DAVIDOVITCH
JEAN   DUPUY
JANA   HAIMSOHN
ELAINE   HARTNETT
JULIA   HEYWARD
SUZANNE   HARRIS
POOH   KAYE
GERALD   LINDAHL
TONY   MASCATELLO
TIMOTHY   MAUL
DICK   MILLER
LARRY   MILLER
DONALD   MONROE
ILHAN   MIMAROGLU
CHARLEMAGNE PALESTINE
NAM JUNE   PAIK
RICHARD   PRINCE

Grommets #3

By JEAN DUPUY

The first time I used grommets was at the Kitchen in Nov. '74—there, I showed a work of mine called i & j which was spelled out in grommets on a piece of canvas. Through them could be seen another large screen, 7 feet × 10 feet, with a video monitor inserted in it at lower right. Taken from the video-tape, black and white slides of i & j making love were projected on the screen. This installation of i & j was the only practical and effective way I had found to show this boring video-tape.

The second time I used grommets was at P.S.1, in Sept. '76—On a Sunday afternoon, I invited 10 artists to perform in one room at the same time, behind a translucid screen. This particular "live installation" has stimulated me to do another one, on a larger scale in my own place, on two floors; to do that I had to cover the front part of the mezzanines from floor to ceiling with a thick canvas (80 feet × 14 feet) and build a set of 6 stairs to give 6 points of access to have a peep at the actions on the second floor, the mezzanines. One of my problems was the choice of the size of the grommets—the diameter of which gives a certain angular view which grows according to the depth of the field. These technical problems having been solved in my mind, I had still to get the money for the realization of that show. At first I asked Oldenburg and Rauschenberg to provide together a fund to help out the 22 young artists involved in it; then, after having received a negative answer, I asked each artist to contribute and fortunately most of them were able to send me $20.

What happened in the third grommets show was that each artist had a room to perform in; which was a different situation from the second grommets show where everybody was performing in the same room and one had a general view of each performer through only one grommet. In the third grommets show, one of the difficulties was that the public had to wait in line in order to peep into each room, an uncomfortable and frustrating situation as there was not enough time to take in what was going on in certain rooms, even if the general view in the public room was interesting since one could see some of the performances through shadows on the canvas. It was also a difficult situation for the artists because they had to perform without knowing what was going on behind the grommet and without intermission during one hour and a half.

By SALLY BANES

A few blocks up from Canal, in Jean Dupuy's loft, another performance turning private into public action was going on all weekend. But while Geoff Hendrick's activity was a 12-hour process available for continuous viewing, *Grommets* presented around 20 different events simultaneously for an hour. Each event, taking place in its own discrete area of a two-story structure, was masked by muslin and visible only through a grommet.

A grommet is a metal eyelet which reinforces a hole in fabric. This is the second of Dupuy's grommet pieces; the first, at PS 1 earlier this fall, presented simultaneous activity in one room which could be viewed through grommets in the canvas doorhanging.

Because the structure generated an aura of voyeurism, it's not surprising that many of the pieces were about private activities, or private parts. Elaine Hartnett, surrounded by stuffed animals, flowered curtains and pillows, chatted to Charlemagne Palestine, visible only on a video monitor, about being watched. Larry Miller hypnotized each willing viewer via rotating fans, and unblinking eye at the end of a spiral tunnel, and a seductive voice over earphones. Suzanne Harris sat among arcane objects muttering about dance and revolution while two dancers moved in and out of vision so close to the grommet that you could only see flashes of the edge of an eye, the crease of an elbow, an expanse of back.

Olga Adorno's two grommets were focussed on her face and bare crotch. As she whispered obscene messages, one looked from one disembodied part to the other, both distorted by lenses corresponding exactly to the grommets. Maureen Connor's silhouette, hanging upsidedown in gynecologists' stirrups, was backed by a field of huge flies. Jana Haimisohn, in boots and workclothes, did a sober dance punctuated by the bored, vagina-framing gestures of a 42nd Street stripper.

But some of the cubicles created other universes entirely, universes made huge by the telescope-like perspective of the grommet. Julia Heyward sang old songs into your ear as you looked back through a seemingly infinite room containing courtyards and windows; Carmen Beuchat seemed to exist on several planes, as dancing among mirrors her body could be seen in the distance and then her face, suddenly, right in front of you.

Thursday night I heard Pooh Kaye was throwing dirt around with some kind of fantastic machine, and I saw Laurie Anderson's tiny 3-D projection of *Mary Hartman*. Saturday night, Anderson was playing one violin note, obsessively, and the *Mary Hartman* grommet was taped over. Kaye was throwing punches, moving her body around abruptly, moving close to the grommet, punching at it, moving away.

The place was getting crowded. There wasn't enough time to see everything, since everything only lasted an hour, and only one or two could look at a time; standing on lines sometimes for 10 minutes at a time required blind judgment and haphazard strategizing, especially since those exhibits with the shortest lines were static, but the changing exhibits one *wanted* to review, yet in the limited time had the least chance to. *Grommets* tantalized, but couldn't fully gratify.

Dear SWN:
In Sally Banes article called "Roots and Rituals" December 9, the Grommets show in which she stated I was whispering obscene messages—
Here are the whispered words—
What are the deep dark secrets that make the shadows on my puss?
Why are the deep dark secrets on my puss?
What makes the deep dark secrets on my puss?
What makes the shadows?
Why are the deep dark secrets on my puss like shadows?

The shadows on my puss—
What are the deep dark secrets faced with?
I will be happy if you would clear it.

Thank you,
Olga Adorno

Soho Weekly News (Dec. 9, 1976), repr. by permission.

OLGA ADORNO

LAURIE ANDERSON

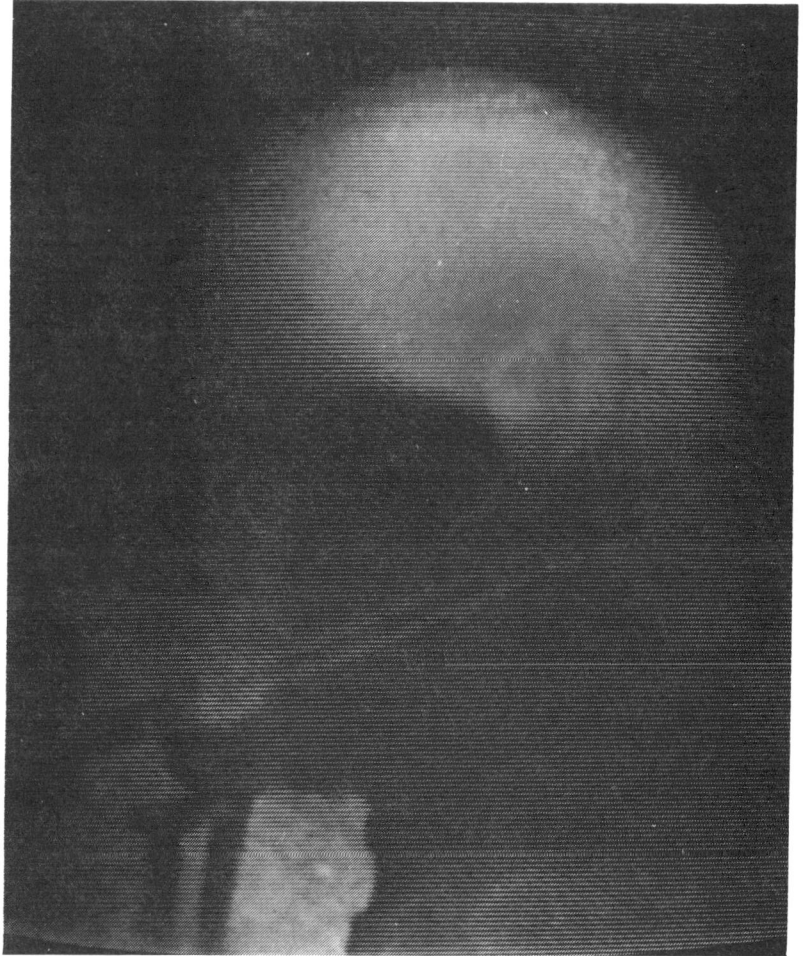

Babette Mangolte

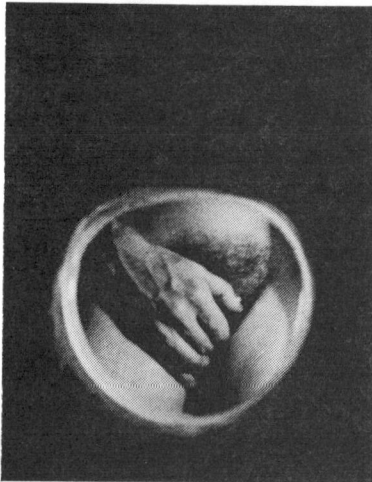

Babette Mangolte

JAMES BARTH

CARMEN BEUCHAT

50

MAUREEN CONNOR

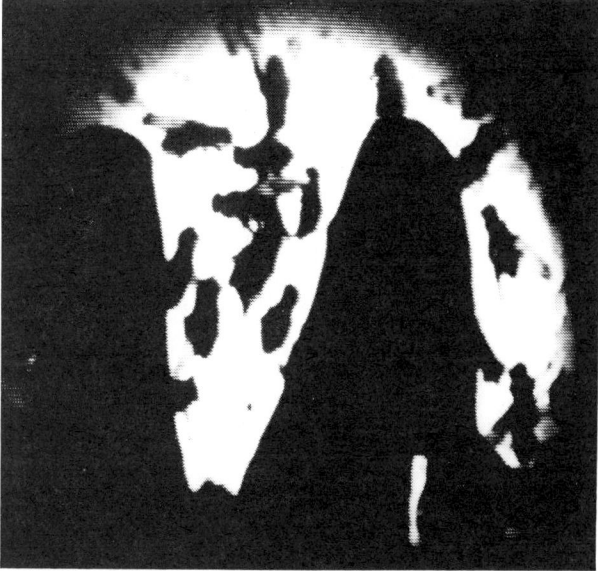

JAIME DAVIDOVITCH

SUZANNE HARRIS

JANA HAIMSOHN

ELAINE HARTNETT/CHARLEMAGNE PALESTINE

JULIA HEYWARD

Babette Mangolte

JULIA HEYWARD

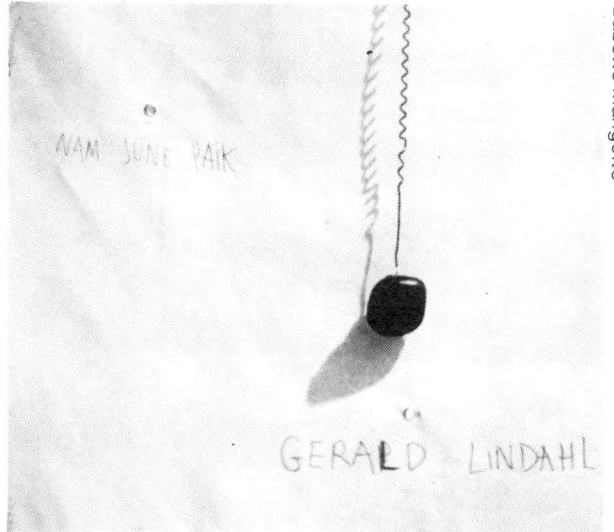

Babette Mangolte

GERALD LINDAHL

POOH KAYE

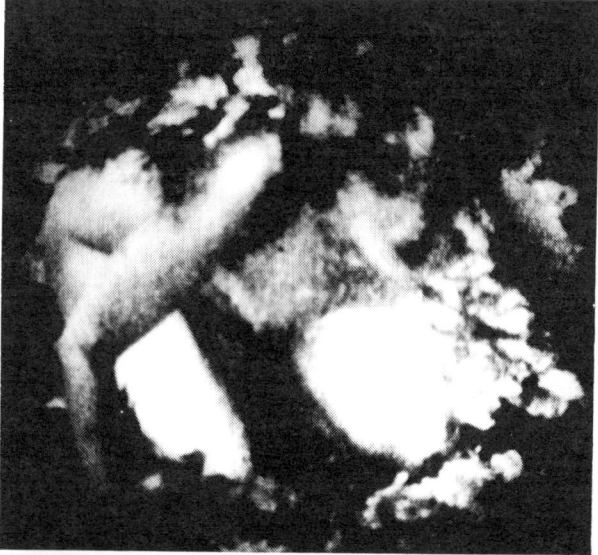

TONY MASCATELLO

TIM MAUL

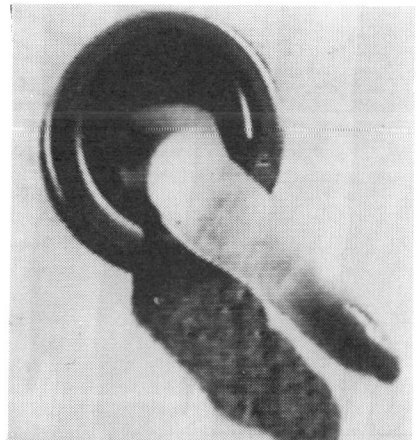

DONALD MUNROE

LARRY MILLER

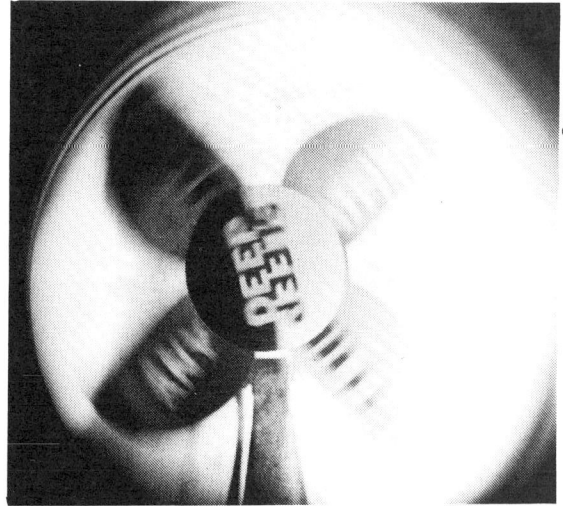

CHARLEMAGNE PALESTINE

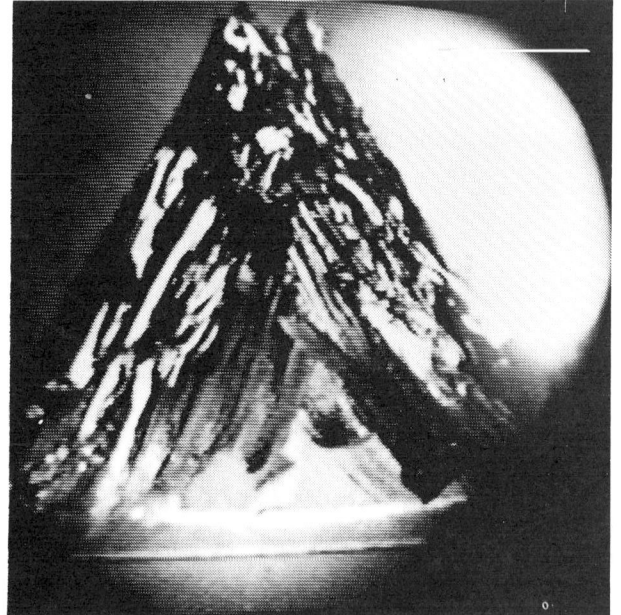

NAM JUNE PAIK

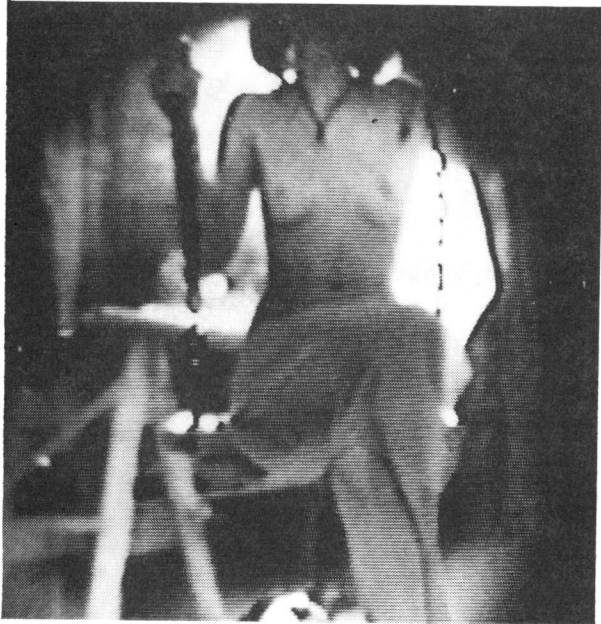 

— RICHARD PRINCE

GENERAL VIEW —

17 SIMULTANEOUS ART PERFORMANCES

537 B'WAY (1 FLT UP)

⦿ GROMMETS 4

MEL ANDRINGA   DAVID APPEL   JEAN DUPUY
JARED FITZGERALD   KIT FITZGERALD &
JOHN SANBORN   WENDY GREENBERG
JANA HAIMSOHN   GEOFF HENDRICKS &
BRIAN BUCZAK   ALISON KNOWLES &
JESSIE HIGGINS   GEORGE MACIUNAS
ANDREW & VARIETY MOSZYNSKI
LUCIO POZZI   STUART SHERMAN &
POWER BOOTH & KAREN GREENBLATT &
NISI JACOBS & JOHN MATTURRI &
MARIE CLAIRE TABARD   MICHAEL SMITH
DOUGLAS TURNBAUGH   JOHN ZORN

APRIL 15, 16 & 17 1977

FROM 8 pm to 9:30 PM   CONT: 2.50

Grommets #4

MICHAEL SMITH

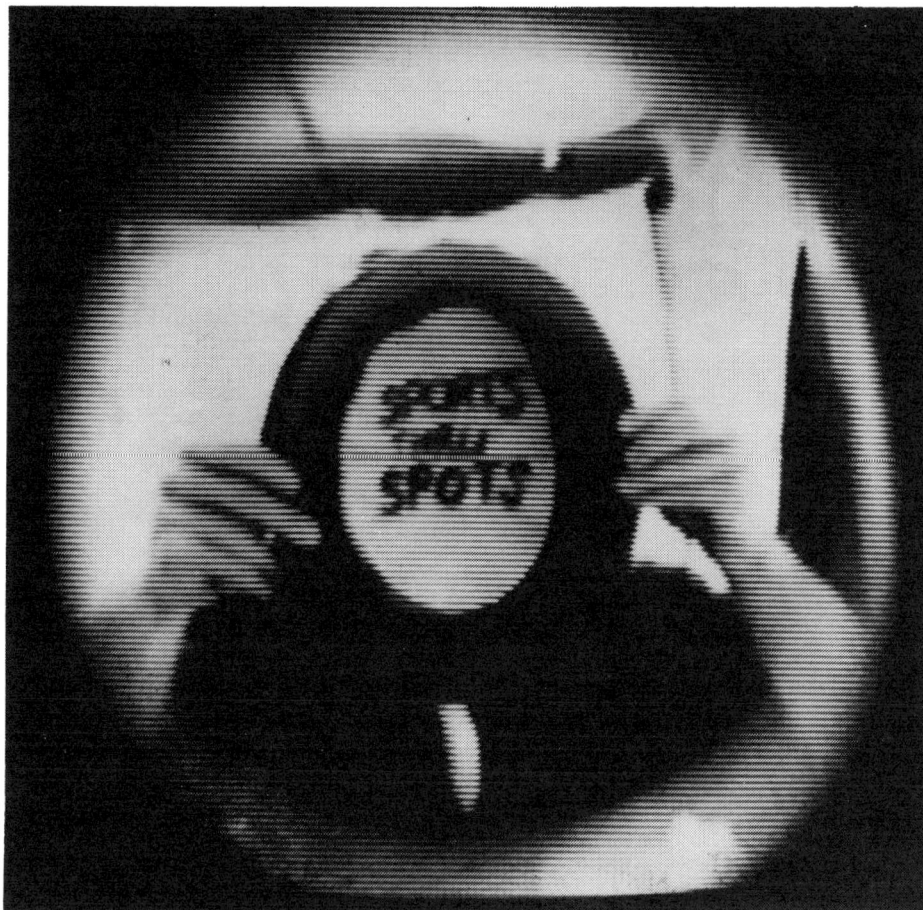

Babette Mangolte

MEL ANDRINGA

Babette Mangolte

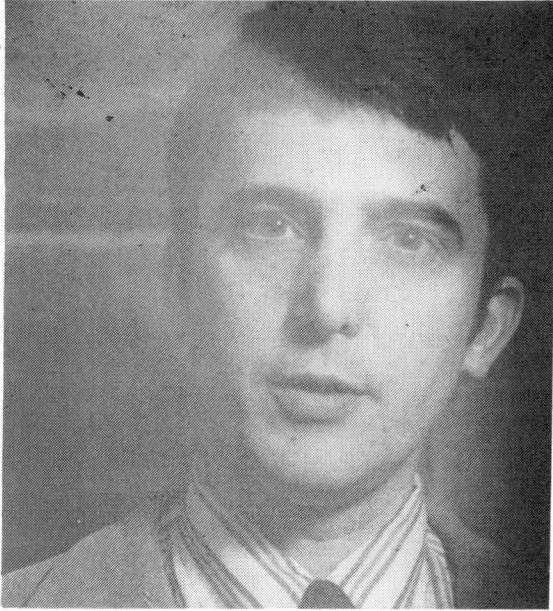

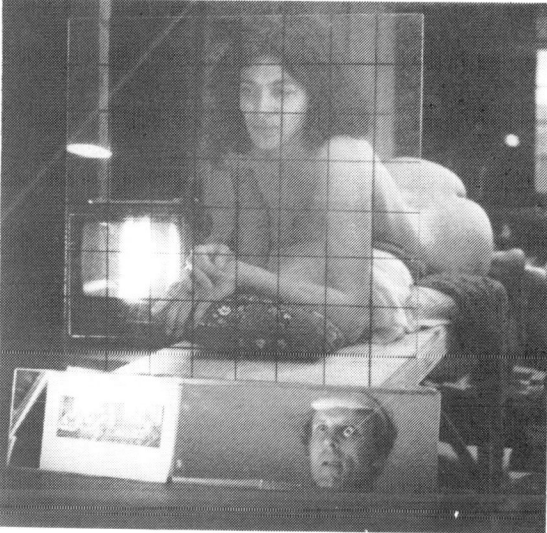

DAVID APPEL with GAIL TETON

Babette Mangolte

**JEAN DUPUY
with OLGA ADORNO**

JARED FITZGERALD

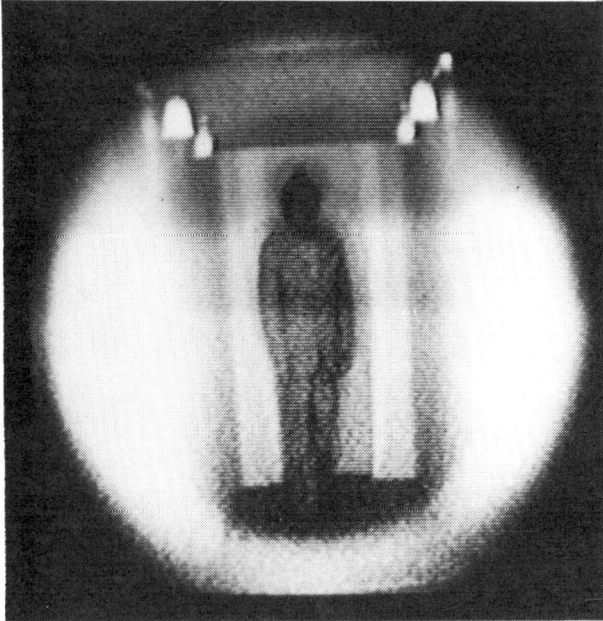

WENDY GREENBERG

Babette Mangolte

GEOFF HENDRICKS

JANA HAIMSOHN

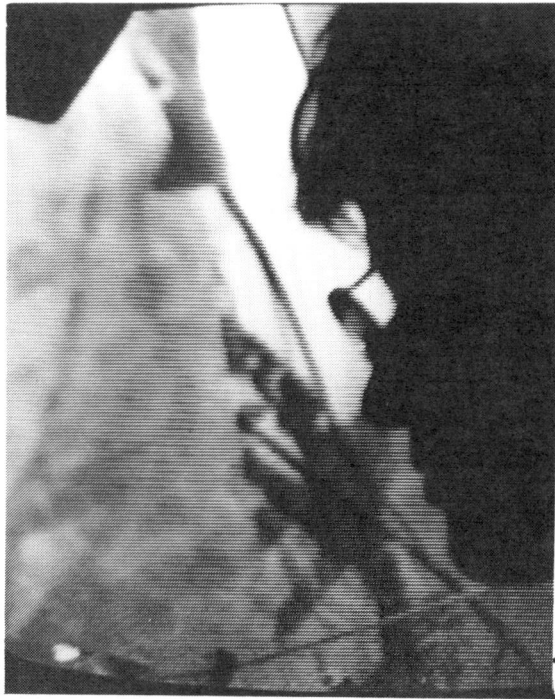

— ALISON KNOWLES

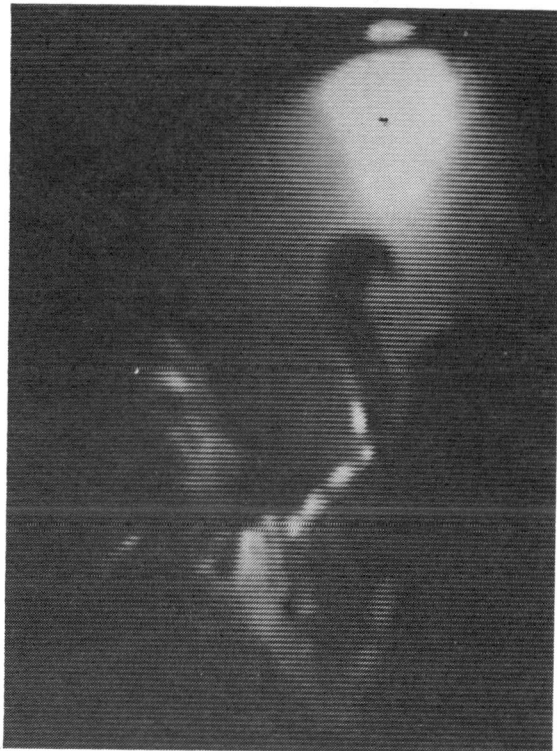

LUCIO POZZI

ANDREW MOSZYNSKI

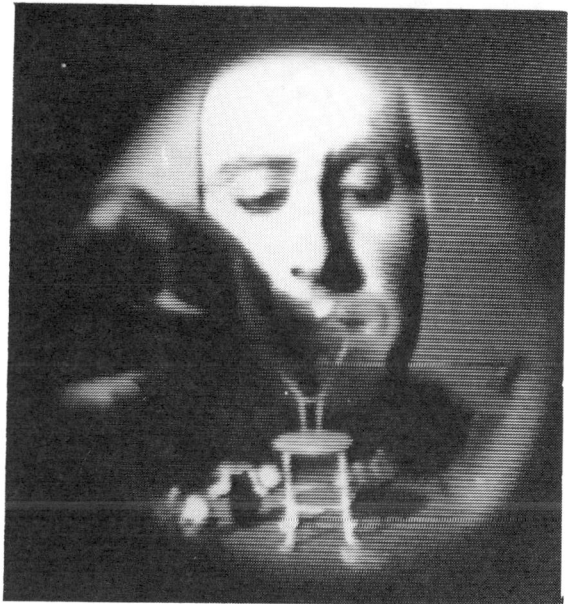

CHANT
A CAPELLA

with: OLGA ADORNO   LAURIE ANDERSON   DON CHERRY
JEAN DUPUY   ROBERT FILIOU   WENDY GREENBERG
JANA HAIMSOHN   ELAINE HARTNETT   RICHARD HAYMAN
JULIA HEYWARD   DICK HIGGINS   DAVID HYKES
TOM JOHNSON   LES LEVINE   GEORGE MACIUNAS
TONY MASCATELLO   CHARLEMAGNE PALESTINE
NAM JUNE PAIK   CHRISTIAN XATREC

AT: JUDSON CHURCH
55 WASHINGTON SQ. S.
NOV. 18, 19 + 20 1977   8:00 P.m.

RESERVATION : 777 0033
CONTRIBUTION : $3.50 TDF $1

Chant a Cappella

JEAN DUPUY: Impresario, Magician, Family Man

By WENDY PERRON

"When I was a child, I did short skits with my sister, brothers and cousins to celebrate special occasions . . . at my grandfather's house in Auvergne. One of us had to tell one of La Fontaine's fables, another a Victor Hugo poem . . . Most of the time I sang a song. We generally performed at the end of lunch in front of the family, still around a table."

—Jean Dupuy

The smorgasbord performance situations that Jean Dupuy has directed in the last four years descend directly from his days in Auvergne. Not that he is trying to relive that life — in fact, he lives very much in the present. But he wants to carry over from those days the love and sharing that are the best parts of the best families. The artists whom Dupuy invites to perform in his projects speak affectionately of his warmth and openness. Clearly, he is the ideal father. "I give freedom to the artists. My time limitations are the only ones. I don't feel to be fascistic."

He chooses the artists democratically. Mostly, he goes by the guidelines of chance and good feeling. Among the hundreds who have performed in his productions (seven since '73), are some big name artists like Claus Oldenburg, Larry Rivers, Philip Glass, and Yvonne Rainer, but it's all the same to Dupuy. They all get equal time, whether it's two minutes, as in Soup & Tart (1974), or one hour, as in Grommets (1976). For his next project, which will probably be at P.S. 1 in February, he will just ask people he sees on the street. When he gets 30 OKs, he will have finished casting.

In the years between his boyhood in Auvergne and his Soho family of today, Dupuy has conducted many fascinating projects. As a painter in France, he was doing, by his own description, dripping type stuff influenced by Jackson Pollock. For years he belonged to a collective of artists involved in Zen Buddhism. "After seven years I was tired and empty. I had been sending work to American collectors so I decided to come here. I arrived here in September '67 and decided not to make paintings any more. By chance I met an engineer . . ." and here begins the story of his extraordinary sculpture Heart Beats Dust (now called Cone-Pyramid), which won him so much attention from critics, galleries, and the public that, within months of his arrival, he became one of the most famous artists in New York.

After trying out my own heart on this "sculpture," I can see why. In a box taller than a person, a cone of red light illuminates the motions of dust above a surface of stretched rubber. Dupuy held a stethoscope to my heart and I watched the dust jump and repattern itself according to the amplified heartbeat. The formations were mostly symmetrical, and beautiful. The sculpture/event makes you want to thank your heart for being so dependable, and for giving you something magnificent to hear and see. It's mesmerizing.

Dupuy thinks that having a father and grandfather who were doctors gave him his interest in anatomy. Looking at, testing, the pieces in his loft is like a ride through a funhouse of bizarre sights, only the sights are parts of oneself. By an arrangement of mirrors and periscopes, you can look through a hole and see your own ear; through another you see the top of your head. Dupuy's curiosity for "secret" parts extends to objects as well. A small mirror leaning against the wall where there's a hole in the floor reflects another mirror across the room in such a way that you can see the beams underneath the floorboards. I think it's magic, but Jean asures me that it's simple technology. Tricks with perspective.

Between 1968 and '72, Dupuy was sought after by the top galleries, but in '72 "conceptual art" was in and "technological art" was out. Dupuy was suddenly abandoned; the feeling was mutual. He felt he could never count on the gallery or museum people to keep up their end of an agreement. He distrusts the entire gallery/museum/grants network, preferring to work outside of it, and encouraging younger artists to avoid it too. He is optimistic about this trend: "The new generation of performance artists is great. They don't make objects, so they don't deal with museums and galleries. They have real problems making a living, like all other people. Some of them clean houses. For me, I survive now by giving cooking classes. We are not controlled by the classical structure of artist-gallery-collector-museum. In that structure, when you reach the museum, you are finished—you don't make anything new anymore." Having had his bout with sucess in 1968, Dupuy feels strongly about this. Except for some of the Fluxus artists, like George Maciunas and Dick Higgins, he is no longer interested in the artists of his own generation. Now he's interested in the younger, performance artists. His belief in these people gives his the energy to take on huge projects like *Chant A Cappella,* performed two weeks ago by about 35 artists at Judson Memorial Church. There were 18 pieces, none over five minutes long and most of them solos.

Dupuy admits that "there is a good aspect and a bad aspect, which is that you have to digest many minds in a short time. This is difficult. Some people can't handle it." Another disadvantage is that it obliges the participating artist to choose the most memorable or outrageous moment from his repetoire and perform it out of context. But this is a legitimate challenge to a performing artist and, needless to day, there are as many solutions to the problem posed as there are participants.

For the audience, the value of an evening like this is in the array of performers—where else can you see such a diversity of performance approaches in one sitting? But for Dupuy, the value is in the nourishing of the community of artists sharing ideas, being affected by the proximity to each other. "What is important in our performance is, from one evening to the next, the influence of one artist on another. That was so clear and magnificent. They performed differently on the second and third nights, having been changed by each other. That is only possible in this meeting of artists together."

A single theme holds sway over the artists' choices in each of Jean Dupuy's performances. The last one was called *Chant A Cappella,* and the theme was just that: All the invited artists were asked to chant or sing without musical acompaniment. The instructions were carried out with imagination, humor and seriousness. The vast range of vocal and conceptual material delighted the audience. After a duet by Charlemagne Palestine and a group piece by Dupuy, the following artists performed solos in nearly alphabetical order: Olga Adorno, Don Cherry, Robert Filliou, Jana Haimsohn, Elaine Hartnett, Julia Heyward, Dick Higgins, David Hykes, Tom Johnson, Les Levine, George Maciunas, Tony Mascatello, Nam June Paik, Christian Xatrec and Wendy Greenberg.

In "Elle Aimait Bien Les Frite, Margueri, i te," 20 people sang a song of the same name — it's a wonderful tune that *grand-père* Dupuy used to sing as a marching song — each at his or her prescribed time. They stood behind a row of six square canvases on stretchers, slowly making incisions wherever they wished. Eventually they stuck unlikely body parts through the rips.

That piece set the tone for anyone who didn't already know that Anything Can Happen in these events, which included two hilarious duets by Palestine for Judith Greentree and Penelope Rockwell, a mysterious operation by George Macuinas, audience choral singing directed by Dick Higgins, intriguing performances by Tom Johnson and Julia Heyward (more about these two next week). Elaine Hartnett screamed for five minutes solid as an interpretation of Pennsylvanian "hooting," and Olga Adorno slid her shoes off and on again as her voice slid through the syllables "Ah Ha." And more.

Stay tuned for the P.S. 1 project in February — Dupuy is planning to build little towers for each artist. It might even be the last of these family get-togethers.

Soho Weekly News (Dec. 8, 1977), repr. by permission.

OLGA ADORNO

DON CHERRY   MOCKY CHERRY

**ROBERT FILLIOU
with OLGA ADORNO**

JANA HAIMSOHN

JEAN DUPUY

WENDY GREENBERG

RICHARD HAYMAN

DAVID HYKES

— ELAINE HARTNETT

JULIA HEYWARD

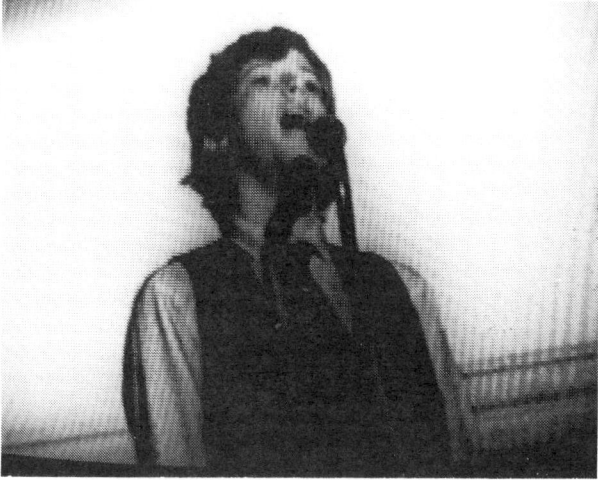

Peter Moore

DICK HIGGINS

Harry Shunk

Peter Moore

Peter Moore

Harry Shunk

CHRISTIAN XATREC

TOM JOHNSON

DICK HIGGINS

TONY MASCATELLO

Harry Shunk

GEORGE MACIUNAS
BILLIE HUTCHINS

Peter Moore

Harry Shunk

Harry Shunk

CHARLEMAGNE PALESTINE

Harry Shunk

NAM JUNE PAIK

Feb. sat 4	Feb. sun 5
1:00 Charlie Morrow	1:00 Heloise Gold
1:25 David Appel	1:25 Elaine Hartnett
1:50 Maureen Connor	1:50 Charlie Morrow
2:15 Elaine Hartnett	2:15 Yoshisama Wada
2:40 Dicky Landry	2:40 Dick Landry
3:05 Nancy Lewis	3:05 Nancy Lewis
3:30 Tina Girouard	3:30 Tina Girouard
3:55 Carmen Beuchat	3:55 Tim Maul
4:20 Marchalore	4:20 Marchalore
4:45 Jerry Hovagamyan	4:45 Jerry Hovagamyan
5:10 Yoshisama Wada	5:10 Andrew Moszynski
5:35 Jean Dupuy	5:35 Jean Dupuy

Feb. sat. 11	Feb. sun. 12
1:00 Christian Xatrec	1:00 Christian Xatrec
1:25 Olga Adorno	1:25 Olga Adorno
1:50 David Appel	1:50 David Appel
2:15 Scott Johnson	2:15 Phil James
2:40 Dicky Landry	2:40 Heloise Gold
3:05 Nancy Lewis	3:05 Elaine Hartnett
3:30 Tina Girouard	3:30 Tim Maul
3:55 Jon Hassel	3:55 Cara Brownell
4:20 Cara Brownell	4:20 Kit Fitzgerald
4:45 Marchalore	John Sanborn
5:10 Andrew Moszynski	4:45 Maureen Connor
5:35 Colette	5:10 Andrew Moszynski
	5:35 Jean Dupuy

Feb. sat. 18	Feb. sun. 19
1:00 Alison Knowles	1:00 Alison Knowles
RICHARD HAYMAN 1:25 ~~Scott Johnson~~	1:25 Carmen Beuchat
1:50 Phil James	1:50 Jon Hassel
2:15 Janelle Winston	2:15 ~~Larry Miller~~ MITCH CORBER
2:40 Heloise Gold	2:40 Janelle Winston
MITCH CORBER 3:05 ~~Anne Hamburger~~	3:05 John Dino (SAVAS)+IAN ROSENFIELD
3:30 John Dino (SAVAS)+I.R.	3:30 Yoshisama Wada
RICHARD ZIGUN 3:55 ~~Maureen Connor~~	3:55 ~~Anne Hamburger~~ DUPUY
4:20 Mary Lucier	4:20 ~~Wendy Perron~~ NINA
NINA LUNBORG 4:45 ~~Wendy Perron~~	4:45 Jerry Hovagamyan
5:10 Peter Van Riper	5:10 Mary Lucier
DOFFY & CLAIRE 5:35 ~~George Maciunas~~	5:35 Heloise Gold
6:00 ALBANO QUATTI	Phil James
	6:00 ALBANO QUATTI

Feb. sat. 25	Feb. sun. 26
1:00 Peter Van Riper	1:00 Peter Van Riper
1:25 Carmen Beuchat	1:25 Olga Adorno
1:50 Scott Johnson	1:50 Charlie Morrow
2:15 Janelle Winston	2:15 ~~Larry Miller~~ SCOTT JOHNSON
2:40 Larry Miller	2:40 Alison Knowles
MITCH CORBER 3:05 ~~Anne Hamburger~~	3:05 Tim Maul
3:30 Jon Hassel	3:30 Colette
3:55 Christian Xatrec	3:55 Cara Brownell
4:20 Colette	4:20 ~~Wendy Perron~~ NINA LUNBORG
4:45 Mary Lucier	4:45 Kit Fitzgerald
5:10 Phil James	John Sanborn
5:35 Kit Fitzgerald	5:10 John Dino (SAVAS) with IAN ROSENFIELD
John Sanborn	5:35 George Maciunas
	6:00 ALBANO QUATTI

A TOWER IN THE AUDITORIUM OF P.S.I

A wooden tower 20 feet high with two ladders
reaching to platforms at 7 feet & 14 feet high,
placed against the west wall of the auditorium
at P.S. 1.
A series of 12 performances, lasting 25 minutes
each, will be presented each sat. & sun. during
February, 1978, between 1:00 PM – 6:00 PM.
These performances are based on a space limitation. The stages are 4 square feet each, situated in a vertical perspective.   —Jean Dupuy

This program is made possible with
assistance from N.E.A.

72

A Tower at P.S. 1

By JEAN DUPUY and PHIL JAMES

Feb. 27, 1978

To whom it may concern:

I was invited by the Institution for Art and Resources to make art performances during the month of February in the auditorium of P.S. 1. I decided to build a 21-foot-high tower with two platforms against the east wall of the room, midway between the north and south walls which are almost entirely windows. Last July I invited 31 artists to perform, giving them enough time to conceive of pieces for this situation.

On January 31 I went with two carpenters to build the tower and I discovered that a 12-foot-high sheetrock partition had been built several feet in from the original structure, decreasing the size of the space and totally obscuring the windows. I asked Linda Blumberg, an executive officer, to have these partitions removed. She said she could get two people to help me take them down but to keep them intact. When we met to do the work we realized it was impossible to achieve this in time for rehearsals and the first performances on February 4. Accidently a small hole was made in the east wall during rehearsal and another larger hole in the south wall during a performance. An artist decided to add two more holes as part of a piece and the audience joined the artist in making more holes in the south wall, intuitively responding to the artist intention in discovering the windows and filling the spaces once again with light, destructive art as a positive force.

The executive director then asked me: "Who is responsible? Who is going to pay?" Not only were the executive officers of the Institution for Art and Urban resources not present for this performance, but only one of them ever showed up and then only for a couple of hours our of a total of forty performing hours. Perhaps if they had showed more interest in performance art, they would have understood the real meaning of what happened. Perhaps, too, they would have taken more care to insure the comfort of the participants in the events. For fifteen of the performing hours there was no heat: several artists simply could not perform and those who did performed to emply chairs because nobody in the audience could stand the cold for more than a few minutes.

Jean Dupuy/Phil James

P.S. This is a paragraph sent to me on June 10,'77 from the Institute for Art and Urban Resources and signed by the program director: "We have not yet received word of funding for honorariums or advertising for the performer an honorium (maximum of $300). We do not expect to know until the fall. If we do receive this funding, it will of course be applied to the program." In fact we didn't get paid . . . not even the cost of the tower: $600.

CARMEN BEUCHAT

DAVID APPEL

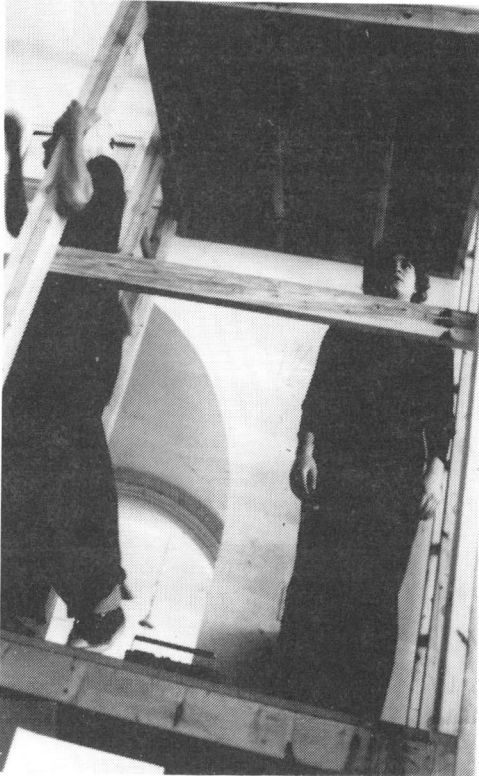

OLGA ADORNO

**MITCH CORBER
with JIM SUTCLIFFE**

CARA BROWNELL

75

JEAN DUPUY

ELAINE HARTNETT

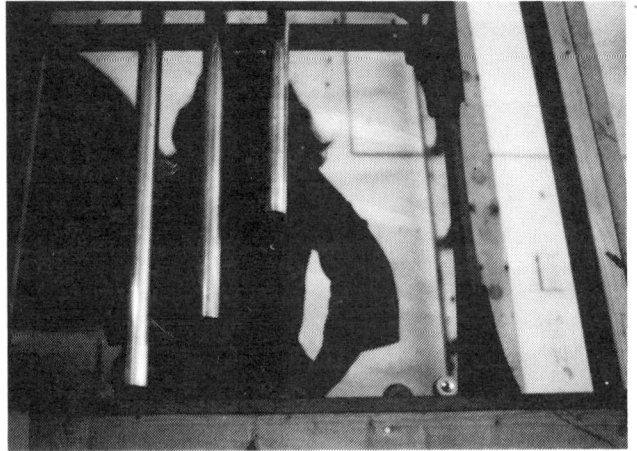

RICHARD HAYMAN—

JON HASSEL

76

SCOTT JOHNSON
with CHARLES MOULTON

← ALISON KNOWLES

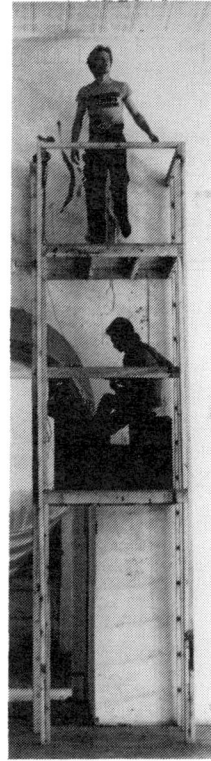

HELOISE
GOLD

PHIL JAMES

JERRY HOVAGIMYAN

NINA LUNDBORG

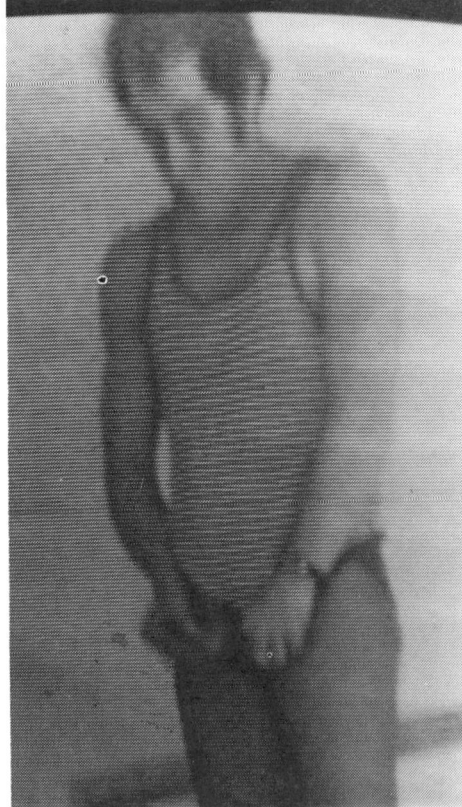

TIM MAUL

LARRY MILLER

PETER VAN RIPER

78

STUART SHERMAN

JOHN SANBORN

CHARLIE MORROW

YOSHIMASA WADA

JANELLE WINSTON

JOHN SAVAS

CHRISTIAN XATREC

Peter Moore

PHIL JAMES (Destruction of Wall)

Babette Mangolte

Wall after Destruction

80

MUSÉE DU LOUVRE

GRANDE GALERIE ET SALLE DES ÉTATS

16 OCTOBRE À 14 H. (LUNDI)

40 ARTISTES

ART - PERFORMANCES / MINUTE

AVEC LA COLLABORATION DU CENTRE GEORGES POMPIDOU

Art Performance/ One Minute

Musee du Louvre

Photographs by André Morain

J. D. TALKS WITH CHRISTIAN XATREC

X- FIRST,ALL THOSE COLLECTIVE SHOWS AND PERFORMANCES
IN NEW YORK DURING THE LAST TEN YEARS..THEN,WHY
IN PARIS NOW AND WHY AT THE LOUVRE ?

D- PARIS,WELL,FIRST OFF,IN JANUARY OF 78 I MADE A
VIDEO TAPE WITH 24 ARTISTS WHO WERE LIVING IN
FRANCE,CALLED:"ARTISTES PROPAGANDA" AT BEAUBOURG
WHICH ENCOURAGED ME TO COME "DO MY THING" IN PARIS
AND IN FRANCE. NOW,WHY THE LOUVRE ? WELL THAT GAVE
THE"NON-PERFORMING" ARTISTS THE CHANCE TO PERFORM..
BECAUSE IT WAS A MATTER OF RELATING THE WORK TO A
PAINTING..JUST FOR ONE MINUTE..A PERFORMANCE RELATED
TO A WORK OF ART CHOSEN FROM THE PAINTINGS IN THE
MUSEUM(WE HAD TO LIMIT OURSELVES TO JUST TWO ROOMS
IN THE PAINTING SECTION FOR PRACTICAL REASONS).

X- HOW DID YOU MANAGE TO GET IN TOUCH WITH THE LOUVRE?

D- THANKS TO BEAUBOURG..FIRST J.H.MARTIN PUT ME IN
CONTACT WITH MR.CUZIN AT THE LOUVRE-WHOM I MET IN
JUNE-AND HE IN TURN,GAVE ME PERMISSION TO PERFORM
ON THE FOLLOWING OCTOBER I5,A SUNDAY,WHEN ENTRANCE
IS FREE AND THE MUSEUM IS CROWDED,IN THE "SALLE DES
ETATS" AND IN THE "GRANDE GALERIE"-PERMISSION GRANTED
TO 40 ARTISTS AND 2 TECHNICIANS OF BEAUBOURG (FOR
THE VIDEO). SO THEN I INVITED 45 ARTISTS WITH THE
HELP OF A.LEMOINE- DURING THE SUMMER 39 ARTISTS
ACCEPTED.
THEN AROUND SEPTEMBER 20TH, AFEW WEEKS BEFORE THE
PERFORMANCES, CUZIN INFORMED ME THAT MR.LANDAIS
(DIRECTOR OF THE NATIONAL MUSEUMS OF FRANCE) WOULD
AGREE TO TAKE ONLY I5 PERFORMANCES BUT ONLY ON
CONDITION THAT THESE PERFORMANCES BE HELD ACCORDING
TO THE RULES IMPOSED ON TOURISTS,WHICH MEANS :
NO PERMISSION TO BRING ALONG ANY OBJECTS, NO
DISTURBING NOISE, NO ACTION WHICH MIGHT HOLD UP
THE FLOW OF VISITORS OR WHICH MIGHT PROVE MORALLY
SHOCKING,ETC...
I ACCEPTED THESE NEW CONDITIONS (I HAD NO OTHER
CHOICE) AND I SENT THEM 20 SYNOPSIS WHICH RESPECTED
THE RULES IMPOSED, AND WHICH I WROTE UP MYSELF AS I
DIDN'T HAVE THE TIME TO CONTACT THE ARTISTS(AS A
MATTER OF FACT, HOWEVER,I HAD DECIDED THAT THERE
WOULD BE 39 OF US AND THAT EACH PROJECT WOULD BE
CARRIED OUT AS PREVIOUSLY PLANNED ON SUNDAY THE I5TH
WITHOUT THE RESTRICTIONS IMPOSED BY LANDAIS,(WHOM,
AS A MATTER OF FACT,HAD MOVED THE DATE BACK TO THE
I6TH,A MONDAY).

X- TOUT D'ABORD,TOUS CES SHOWS COLLECTIFS,CES
   PERFORMANCES A NEW YORK..DEPUIS UNE DIZAINE
   D'ANNEES..ALORS POURQUOI PARIS MAINTENANT,ET
   POURQUOI AU LOUVRE ?
D- PARIS- D'ABORD EN JANVIER 78,J'AI FAIT,AVEC
   24 ARTISTES QUI VIVAIENT EN FRANCE UN VIDEO-
   TAPE:"ARTISTES PROPAGANDA",A BEAUBOURG..CE
   QUI M'A ENCOURAGE A VENIR"TRAVAILLER"A PARIS
   ET EN FRANCE..POURQUOI LE LOUVRE ? CELA OFFRAIT
   UNE SITUATION QUI PERMETTAIT AUX ARTISTES "NON
   PERFORMEURS" DE FAIRE UNE PERFORMANCE..CAR IL
   S'AGISSAIT DE FAIRE UNE RELATION AVEC UNE
   PEINTURE..UNE ACTION D'UNE MINUTE..LIEE A UNE
   OEUVRE CHOISIE PARMI LES PEINTURES DU MUSEE
   (IL FALLAIT SE LIMITER A UNE OU DEUX SALLES
   DANS LA SECTION PEINTURE..POUR DES RAISONS
   PRATIQUES.).
X- COMMENT ES-TU ENTRE EN CONTACT AVEC LE LOUVRE?
D- GRACE A BEAUBOURG-D'ABORD J.H.MARTIN M'A MIS
   EN CONTACT AVEC MR.CUZIN DU LOUVRE..QUE J'AI
   RENCONTRE EN JUIN..ET LEQUEL M'A DONNE LA
   PERMISSION DE FAIRE DES ACTIONS DANS LA "SALLE
   DES ETATS" ET DANS LA"GRANDE GALERIE"..UNE
   PERMISSION ACCORDEE POUR 40 ARTISTES ET DES
   TECHNICIENS(POUR LE VIDEO ET LES PHOTOS)..LE
   I5 OCTOBRE SUIVANT..UN DIMANCHE(C'EST GRATUIT)
   ET IL Y A DU MONDE. DONC,J'AI INVITE 45 ARTISTES
   AVEC L'AIDE D'A.LEMOINE-DANS LE COURANT DE L'ETE
   NOUS AVONS RECU 39 REPONSES POSITIVES.
   OR,VERS LE 20 SEPTEMBRE,QUELQUES SEMAINES AVANT
   LES PERFORMANCES,CUZIN M'A ANNONCE QUE MR.LANDAIS
   (DIRECTEUR DES MUSEES DE FRANCE)ACCEPTERAIT DE
   MONTRER UNE QUINZAINE D'ACTIONS SEULEMENT,ET A
   CONDITION QUE CES ACTIONS SOIENT ACCOMPLIES DANS
   LES REGLES QUE LE MUSEE IMPOSE AUX TOURISTES..
   C'EST A DIRE : AUCUN DROIT D'APPORTER DES OBJETS,
   AUCUN BRUIT GENANT,AUCUNE ACTION QUI INTERROMPERAIT
   LE TRAFFIC OU QUI CHOQUERAIT LA MORALE..ETC..
   J'AI ACCEPTE CES NOUVELLES CONDITIONS(JE N'AVAIS PAS
   LE CHOIX!)ET J'ENVOYAIS UNE VINGTAINE DE " SYNOPSIS",
   QUI RESPECTAIENT LES REGLES IMPOSEES,QUE J'ECRIVAIS
   MOI-MEME..CAR JE N'AVAIS PAS LE TEMPS DE CONTACTER
   LES ARTISTES(EVIDEMENT,JE DECIDAIS EN MOI-MEME QUE
   NOUS SERIONS 39 ET QUE CHAQUE PROJET SERAIT REALISE
   COMME PREVU,LE DIMANCHE I5 ,SANS LA CENSURE IMPOSEE
   PAR LANDAIS..QUI D'AILLEURS A REPOUSSE LA DATE
   AU I6,UN LUNDI...

MY SOLE CONCERN WAS TO GET THE AUTHORIZATION
BUT THERE WERE 40 ARTISTS ANNOUNCED ON MY
FLYER ! WHICH I HAD TO EXPLAIN BY SAYING THAT
20 ARTISTS HAD BEEN INVITED TO PERFORM WITH THE
HELP OF 20 OTHERS (THE PAINTERS OF THE WORKS CHOSEN
FROM AMONG THOSE ALREADY IN THE MUSEUM) 20+20=40
WE WERE ALSO HELPED BY THE FACT THAT 2 ARTISTS
HAD ALREADY PERFORMED IN THE LOUVRE IN PREVIOUS
YEARS(R.FILLIOU AND A.CADERE)-MOREOVER P.HULTEN
AND G.VIATTE PUT PRESSURE ON LANDAIS TO GET
PERMISSION.

X- THEN WHAT ABOUT THAT DAY IN THE LOUVRE ?

D- I THINK THERE WERE ABOUT 300 PEOPLE FROM THE ART
WORLD AND A LOT OF TOURISTS.OBVIOUSLY RATHER
SURPRISED..A LOT OF TENSION..THE CONSTANT THREAT
OF THE POLICE ..THE FLOW OF VISITORS HELD UP BECAUSE
WE HAD THE SPECTATORS SIT DOWN DURING THE PERFORMANCES
..ONE DISAPPOINTMENT ! NO VIDEO CAMERA-I DON'T KNOW
WHY THEY LET US DOWN..ALSO AN UNPLEASANT SURPRISE !
3 SMALL SMOKE BOMBS INTERRUPTED A PERFORMANCE WHICH
CAUSED THE MUSEUM DIRECTOR TO CLOSE ABRUPTLY THE
SALLE DES ETATS..NEVERTHELESS WE WENT ON WITH OUR
PERFORMANCES UNDER INCREDIBLE PRESSURE AND FINALLY
23 OUT OF THE 39 SCHEDULED PERFORMANCES WERE
CARRIED OUT. THE POLICE WERE WAITING FOR US AT THE
DOOR- BUT THERE WAS ACTUALLY NOTHING VERY SERIOUS.

X- SO,IN SHORT ?

D- A UNIQUE GATHERING OF ARTISTS AND SOME VERY IMPRESSIVE
PERFORMANCES,GIVEN THE SITUATION.
TOO BAD THAT WE DIDN'T HAVE THE VIDEO!
A LOT OF ARTISTS FROM PROVINCES,FROM PARIS AND
EVEN FROM NEW YORK MET EACH OTHER FOR THE FIRST TIME-
CONTACTS WERE MADE -THE MEDIA PERFORMANCE(ACTION)
WAS UNDERSTOOD THAT VERY DAY BY A QUITE A FEW ARTISTS
IN FRANCE AND BY SOME TOURISTS,I SUPPOSE.
AND THEN,TOO, A DATE WAS SET FOR THE FUTURE IN NEW YORK.
IN THE SHORT RUN HOWEVER "LE LOUVRE" WENT BY
UNNOTICED AND WAS SQUELCHED.
STRANGE,DON'T YOU THINK ?

TRANSLATED BY WARD SMITH,DEPT OF ROMANCE LANGUAGES
                      CITY COLLEGE OF NEW YORK.

DONC,LE TOUT ETAIT D'AVOIR L'AUTORISATIO..ET
MON AFFICHETTE ANNONCAIT 40 ARTISTES!..J'AI DU
"EXPLIQUER" EN DISANT QU'IL Y AVAIT 20 ARTISTES
INVITES A FAIRE DES ACTIONS EN COLLABORATION
AVEC 20 AUTRES (LES AUTEURS DES PEINTURES CHOISIES
DANS LES SALLES DU MUSEE)...20+20=40
CE QUI NOUS A AUSSI AIDE,C'EST QUE 2 ARTISTES DEJA
AVAIENT FAIT DES ACTIONS AU LOUVRE,DANS LES ANNEES
PRECEDENTES(FILLIOU ET CADERE)ET P.HULTEN ET
G.VIATTE ONT "POUSSE" POUR AVOIR LA PERMISSION DE
LANDAIS...

X-ALORS CETTE JOURNEE AU LOUVRE ?

D-JE PENSE QU'IL Y A EU ENVIRON 300 PERSONNES
"SPECIALISEES" ET BEAUCOUP DE TOURISTES..EVIDEMENT
ASSEZ SURPRIS..BEAUCOUP DE TENSION..UNE MENACE
CONSTANTE DE L'INTERVENTION DE LA POLICE..LE TRAFFIC
INTERROMPU!..CAR NOUS AVONS FAIT ASSEOIR LES
SPECTATEURS PENDANT LES ACTIONS..UNE DECEPTION :
PAS DE CAMERA DE VIDEO..JE NE SAIS PAS POURQUOI ON
NOUS A LAISSE TOMBER ?..UNE MAUVAISE SURPRISE : 3
PETITES BOMBES FUMIGENES QUI ONT INTERROMPU UNE
PERFORMANCE ET QUI ONT POUSSE LA DIRECTION DU MUSEE
A FERMER BRUSQUEMENT LA SALLE DES ETATS..QUAND MEME
NOUS AVONS POURSUIVI LES ACTIONS..DANS UNE TENSION
INIMAGINABLE..ET FINALEMENT 23 ACTIONS ACCOMPLIES
SUR 39 PREVUES..LA POLICE A LA SORTIE MAIS RIEN
DE GRAVE ,VRAIMENT

X- BREF ?

D- UNE REUNION D'ARTISTES..UNIQUE..DES ACTIONS TRES
FORTES DANS UNE TELLE SITUATION..
DOMMAGE QU'ON N'AIT PAS EU LE VIDEO..
BEAUCOUP D'ARTITES DE PROVINCE,DE PARIS ET MEME DE
NEW YORK SE SONT RENCONTRES POUR LA PREMIERE FOIS..
DES CONTACTS ONT ETE PRIS..LE MEDIA"PERFORMANCE" OU
"ACTION" A ETE COMPRIS, CE JOUR-LA,PAR UN CERTAIN
NOMBRE D'ARTISTES EN FRANCE.ET PAR QUELQUES TOURISTES!
ENFIN UN RENDEZ-VOUS A ETE PRIS,A NEW YORK,POUR LE
FUTUR..
A COURT TERME ,CEPENDANT, LE "LOUVRE" A PASSE
INAPERCU,A ETE ETOUFFE..
BIZARRE ?

JEAN DUPUY (Oct. 16, 1978)

I should like to express my thanks to the administration of the Musee du Louvre, whose role and whose principal concern, as they themselves confided to us, is to conserve.

Here are a few practical suggestions for them:

Let's lock up the Mona Lisa and forget about her! With a telescope system that I have invented each visitor could view her individually—and with one eye. Let's open the eye to the security of the property of the State! Let's provide Mona Lisa-type glass cages for all the art works displayed in the museum. The glass industry would thus stand to gain for it, as would the artists who could be hired as "Saint Gobain Cleaners." Better still, let's replace all the art works of the museum with copies made by the artist according to their own specialities. Fakes could be slipped in with copies, both to fill up empty spaces and to enrich the appearance of the national heritage.

Let's place all the original works in the vaults of the Bank of France after first re-modeling it in such a way that the works could be viewed through the telescope of my invention, mentioned above.
Conservez! con servez!

Je tiens à remercier la conservation du musée du Louvre, dont le rôle et le souci prin-cipal, nous a-t-elle confié, sont de conserver.

Pour elle, voici quelques suggestions d'ordre pratique:

Mettons la joconde dans un coffre fort et n'en parlons plus!—Avec un système télescopique de mon invention, chaque visiteur pourrait la voir—en solitaire—et d'un seul oeil—ouvron l'oeil sur la sécurité de la propriètè de l'ètat Français!

Multiplions les cages de verre du type joconde poor toutes les oeuvres esposèes dans le musèe—l'industrie du verre y gagnerait ainsi que les artistes qu'on pourrait engager comme "Laveurs de Saint Gobain."

Mieux encore! Rem plaçons toutes les oeuvres du musée par des copies faites par les artistes suivant leur specialitè—des faux paorraient même se glisser parmi les copies pour *et* combler les vides *et* enricher en apparence le patrimoine national.

Tous les originaux dans des coffres à la Banque de France, rebatie et aménagèe de telle sorte que l'on verrait les oeuvres grâce au systéme télescopique de mon inven-tion, dont j'ai déjà ,parlé. Conservez! Con servez!

BEFORE THE PERFORMANCES

MARTINE ABALLEA

OLGA ADORNO

ARTHUR AESCHBACHER

JACQUELINE DAURIAC

FUTURO

CESAR COFONE

PHILIPPE DEMONTAUT

JEAN DUPUY

LEA DOUGLAS

CHARLES DREYFUS

ROBERT FILLIOU

JACQUES HALBERT

TIMOTHY HENNESSY

JOEL HUBAUT

TIM MAUL

JACQUES MONORY

COME MOSTA-HEIRT

GREGORY MOLNAR

ANDREW MOSZYNSKI

JACQUES OHAYON

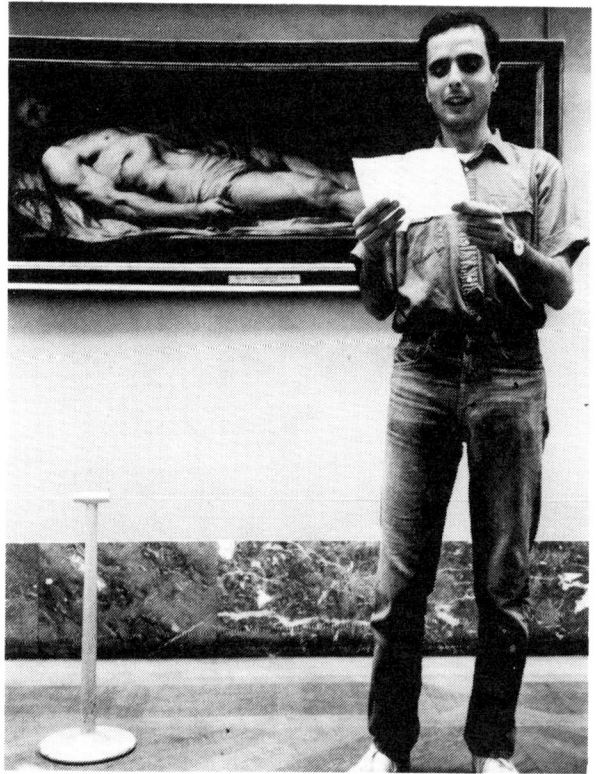

ORLAN

UNTEL

JEAN ROUALDES

MARTIAL THOMAS

95

SMOKE BOMB

**WITH THE POLICE AFTER THE
PERFORMANCES**

96

ABOUT
405 EAST 13 STREET
BY:

Joseph Alessi. Brendan Atkinson. Charles Atlas.
Claudio Badal. Michael Breed. Norvie Bullock.
Stephen Crawford. Juan Lowney. Jean Dupuy. Karen
Edwards. Dana Egan. Jeanne Gollobin. Paul Jay.
Fred Krughoff. Shigeko Kubota. Gianfranco Mantegna.
Lizbeth Marano. Gordon Matta Clark. Antoni Miralda.
Charlotte Moorman. Antoni Muntadas. Chris Murphy.
Nam June Paik. Marc Rattner. Larry Rivers. Richard Squires. Fred Stern. Terry
Stevenson. Patrick Waters. Irene Winter.

405 East 13 Street, one flight up
from May 4 to 14
1 pm-7pm
opening Friday 4, 4 pm

About
405 East 13th Street (#1)

By LAURIE ANDERSON

"Spatializing" and its implications were the premises on the 34 artists who participated in Jean Dupuy's show "About 405 East 13th Street" early this summer. "About" dealt with various interior, exterior, and interfacial aspects of Dupuy's loft in terms of description and manipulation. Microscopic and telescopic realignments undermined the standard subject-object relationship. The show's site, a living and working loft, dramatized this "spatializing" approach. Psychological and visual conditions imposed on the viewer in gallery space did not exist. The murky and raw space contributed to the intial impression of casual disarray rather than that of a carefully spotlighted area for the display of discrete objects.

Several of the artists operated on the premises of near-invisibility. The most obstinately flat-footed piece was that of Gordon Matta Clark who washed one of the windows, a barely perceptible change in the overall scheme of things but one that literally allowed for more visibility. In a counter move, Brendan Atkinson almost sealed off a window by building a curved wooden wall extension the texture and color of the brick wall on either side of the window. This trompe-l'oeil extension came off as a kind of private, practical joke on Minimalism: its function was to extend and block, but its look was architectonic. Preoccupation with "negative space," the wall, were overcome by occupying and amplifying that space. Although the window was blocked or closed, the extension left a narrow slit on one side. The interior edge was painted blue, a metaphorical compensation for the blocked-out strip of sky. Being opened and closed simultaneously—a paradox the Duchamp made operative in his New York studio—is realized in Atkinson's piece in a less analytical, more massive way similar to the Egyptian impulse to seal off the pyramids.

Three pieces that made slight readjustments and realignments in the ceiling, wall, and floor did so by shifting and relocating surfaces. There is a broad green stripe that runs the length of the loft (135'). Fred Krughoff isolated a rectangular section on the floor with taped lines. Half of the section was brown (floor) and the other half green (stripe). Then he painted the brown half green and the green half brown. In context, this visual detour ruptured the continuity of the streamlined stripe. Another piece that had a pointing function was Marc Rattner's small piece of waxed paper attached to the wall. Punctures were made in the surface of the wall. As the ultimate step in the dialectics of drawing, the paper expressed only its physical placement. Its transparency outflanked recent investigations of the implications of being flush with the wall. Rattner gets around the mechanics of "the drawing which makes itself" by literalizing the metaphor of "a painting is a window on space." Nam June Paik, in a move similar to Rattner's, projected a videotape of the ceiling onto the ceiling.

Chris Murphy placed rubbings of the slightly coffered ceiling on the floor below. This inversion—giving the viewer the same visual experience when looking up as when looking down—forced an awareness of an obvious but still surprising optical fact: visual information is typically acquired at a height of five to six feet below the ceiling. Identical views above and below located the viewpoint in terms of anatomy.

Two pieces that dealt with light used the loft situation as a starting point. Jeanne Gollobin placed a long candle along the wall parallel with some electric wiring. The lit paper burned gradually in a kind of parody of the lightproducing electricity moving along the wire. Nancy Harris focused on the shadow cast by a suspended lamp. She painted the shadow gray, effecting a visual double take when the lamp swayed or another light source relocated the lamp's shadow.

The window as a frame for opening out onto other spaces was used figuratively in several pieces. Paul Cinelli placed a Filippo Lippi print (*Madonna and Child in a Landscape*) on the ceiling where its function as a window was thwarted. Karen Edwards put a narrow mirror in a window frame which reflected a film of the ocean. Jean Dupuy projected films of people walking and skating onto the floor. These rectangular and opening-out framing devices relocated the position and function of the window.

Similarly, Antoni Muntadas isolated extra-loft situations in his drawers of smell piece. "May 1 '73, I went through all the areas between 11th and 14th Streets and 1st and A Avenues. Four spots were considered as characteristic because of their particular smells. These four locations show an itinerary and describe an environment that surrounds 405 East 13th Street." Muntadas then collected characteristic objects from each location (e.g. shoes from a shoe repair shop) and installed them in labeled drawers. Two of the pieces hinged on movement as a modulating factor of perception. An accordionlike stretching of perception was most clearly demonstrated n the swing which Joseph Alessi installed in the loft.

Larry Rivers' videotape of the building's elevator recorded vertical movement, but the basic thrust of the tape seemed reminiscent of the carnival aspect of Happenings. Crowds of people drinking tea, potted plants, rugs, and chairs were crammed into the elevator; a girl appeared nude, then dressd, then nude again in a series of sight gags, slapstick, and mugging for the camera that got in the way of what seemed to have been a clear idea.

Lizbeth Marano's photograph of the door to the loft was an exact-scale duplicate of the door mounted on the door itself—an exercise in illusion that couldn't have been experienced in a less functional situation. Expectancy and surprise, qualities that photorealists trade on, were strictly and directly applied.

The announcement of "About" was circumscribed by a floor plan of the loft and two artists chose to deal with the entire space. Richard Squires built a model of the loft which was suspended int the center. The clear proposition (let ½" = 1') slipped around minimalist rhetoric about scale and eluded the coy miniaturization of artists who work with the diminutive. When something is scaled down from its standard size, whether it's a midget, a doll, or a Coke bottle, it often elicits a mixture of patronization and dismissal. Squires' model, on the other hand, had none of the coquetry of the maquette. In fact, its crafted look rendered the actual loft look like a gross blow-up.

Another piece of Jean Dupuy's dealt with the space as a whole but took a more prosaic, reportorial tack. A large wooden map of the loft was set up vertically and several square holes were cut out in parts of the diagram. Slides of activities peculiar to each area were projected through the holes from the back. The didactic premise was similar to a museum display, but the chosen activities were small, random moments of domestic life: washing hands, turning a page, testing a sauce. Anne Tardos was also interested in connecting the private parts (kitchen, bathroom, bedroom) with the public space. She placed a monitor in Dupuy's map that recorded what was going on in the kitchen and placed a microphone over the kitchen table. These bugging devices seemed to accept the distinction between public and private while subverting it.

A later addition to Dupuy's map was a peephole in the center. Through this peephole was a slide of the wooden diagram. The sudden shock of seeing the scale model of the scale model it was set In made the viewer something of a voyeur, focusing on the very act of seeing itself as a highly self-conscious activity.

Other of Dupuy's pieces had the function of opening up space in unpredictable ways. An arrow of tape on the floor pointed to a small mirror leaning against a wall. This reflected the image caught by another mirror attached to the ceiling opposite an airduct that led up through the chimney to a small patch of sky. Thus, by looking down at the mirror on the floor, you were looking into a narrow shaft and up at the sky 60 feet away. This stretching and inversion became the jumping off point of another mirror piece. A narrow mirror was set at an angle on a window sill. The window was opposite the brick wall of another building but the image in the mirror was a long tilting shaft with a strip of sky at the bottom.

Another of Dupuy's pieces, in many ways the most vivid, was the most invisible. The loft is back to back with a beauty parlor, and Dupuy placed microphones in the shop. The sounds were then piped in and amplified. Bits of gossip, scissor snipping, the exhaust of hair spray cans, and banal beauty parlor shoptalk were blown up. This transfer of the minute over distance was the principle behind Dupuy's dust piece as well. The loft was swept daily and the accumulated pile of dust was spotlighted from above. Thirty feet away a telescope focused on the pile. The first impression of the telescope view was that of a rugged, mountainous landscape. Suddenly, what appeared a gargantuan cigarette butt loomed up; the telescope had become, in a sense, a microscope.

These rapid switches of viewpoints informed much of the work in the show. Many of the artists have been deeply influenced by Dupuy's unique and visionary sense of scale and visual transformations. Dupuy denies this influence and says only, "I wanted to design a trap, to make limitations to work within. It's like a joke, really, but a joke on a level I like to be."

Several pieces in the show concentrated on measurement and opted for a more or less mathematical definition of "About." the geographic location of the loft in terms of the neighborhood and city was pinpointed in Irene Krugman's piece. She transported a rod from 310 Riverside Drive to the loft and wrote, "I wanted to give some measurements for comparison to get people thinking about the space between 310 Riverside Drive and 405 East 13th Street as well as the relative positions of the hanging rod 1) in the former space 2) and now inclined and touching wall and floor. For instance, it is now installed 25' off the ground 33' lower than formerly." The original function of the rod — hanging paintings — was transformed by the move into a kind of yardstick that located one space in terms of another. Juan Downey's videotape "From Loft to Loft" recorded a walk from Downey's loft to Dupuy's and the "footage" — taken literally — measured distance in terms of steps.

Two artists who dealt with measuring and recording lines of sight were Gianfranco Mantegna and Bob Fiore. Mantegna took a photograph from the roof of the Con Edison plant that looms over the east side of 14th Street. He took the photograph to a mathematician who calculated the exact distance from roof to plant working only with data provided by the photograph. The thrust of the piece, the transformation of pure visual data into precise measurement via mathematical procedures, underlined the almost unconscious, quasi-mathematical operations of everyday seeing, the little calculations that allow us to say, "I see a man standing approximately 20 feet in front of a building which is two blocks away." Bob Fiore used the line of sight to demonstrate an erratically funny brand of existentialism. He took a photograph from the window of his fourth floor loft (two floors above Dupuy's) of the building opposite. (At the time, four firemen were in the act of trying to extinquish a small blaze.) In Dupuy's loft, he placed the photograph on the window which was directly below the window from which the photograph was taken. The view from the second floor window could only roughly correspond with the architectural elements in the photograph because of radical foreshortening, thus situating the viewer 20' below the chosen view and forcing acknowledgemnt of his 'arbitrary' viewpoint. The presence of the firemen added something of a Marx Brothers touch that lightened the impact.

Three artists chose to deal with "About" in terms of time. Each day of the show, Gianfranco Mantegna posted a photograph and descriptions of events that occurred exactly five years previous to the present date (e.g. the '68 uprisings at the Sorbonne). The calendar as a devise for separating and organizing time was collapsed into a double-barrelled instrument that zeroed in on the concept of time itself as merely a mechanism that prevents everything from happening at once. Irene Winter's piece adhered more strickly to the premises of "About." She placed a terracotta potsherd (c. 2000 BC) on the terracota brick wall (c. 2000 AD) of the loft. The grand scale of archaeological approximations of time (rounding off to the nearest thousand) was in sharp contrast with the modesty of the artifacts. The four millennia that separated the terracottas were telescoped by their physical proximity via a sensitivity to time and distance.

Three artists defined "About" in terms of words. Dana Egan wrote the names of participating artists on a piece of tape stuck to the wall. As straightforward enumeration, it had some interest but its main point seemed to be a comment on the show as a group effort. There was no indication of who did what in "About." The absence of name tags underlined the problem character of the show and the impression that several of the pieces seemed to be the products of a single sensibility. Andrea

Halpern's Latin inscription in foot-high Roman type ("Decorationes Domus Amici Frequentantis") playfully stressed the architectural and ironically deflated the scale. Paul Jay took a slide of his own wall on which was written, "I intend to photograph the wall and use it in illuminating Jean Dupuy's wall. Watch the light." This slide was projected at Dupuy's. Beside it was a note, "Helpful Hints on the Projection: The light in this piece works as a vehicle for certain information concerning two specific walls (mine and Dupuy's). This information in its turn acts as a vehicle for certain implications (the art concerns) which may be called (for our purposes) meaning. The light mechanisms via which this implied meaning is transferred stand as a metaphor for the wall verbal meaning (the writing on the wall) is transferred. I am concerned with your reactions but I don't want to know them."

Art Forum (Sept., 1973), repr. by permission.

By ALAN MOORE

Dupuy presented *Table* in the second of two shows in his studio, "About 405 East 13th Street (2)." "About 405 . . . (1)," was held in 1973, and the unexpected response led to this year's exhibition, which included the work of nearly 40 disparate artists, young and old, known and unknown. Dupuy organized these shows, which amalgamated certain underground tendencies, as an alternative to the strictures of a gallery situation. Unlike the galleries—clean, self-effacing marketplaces—the pieces at 405 were crammed together, unidentified, and shown without commercial motive. Like the "Anarchitecture" show at 112 Greene Street gallery, the two exhibitions had the feel of manifestos. Most of the works were loosely related, dealing as they did with the space and/or the architectural facts of 405. The first show pleased Dupuy more than the second because it was nearly invisible, the pieces more subtly in touch with the givens of their site. It was almost, he said, as if a meta-studio had arisen within the real one. Dupuy's own works for "About 405 . . . (2)" are sited within his studio to such an extent that to adapt them to another place would prove difficult.

With these pieces Dupuy enlarges the optical systems (of mirrors, lenses, and lights) he had previously confined to his earlier wooden boxes and collages. For *Floor Mirror*, Dupuy cut two holes in his floor, one at the east and one at the west wall, and stuck a mirror in each. A stage spotlight, shining into the mirror near the east wall, sends a strong beam under the floor. Looking into the hole at the west wall, one sees the long thin corridor formed by the floor joists. Except to carpenters and wreckers, it is a strange sight, and peculiarly scaleless. This dusty region beneath the floor might be a mineshaft, or, an archaeological excavation. It's the first Earthwork in the floor that I've seen.

Floor Mirror, as a lateral section, can be related to Gordon Matta-Clark's *Splitting*, a bisected house in Englewood, New Jersey. Although Dupuy's mirror setup is tiny compared to Matta-Clark's grandly scaled act of art, neither piece relates part to part as a means of underscoring the clarity of architectural structure. Rather, like an anomic archaeology, these works reveal raw tectonic mysteries.

Two other mirrors placed by Dupuy reflect the sky. One stuck in a hole in the wall, catches sky at the top of a bricked-up chimney shaft, the other through ventilation pipes. A third mirror piece, *Window Mirror*, shows something of Dupuy's working method. Two windows in the loft "open" smack into the brick wall of the building adjoining 405. Dupuy was irritated by this architectural absurdity — "It's a Magritte," he said, "and I didn't like it so much. I'm not so Surrealistic." To counter the effect, Dupuy placed a strip of mirror just outside the window to reflect the sky. Beyond the ironic contravention of a Surrealistic reality, *Window Mirror* is striking because it introduces light illogically. The mirror glares during the day like a fluorescent tube. The parts of the optical system become disjointed: a patch of light reflected on some ceiling tiles does not make them seem illuminated, merely cleaner.

Dupuy began *Window Mirror* as part of an optical system that would enable him to know the weather from his bed. At one point, he thought to drill through the adjoining wall to the church beyond so that, as he said, he could watch the Mass in bed like a Spanish king in the Escorial. There were practical problems with this installation—the plaster from the drilling would have fallen conspicuously into the church—so for "About 405 . . . (1)" Dupuy substituted an audial project, placing twin microphones in a back wall to monitor the sounds in an adjoining beauty parlor.

Art Forum (Oct., 1974), repr. by permission.

RICHARD SQUIRES

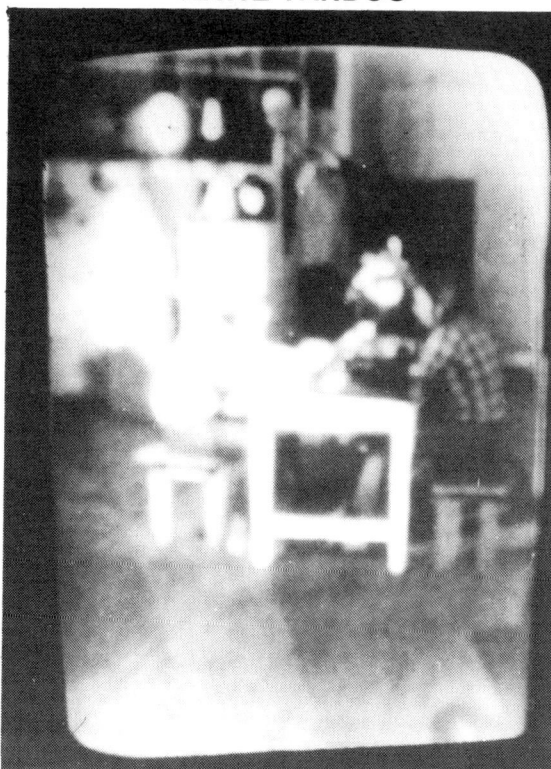

ANNE TARDOS

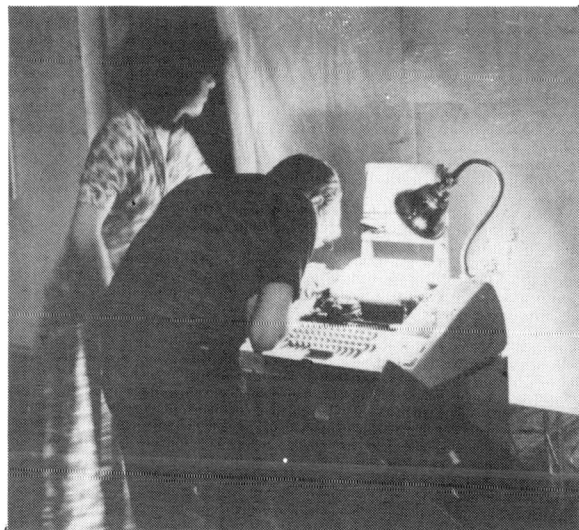

FRED STERN

IRENE WINTER

Gianfranco Mantegna

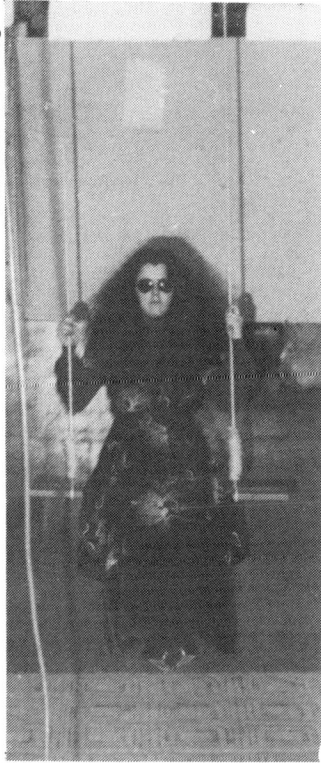

Lizbeth Marano

Gianfranco Mantegna

GOD BLESS THIS LOFT

Lizbeth Marano

106

CLAUDIO BADAL

NORVIE BULLOCK

PAUL CINELLI

STEPHEN CRAWFORD

Juan Downey

JUAN DOWNEY

Juan Downey

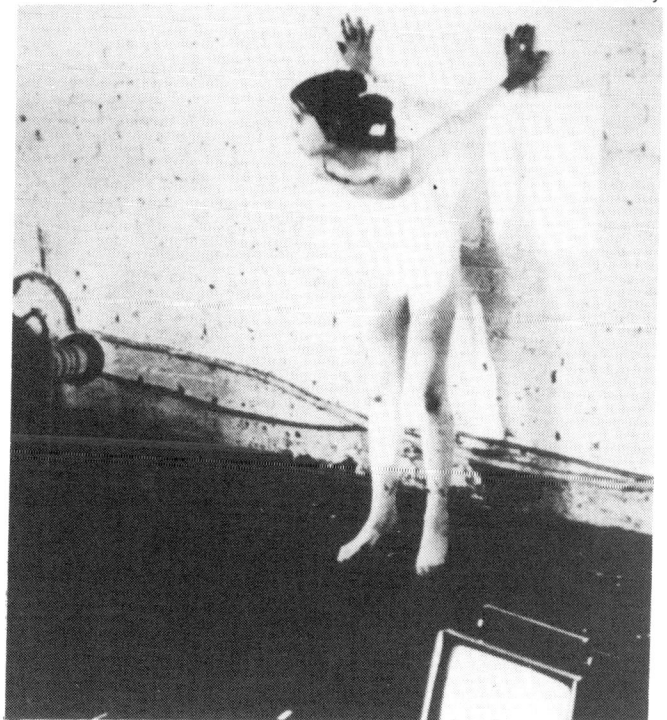

Gianfranco Mantegna

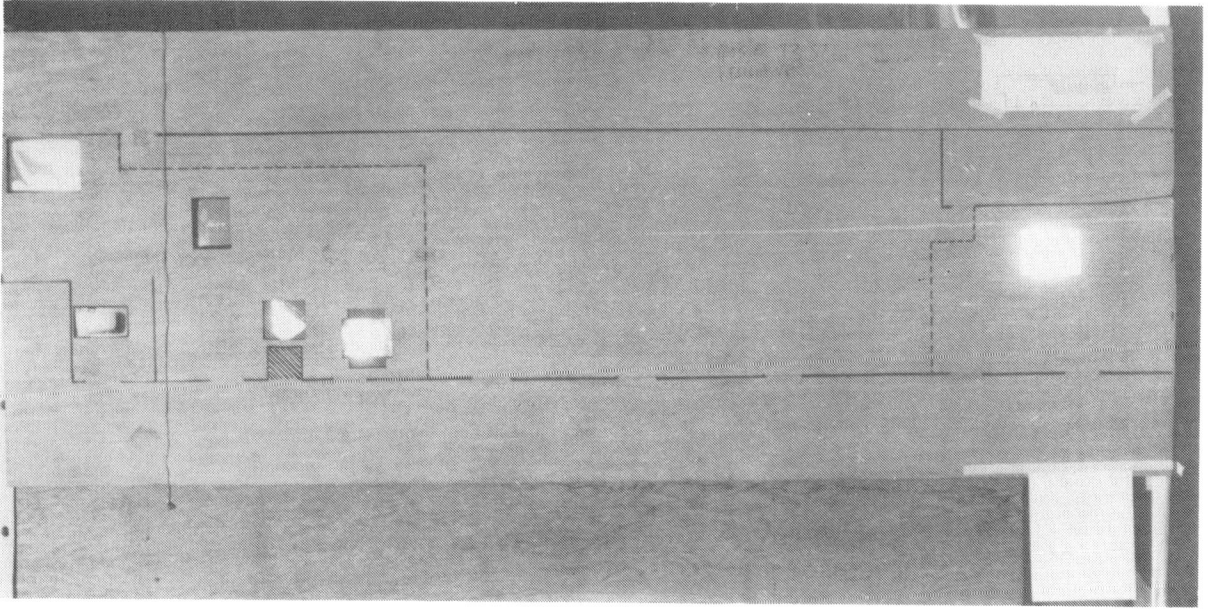

Richard Stern

JEAN DUPUY

Gianfranco Mantegna

GORDON MATTA CLARK

SHIGEKO KUBOTA

Gianfranco Mantegna

FRED KRUGHOFF

GIANFRANCO MANTEGNA

Lizbeth Marano

PAUL JAY

LIZBETH MARANO

NANCY HARRIS

Gianfranco Mantegna

LARRY RIVERS

Lizbeth Marano

BOB FIORE

ANTONI MIRALDA

Gianfranco Mantegna

CHARLOTTE MOORMAN

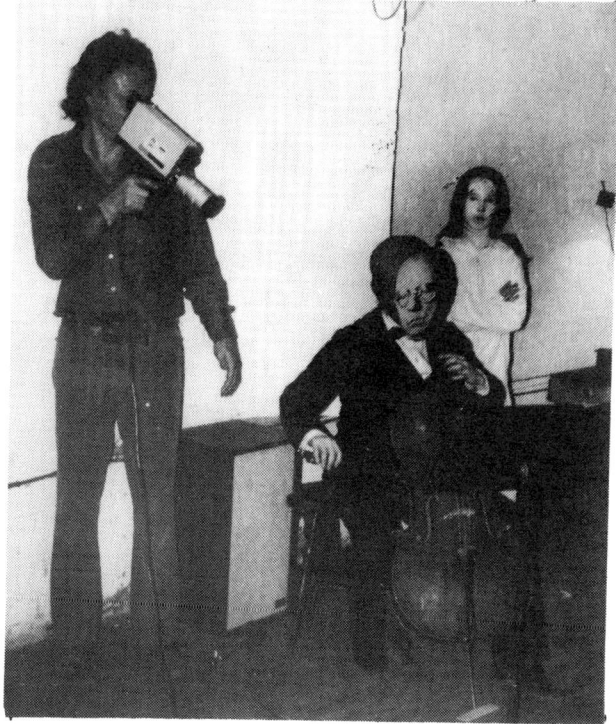

Gianfranco Mantegna

Richard Stern

ANTONI MUNTADAS　　**IRENE KRUGMAN**　　**CHRIS MURPHY**　　111

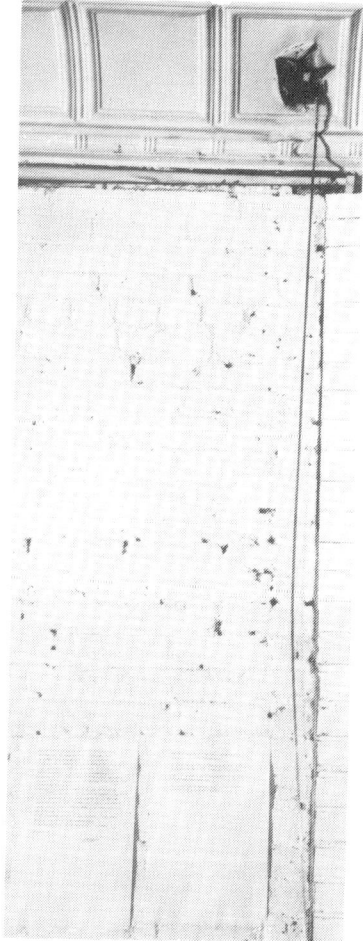

ABOUT 405 EAST 13th STREET (2)

BY:

405 EAST 13th STREET, one flight up

April 18, 19, 20, 21
1 pm- 7 pm
opening Thursday 18, 4 pm

Revolving Stage

Laurie Anderson. Brendan Atkinson. Charlie Atlas. Kathryn
Bigelow. Jim Cobb. Jay Craven. Stephen Crawford. Frazer
Dougherty. Jean Dupuy. Bob Fiore. Jeanne Gollobin. Deedee
Halleck. Susan Hartnett. Gene Highstein. Nancy Holt. Jerry
Hovagimyan. Paul Jay. Poppy Johnson. Philip Kaplan. Shigeko
Kubota. Emile Laugier. Jeffrey Lew. Gianfranco Mantegna.
Lizbeth Marano. Gordon Matta Clark. Antoni Muntadas. Donald
Munroe. Chris Murphy. Claes Oldenburg. Patty Oldenburg.
Nam June Paik. Larry Rivers. Lynda Rodolitz. Joan
Schwartz. Alison Sky. Tony Smith. Irene Winter.

PERFORMANCES:
(contribution $ 2)

Friday, April 26   JEAN DUPUY: Steel,
8.30 pm   PHIL GLASS: Solos (Two Pages, 1968. Music in Contrary Motion, 1969)

Saturday, April 27   ROSALYND FRIEDMAN: Frank Wagner's Body Works,
8.30 pm   JUAN DOWNEY: The Flag

Sunday, April 28   BRENDAN ATKINSON: Taping Up
8.30 pm

112

About
405 East 13th Street (#2)

By P. I. GREENE

For the second year in a row, a show called "About 405 East 13th Street" has been held at 405 East 13th Street, in the loft of Jean Dupuy. Unlike the majority of independent exhibitions tied to no gallery or institution, which generally show the work of a single individual, this is a group show including the works of some 38 persons, six of who live in the building, the rest artists who nonetheless have addressed themselves to the building/loft.

Given the theme implicit in the title, the most successful pieces were precisely those which were most closely related to the space at hand. Different artists, of course, manipulated the space in different ways, a number insisting on the contrast between outside and inside. Gordon Matta Clark, for example, cut a whole in the wall near the entrance and accompanied the hole with a photo of a menacing arm reaching through and up to the spring of the lock on the door; Jeffrey Lew placed one of his plexiglass pentagons imprinted with a huge photograph of a starfish just outside an open window, giving one the sense of an alien presence to the indoor space and connecting one to the out-of-doors; Nancy Holt covered an entire window with white cardboard and via a stage projector and mirror, juxtaposed a circle of artificial light replete with heat waves with a cut-out circle in the cardboard letting in clear day light.

With respect to the space, Dupuy is evidently in a rather privileged position since it is his loft, and his work in the show (seemingly separate pieces which function together toward the same end) probes the limits of the space by several means. Two versions of Vitruvian man (studies by Leonardo da Vinci and Francesco di Giorgio of the porportions of the human body at the same time within a square and a circle, which represent the symbolic structure of the position of Renaissance man in the universe) have been placed on the ceiling, each within a square containing a circle that forms the decorative motif of the tin roofing. From the ceiling we are led to the floor where a light projector illuminates a mirror placed through the floor-boards at an angle of 45 degrees, such that one is able to see in architectural section one's own feet standing on the floor and the emptiness below, from which one is separated only by the narrow flooring. It is a weird feeling—one generally thinks of a floor as "solid," yet here there is rather a sense of the precariousness of this supporting strip that resists gravity and keeps us anchored on the second storey. In the third member of this grouping, Dupuy leads us to the upper floor, again without changing place, via a drawing table on which a portfolio is open to a white page that contains a lens in the center. This lens is connected to a periscope; a mirror just *above* the table sends us through the periscope into the loft above, where—for the duration of the opening at least—Dupuy himself could be seen sitting at a table. At the same time, a video camera is registering the back of the viewer bent over the lens at the drawing table and the image is projected on a television screen upstairs, so that one sees oneself monitored through the periscope as well. That is to say, *you* look through the lens, and *you* have become the canned software, while the upstairs loft becomes the real space you are voyeuristically invading. The strength of these three pieces lies then in the extension of one's perceptions by varying means so that the loft suddenly becomes a rather arbitrary unit within "Universal" space.

Another successful piece within the context of "About . . . " was that of Claes Oldenburg, who lived in the building for several years. Oldenburg blew up a sheet of calculations which documented the vibrations of the building on a given day in January, 1966—his varying perceptions of those vibrations a function of what else he was doing at a given moment. The page was hung about mid-way down the length of the loft, on a wall seared by a long vertical crack, the presence of which served to make the calculations as vital and menacing in 1974 as they had been 8 years earlier.

Brendon Atkinson, who lives in the loft immediately above Dupuy's, also made a

114

very personal piece—a column from floor to celing, marked top and bottom with arrows of the sort used in architectural plans to indicate dimensions. In the center of the column was cut a window in which the fluorescent numbers: 10′9¼″ were visible. The problem set by Atkinson, to sculpturally define the space between Dupuy's loft and his own, is well realized by the wooden column. The addition of the fluorescent numbers illuminated by black light in plexiglass window, however, were rather a distraction than a complement to the column, seducing the viewer into the mysteries of the window rather than emphasizing the vertical space he wished to measure.

The fact of the show's title and the limits posed by the space of the loft provided an opportunity for a number of artists to move outside of the usual structure of their art work in addressing themselves to the loft.

Tony Smith, who is such a perfectionist in the presentation of his finished work, could, in this situation, permit himself the freedom to present disconnected fragments of a model done for a large piece shown at the Los Angeles County Museum—disjointed members composed of the small pyramids and tetrahedra Smith uses as his units of construction. By so doing, Smith, a former architect himself, permits us to share in the architecture of a piece—units joined by tape to form segments of a whole—that is a response to the architectural problem of the space in the loft.

The piece of Fraser Dougherty also fits into the context of a departure from studio works. Dougherty is a painter who generally does large canvases divided into geometric units which also reflect progressions of color. Still using color progressions, but departing from the controlled scale of a stretched canvas, Dougherty in this case has applied a series of pastel-tone color cards in a strip down the center of the ceiling, each card within its own square of the tin-paneled surface. He thus defines the length of the space by a progression of color within geometric units, adding that delicious element of discovery for the viewer in the exploitation of a surface not often used by artists.

The loft, in other words, introduced another factor into the work, which is no longer only about the artist and his medium (the finished product to exist independent of its eventual setting), but is now also about the definition of a specific space. Even works like the "cookies" of Hannah Wilke—36 soft, rose-colored clay cunts, each different, sweetly folding in on themselves—which remain essentially the same pieces as those which left the artist's studio, become allied to the space by virtue of the white stripe the artist painted on the floor on which to set the pieces. Likewise, the quantity of double-headed and double-tailed quarters miraculously fused in a secret process by Kathryn Bigelow become a part of the loft through their situation in the space. The coins were set on a chest-high table beneath a sharply-focused light fixture, and because of their height it was impossible not to interact with them (a number of dinners were won and lost over that table).

Other artists, like Poppy Johnson, tied their work more closely to the loft. Understandably attracted by the potential of brick walls for fresco, her solution (draped cloth and the head of Adam from the Sistine ceiling) is nevertheless too literary and too literal. A less specific choice would in fact have left more for the viewer to get into. In a sense, I feel the work falls into a category of overstatement—an assumption that "more is more" which actually turns out to be "more is less," that is also characteristic of a couple of other pieces in the show. Gianfranco Mantegna incised a spiral in the center of the floor which hits the west (long) wall at a point where three bricks have been taken out of the chimney and an angled mirror inserted through which one can see the sky. On that wall is an enlarged map of Manhattan, and the spiral continues from the rectangle of 405 East 13th Street out into the world.

The idea of Laurie Anderson—to stretch tension wires from floor to ceiling and across the length and width of the loft at the ceiling in such a way that each wire would resonate on a different tone when plucked, based upon the dimensions of the loft—was in theory a fine adaptation to the space.

Also raising the question of overstatement, or, in this case, the alternative of a Duchamp-like esotericism, is the mouse-trap of Philip Kaplan. Baited and set in a hole cut in the floor-boards and covered with clear plexiglass, it is accompanied by the words, "La petite sorciere," which translate into English as "The little witch." In order to understand Kaplan's pun, one must not only be able to translate the original phrase, but also to know that mousetrap in French is "La souriciere." One is left with the supposition that it is more a private joke between Kaplan and Dupuy, or that it has been done precisely because it is the loft of Dupuy, and that this therefore is the one piece that related not only to the loft but also to its owner.

Nevertheless, it is this very attribute: the re-introduction of a literary (extra-structural) reference which has marked the transition from minimalism to post-minimal abstraction in the work of such artists as Bruce Naumann. In a way it is a direct outgrowth of the work of Duchamp, and marks the reinstatement of humor which seemed to have been so lacking in the work of the minimal artists.

Even the piece of Jim Cobb—a rectangular wooden structure creating a passage scaled to the height of a man, with doors closing off three sections—which in shape might have passed for a minimalist construction, is not that at all. For one thing, it is painted brown. Now, no minimal work was ever painted brown. White, grey, or the natural color of the material; essentially the absence of color. Cobb's choice therefore is a statement of opposition, an intellectual reference, for brown is the sum of *all* colors; and movement through the structure, which thereby engages the participation of the public, is a microcosmic movement through space in time.

The richness of Lizbeth Marano's piece is also for me part of the post-minimal tradition, yet the means by which it is realized call to mind some of the later projects of E.A.T. A varnished wooden box, longer than it is high, with a horizontal slit across one long side, is set on a pedestal so that the slit is essentially at nose level. Inside is a veritable jungle of hyacinths, partially visible and overwhelmingly fragrant, helped by the self-contained ventilation and blower system housed in the roof of the box. It is a tangle of green and rosey color; the mysterious garden; that faint whiff you could never quite seize, at last magnified, enough.

It is clearly not possible to describe each and every piece in detail. A thing I particularly liked in this show, however, was the freshness of juxtaposition, the meeting of pieces by artists of different so-called "generations" and "persuasions," who would not ordinarily be shown together (except in Whitney annuals, where nothing is related to anything else). It is that fresh quality that (one finally understands) one had been prepared for outside the entrance by the "piece" of Irene Winter. In the stairwell, to the right of the door, a blow-up of a devastating view of Tom Hoving and the Met, taken from a *New York Times* Book Review, is placed alongside of a blow-up of the announcement of the show (a plan of the space of the loft, with the participants' names contained within). Winter is an art historian, who lives in the building—and this is an academic piece—yet it provides the intellectual framework for the show, with its reference to the contrast between corrupt establishment space and the openness of non-aligned, independent space.

DUPUY LOFT DURING SHOW; NORTH VIEW

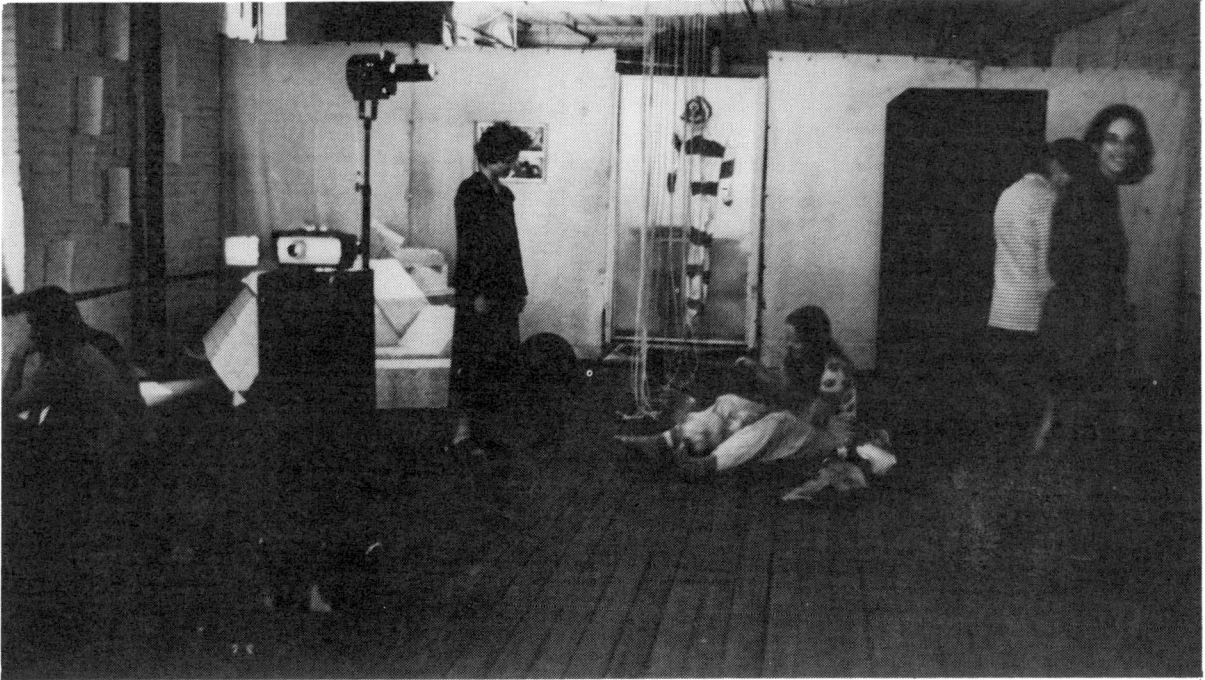

DEEDEE HALLECK

DUPUY LOFT DURING SHOW; SOUTH VIEW

117

KATHRYN BIGELOW

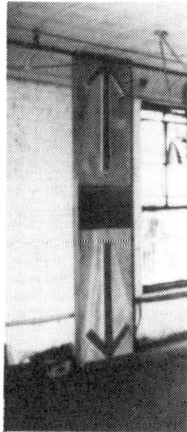

BRENDAN ATKINSON

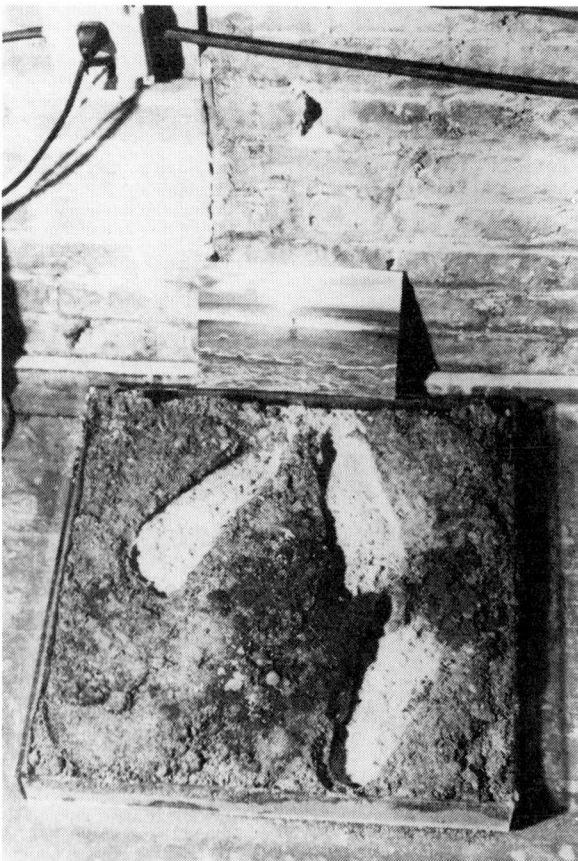

JUAN DOWNEY

STEPHEN CRAWFORD

JEAN DUPUY

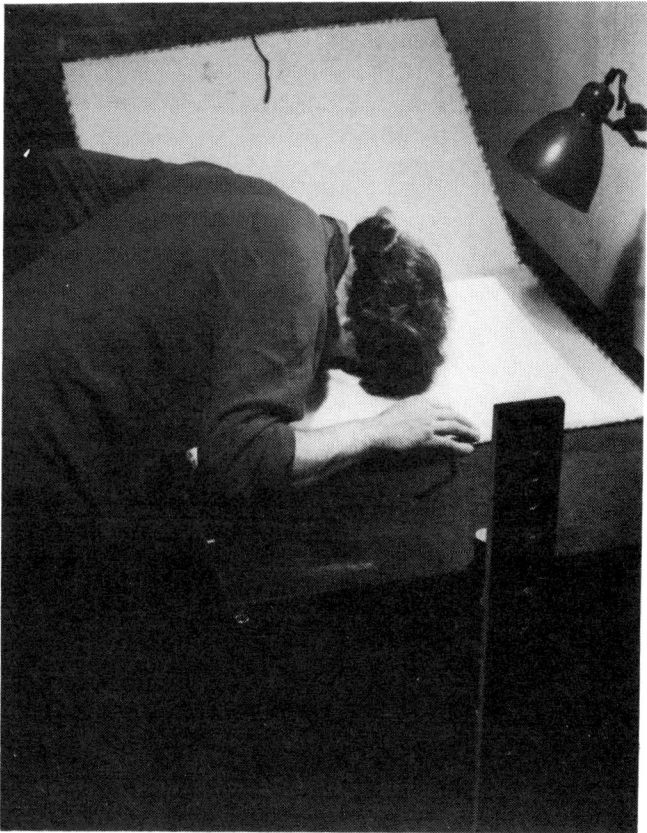

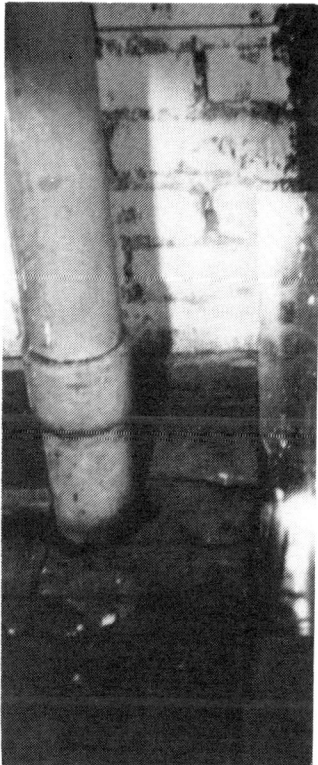

FRAZIER DOUGHERTY

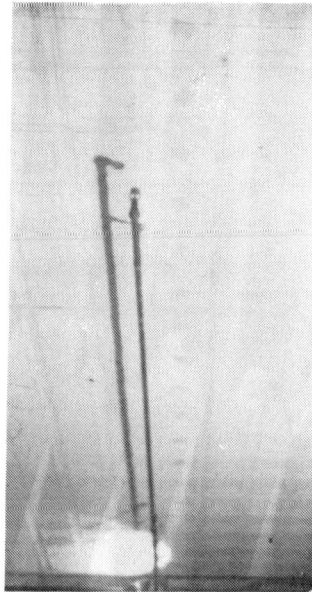

PHILIP GLASS

NANCY HOLT

BOB FIORE

PHILIP KAPLAN

SHIGEKO KUBOTA

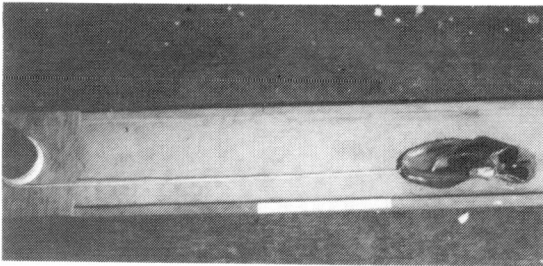

EMILE LAUGIER

JEFFREY LEW

PAUL JAY

LIZBETH MARANO

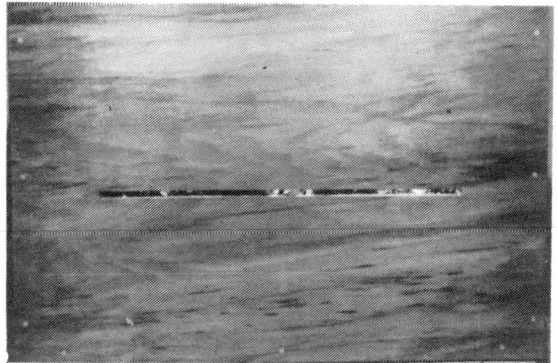

GORDON MATTA CLARK

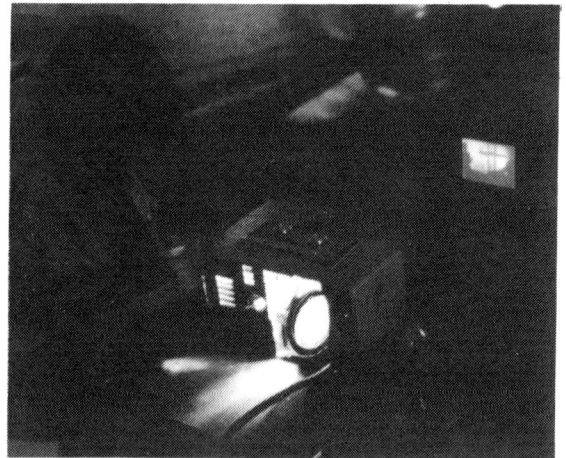

DONALD MUNROE/JOAN SCHWARTZ

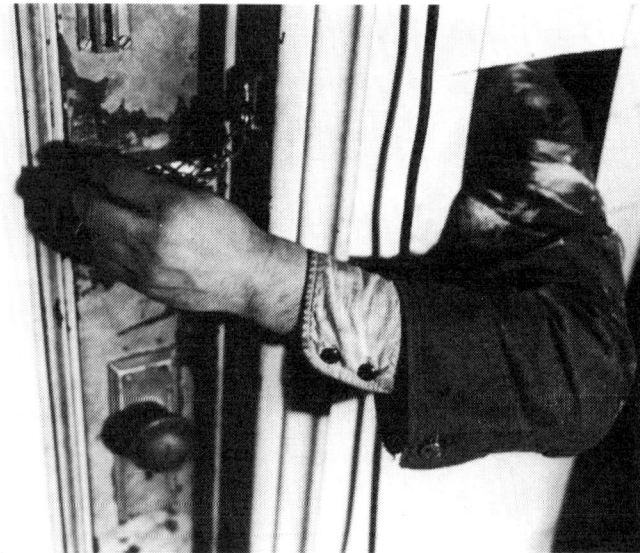

GIANFRANCO MANTEGNA

CHRIS MURPHY

PATTY OLDENBURG

CLAES OLDENBURG

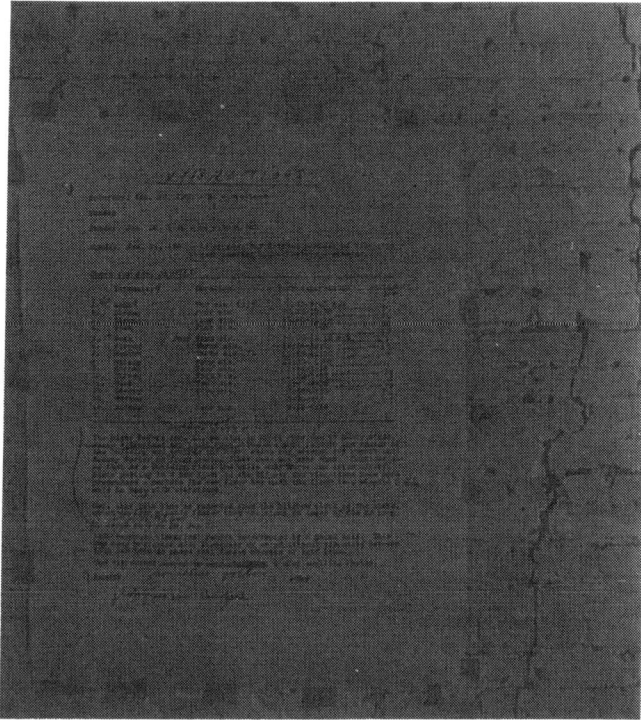

NAM JUNE PAIK

Michelle Stone

ALISON SKY

124

HANNAH WILKE

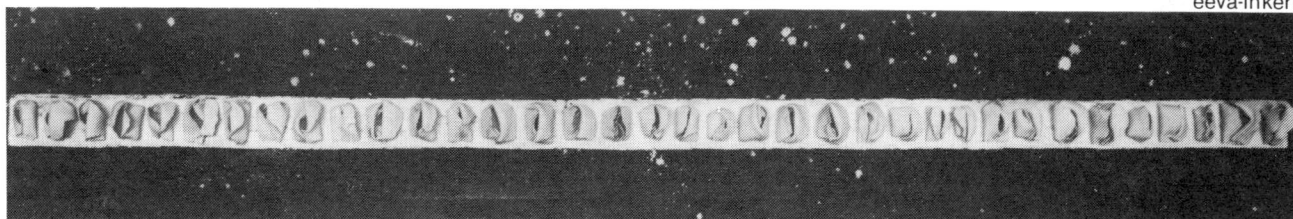

TONY SMITH

ABOUT 405 E 13 ST (3rd and 4th)

: A CONTRADICTION

BY : BRENDAN ATKINSON , EVRIAH BADER , VICTORIA BARR , KATHRYN BIGELOW , JAYNE BLISS , JILL BREAKSTONE , JAY CRAVEN , JIM COBB , STEPHEN CRAWFORD , FRAZER DOUGHERTY , JUAN DOWNEY , JEAN DUPUY , BOB FIORE , ANGELA FRASCONE , JON GIBSON , JEANNE GOLLOBIN , JANA HAIMSOHN , DEEDEE HALLECK , JERRY HOVAGYMIAN , JULIA HEYMAND , KEN JACOBS , PAUL JAY , POPY JOHNSON , SCOTT JOHNSON , BENNIE KIRSCHENBAUM , OLGA KLUVER , IRENE KRUGMAN , MICHAEL KRULMAN , SHIGEKO KUBOTA , JEFFREW LEW , MICHAEL MALOY , LIZBETH MARANO , TONY MASCATELLO , TIMOTHY MAUL , ANTHONY MCCALL , DICK MILLER , CHRIS MURPHY , RICHARD MOCK , CLAES OLDENBURG , PAT OLDENBURG , NAM JUNE PAIK , TONIE ROOS , LARRY RIVERS , EVE SONNEMANN , CAROLEE SCHNEEMANN , WILLOUGHBY SHARP . SUSAN WEIL

AT : JAMES YU GALLERY 247 BROADWAY

JUNE 10 TO 20 , 75

BACK

About
405 East 13th Street (#3)

Also see Jayne Bliss' entry in "Artists' Statements"

JUAN DOWNEY

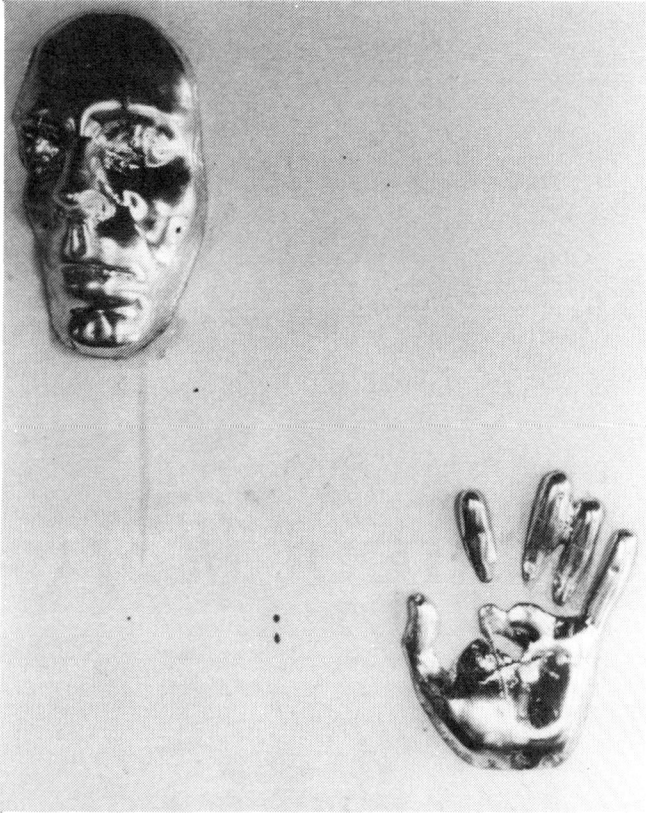

CHARLES DREYFUS

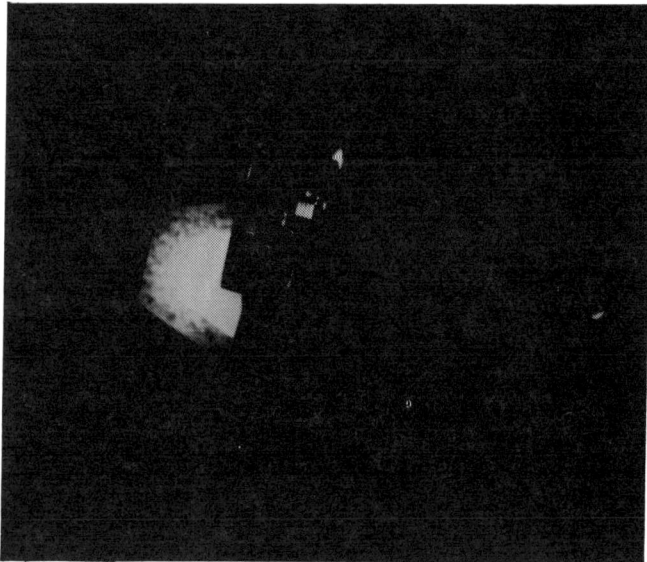

BOB FIORE

JANA HAIMSOHN

DEEDEE HALLECK

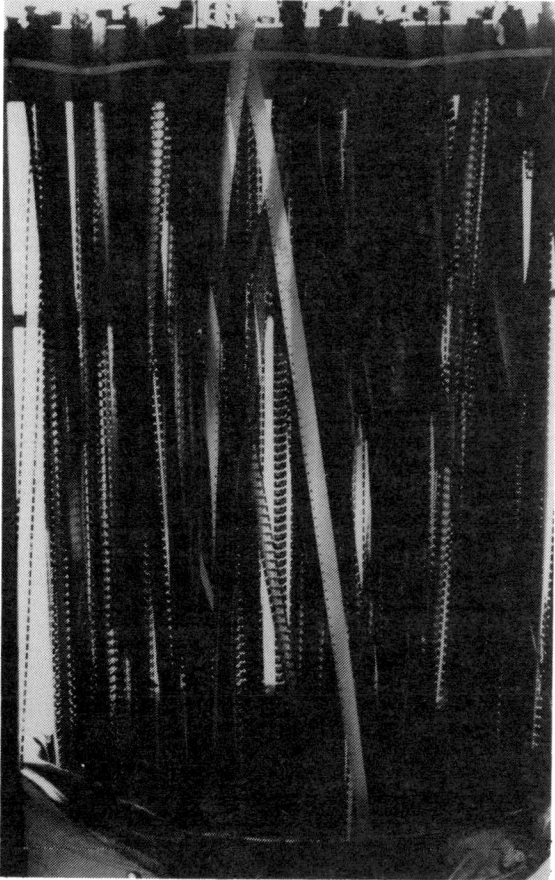

RICHARD MOCK

JULIA HEYWARD

DICK MILLER

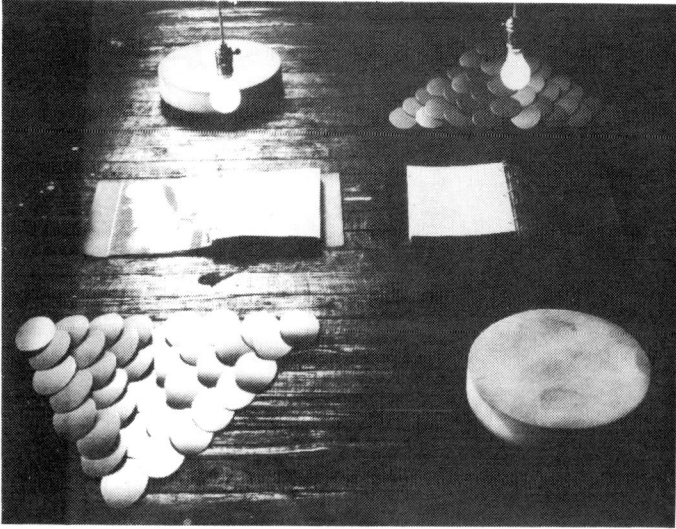

LARRY RIVERS

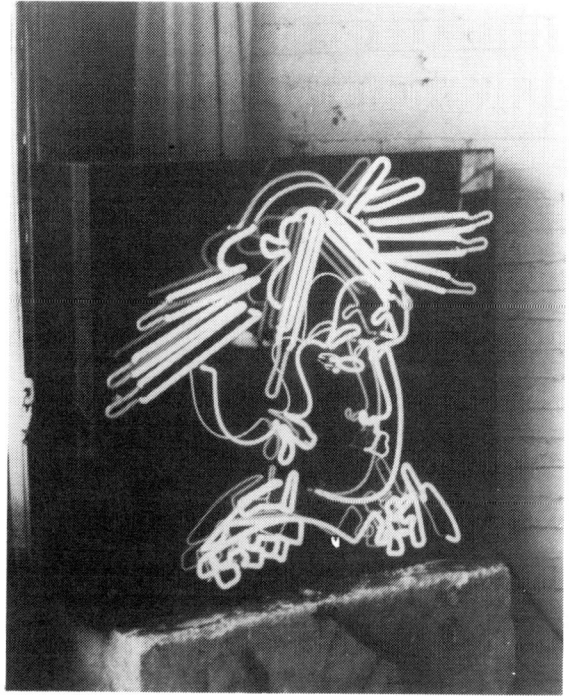

NAM JUNE PAIK

TONIE ROOS

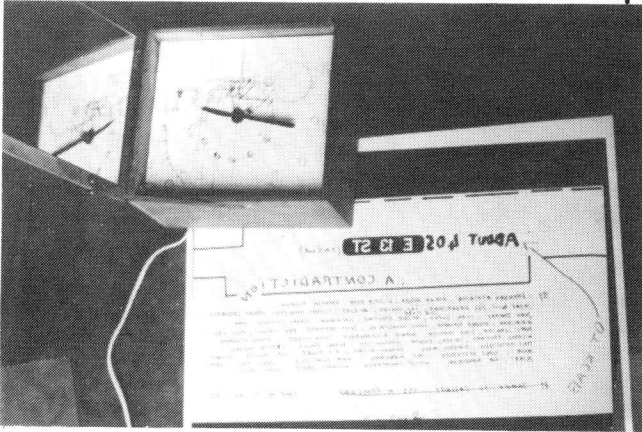

JEAN DUPUY —

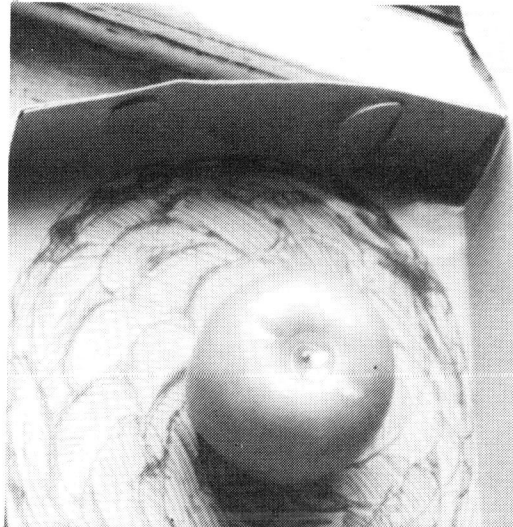

OLGA ADORNO

OLGA ADORNO

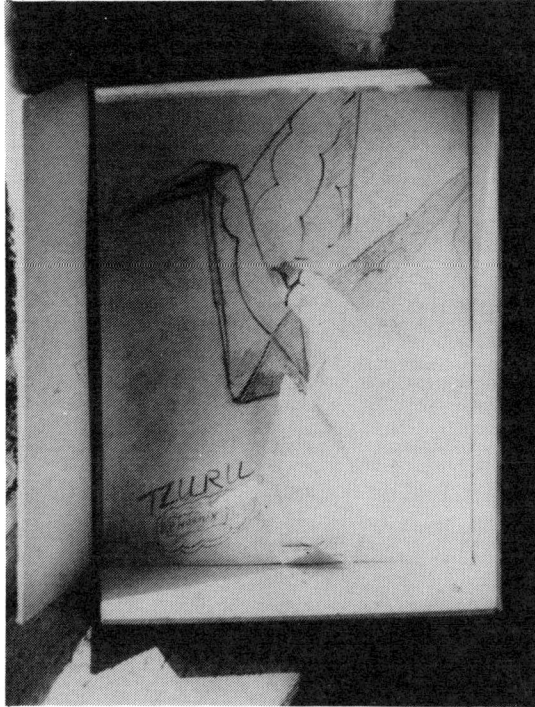

JAYNE BLISS' LOFT

Scale 1/1
(James Yu Gallery)

By JEAN DUPUY and ELLEN SRAGOW

In May '75 I invited Adorno, Atkinson, Highstein, Harris, Hovagimyan, Lew, Matta Clark, Marano, Murphy, Zadikian, to show at Yu Gallery under the title "Sculptors' Drawings Show, Scale One to One." Some of the artists responded to the scale one to one, by retouching, (redrawing) the architecture of the gallery: for instance, Marano built two walls in the south-east corner of the back room, Matta pulled down a part of the north wall, then changing his mind, he rebuilt the wall and wrote the word "withdrawn" on it., and Zadikian spent two days building a pink shutter inside the front room, behind one of the three large windows on West-Broadway, and then he broke the glass from the street side. Some artists used the given space as is: Adorno, drew on a wall the three sides of a scaffolding and placed the scaffolding itself beside the drawing as the fourth side of the scaffolding; like Adorno, I did a two dimensional spatial drawing, using the columns of the gallery as the support for a 110 foot piece of drawing paper (the width was 2 feet) on which I made a 109 foot long drawing with a split pencil. Harris made a "trompe l'oeil" with a post minimalist drawing painted in black on the south wall of the front room, and Atkinson also made a "trompe l'oeil" by means of a post-surrealist image.

In May '76 I invited Adorno, Beuchat, Downey, Haimsohn, Kaye, Mascatello, Miller, Van Ripper and Weese to show drawings under the title "Performers' Drawings" at the Fine Arts Building—there, for practical reasons, we hung from south to north the 30 drawings with clothes-pins to two fifty foot long wires stretched from wall to wall.

The next season I proposed to Ellen Sragow Gallery situated in the same "Fine Arts Building" to have a show under the title "Front/Back" using wires again stretched from wall to wall. The works were seen from the front and from the back. Here is the text Ellen Sragow wrote about it:

How to show a lot of work in a small space.
How to hang a lot of work in a small space.
Hang it *in* the space.

The space consisted of two small rooms. The installation in the first room consisted of wires stretched from wall to wall in a simple grid system eight feet above the floor. The second room had a single wire spanning its narrower space.

Thirty one artists submitted owrk created specifically for the exhibition. The exhibition premise was to create works that could hang freely in the space, suspended from the wire support; works which could be seen from the front and from the back. This took the flat pieces off of the wall and out of the frame. It took sculptural, three-dimensional pieces off of the floor and off of the pedestal.

Once installed, the works became a maze of art to pass through; to pass under; to bump into; to stand in the middle of; to stand in front of; to stand in back of; a ladder (Mary Beth Edelson), a bathrobe (John Sanborn), a snake (Robert Stackhouse), a cat-like paper skeleton (Mark Eisenberg), photographic portraits—full figure (Kathleen Agnoli) and partial face (Marcia Resnick), books (Maureen Connor, Joseph Alessi), a page from a book—telephone (Jean Dupuy).

The work could be viewed as a total environment, lyrical in essence, strong in nature, or as individual pieces demanding consideration.

Front/back people viewing.
Front/back art.

134

OLGA ADORNO

GORDON MATTA CLARK

WITHDRAWN

LIZBETH MARANO

BRENDAN ATKINSON

ZADIK ZADIKIAN

GENE HIGHSTEIN   JEAN DUPUY

JEFFREY LEW   CHRIS MURPHY   SUZANNE HARRIS   BRENDAN ATKINSON

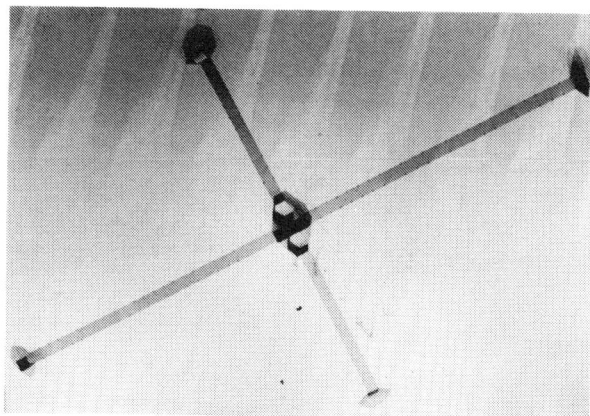

JERRY HOVAGIMYAN

OLGA ADORNO

NANCY BARBER

VILLARD DE HONNECOURT

WALTER DE MARIA

PHILIPPE DEMONTAUT

JEAN DUPUY

JARED FITZGERALD

JANA HAIMSOHN

GEORGE MACIUNAS

TIMOTHY MAUL

KIKI SMITH

BILL STONE

CHRISTIAN XATREC

13 X 33

AT 112 GREENE ST.

FROM MAY 28 TO JUNE 16, 1977 11:30 — 6:00

13 × 33

Photographs by Nancy Barber

FOR IMMEDIATE RELEASE

112 Workshop, Inc. is pleased to present
"13 x 33" a group exhibition conceived and
organized by Jean Dupuy. The show runs
from May 28th through June 16th.

The gallery will be divided into 13 parallel
corridors interconnected to form a maze.
Each artist will present two works located
at the beginning and end of a corridor of
the gallery space which is 33 feet wide.
Thus the whole exhibit experience is spatial,
sequential and cumulative: the viewer sees
the works in forward and reverse.

"13 x 33" features the work of 13 artists:
Olga Adorno, Nancy Barber, Villard de Honnecourt,
Walter de Maria, Philippe Demontaut, Jean
Dupuy, Jared Fitzgerald, Jana Haimsohn,
George Maciunas, Timothy Maul, Kiki Smith,
Bill Stone, Christian Xatrec.

A catalogue will be published in connection
with the exhibition.

112 Workshop, Inc. is supported in part by
grants from NYSCA and NEA.

Contact: Robyn Brentano
         226·8971 or 825·0909

By TIM MAUL

I suspect that Jean's always happiest with the group shows that have asked the most from an audience in terms of participation. Jean believes that artists shouldn't work for free, and in the same sense I think he believes that the relationship between the viewer and the artist's product should not be a casual (free) one either, and that some exchange be demanded.

Jean asked 13 artists to present a single (or two related) works that would appear on opposite walls at 112 Greene St. in May 1977. To assure that the pieces on opposing walls would be perceived as one work, Jean organized the long space by installing a system of corridors that once entered guaranteed that each work was experienced from "wall to wall" as intended. The physical act of element that allowed the works to be viewed sequentially left-to-right and right-to-left. Although all the works existed sequentially, some specifically used elements of superimposition that suggested optical concerns. I think of Christian Xatrec's pair of number 3's, one inverted, drawn on the wall, functioning much like the working of the eye and the sparsest piece in the show. Also Olga Adorno's vertically bisected male/female figures (with shoes) a kind of stereo androgony. Dupuy showed two painted envelopes that had been mailed to the gallery. One image of a mountain when reversed on the opposite wall became an impressionist seashore.

Jana Haimsohn showd two work boots, one normal size and one incredibly tiny, altering perspective by means of a personal talisman. More conventional use of the wall-corridor was represented by Walter De Maria's instructional plaques, Jared Fitzgerald's enigmatic lamps, Phillipe Demontaut's unsettling furniture drawings, Kiki Smith's boatlike structures and Nancy Barber's choice of meat-on-velvet photographs. I liked Bill Stone's back-pack reel device for finding one's way in the forest, the backpack itself on one wall and a photograph of it in use on the opposite wall. I'm embarrassed using my own image in my work, but remembering 112's Body Art past I decide why not, so I offered a lathered portrait of myself staring into a medicine cabinet on the opposite wall, both photographs. Immediately recognizable was George Maciunas's centrally located swing for fording a supposedly freshly painted area in his designated corridor, a different point of view on the show's premise altogether, as was Villard de Honnecourt's speculations concerning angels on the interior and exterior of a certain cathedral.

Jean organizing a show at 112 Greene St. at this time seemed ironic to me for several reasons. The early activities at 112 Greene along with Jean's initial "About 405 E. 13th St." group shows sensibiity which would later run amok at places like P.S. 1. Far from being a funky installation, 13 x33 was probably Jean's most sparely beautiful. The black cord that formed the corridors (supplied by Maciunas) gave the gallery an unexpectedly elegant look which isn't easy. I have a theory that New Yorkers love waiting in line for things and being physically directed (popular movies, worlds fairs, etc.). Anyway, people visiting the show really enjoyed themselves, and it was a pleasure seeing individuals clotted around certain works in a receding horizon of parallel lines. In what could be viewed as a decline in the quality of activities at 112 Greene, 13 x 33 proved that if conditions were right, it could happen all over again.

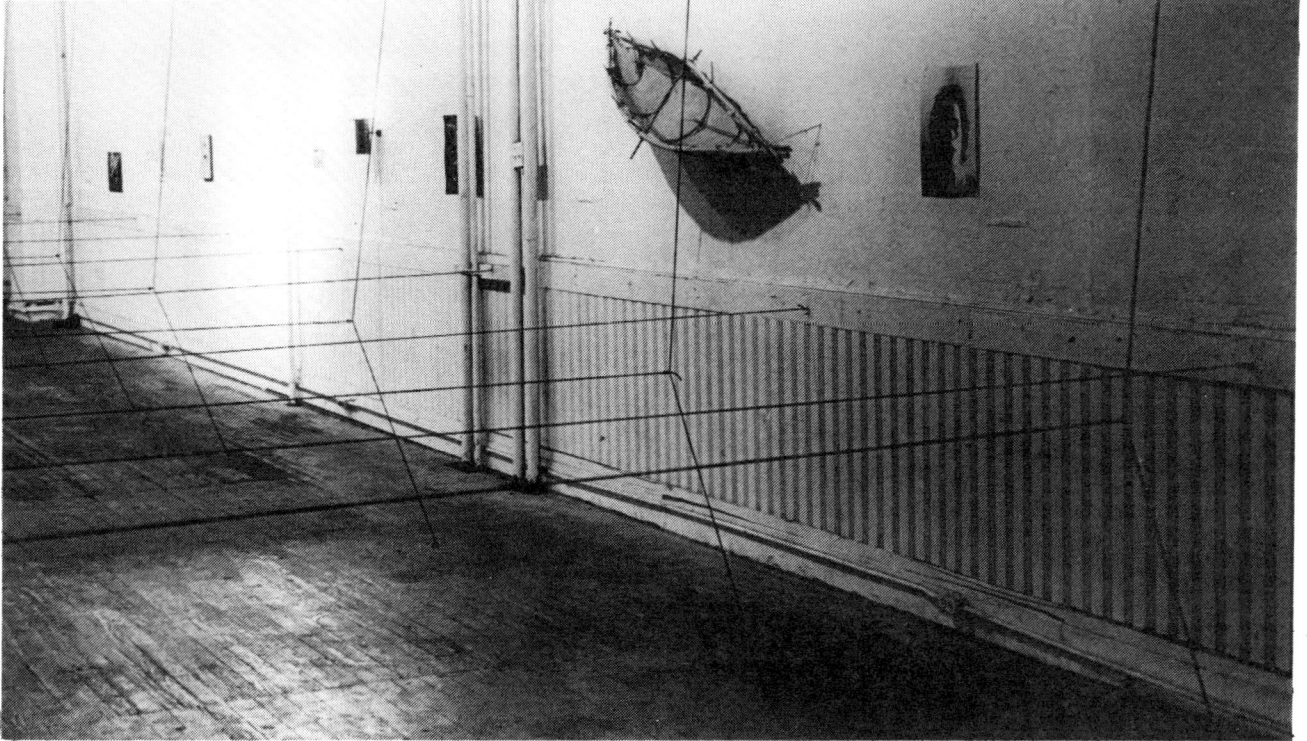

OLGA ADORNO

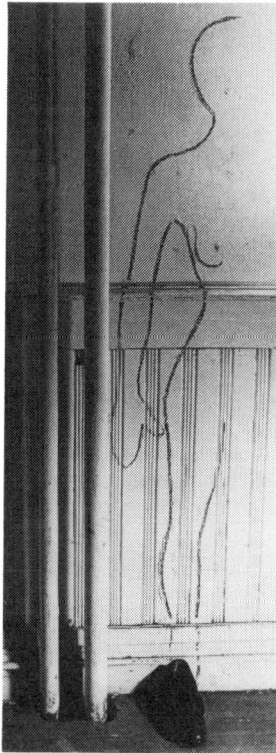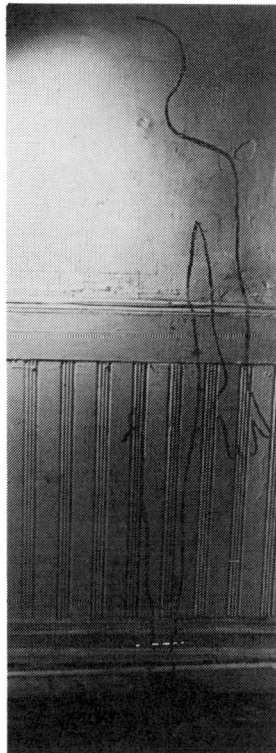

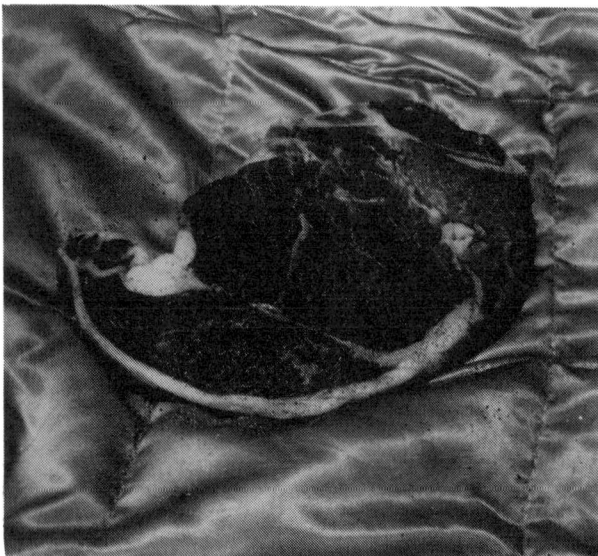

NANCY BARBER

142

While the angels above the buttresses, as you may see now, are clothed and have very short wings, Villard drew them nude with giant wings.

The crenelles ⊓⊔⊓⊔ don't exist anymore— they have been covered in such a way by a balustrade that just enough room for some intermittent horizontal foot supports has been provided in case the roof needs repair.

WALTER DE MARIA

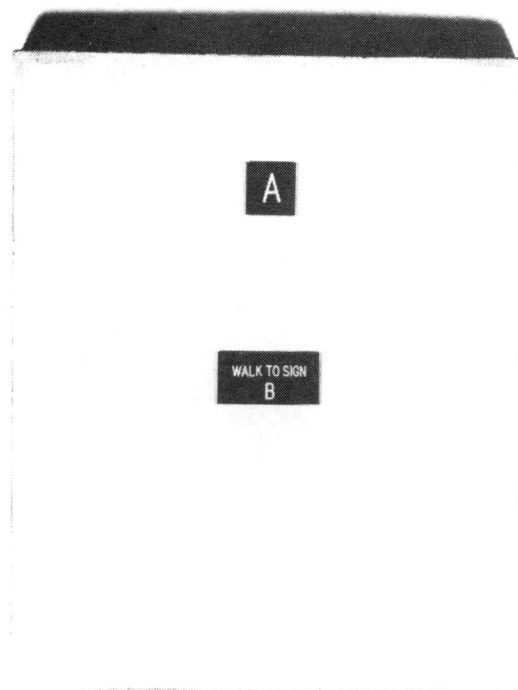

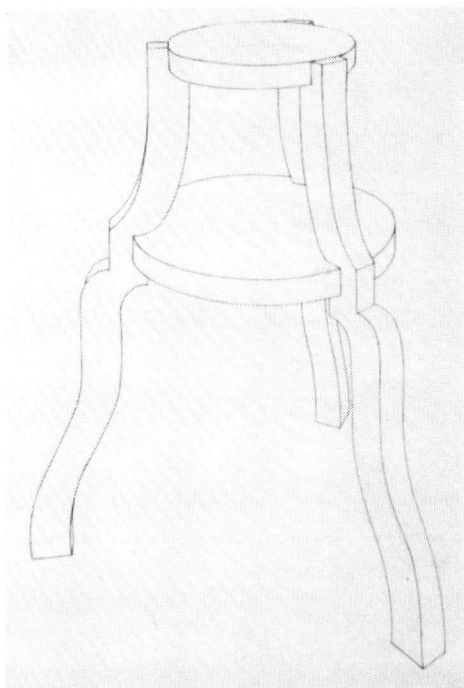

PHILIPPE DEMONTAUT

JEAN DUPUY

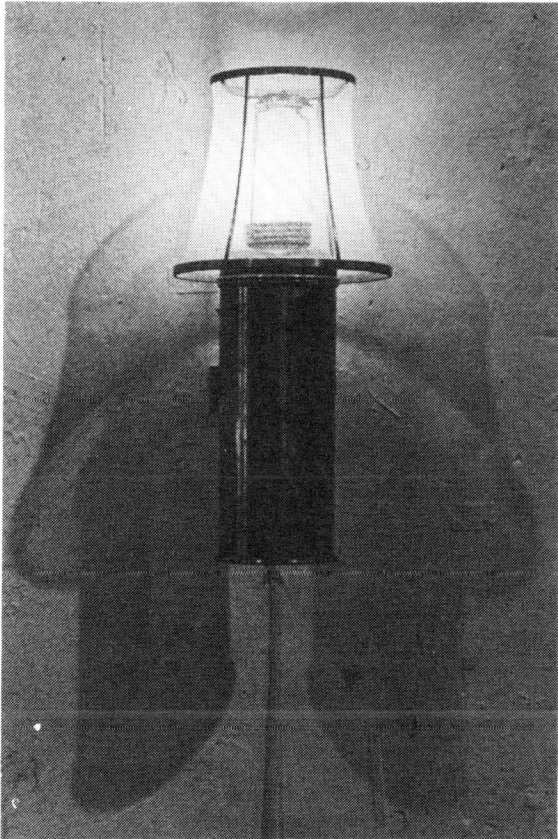

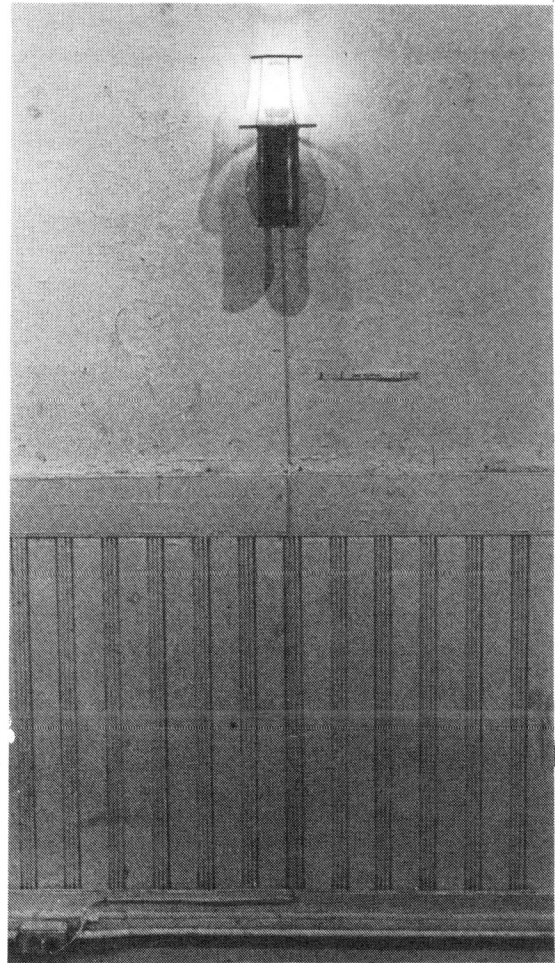

JARED FITZGERALD

JANA HAIMSOHN

FRESH PAINT

GEORGE MACIUNAS

146

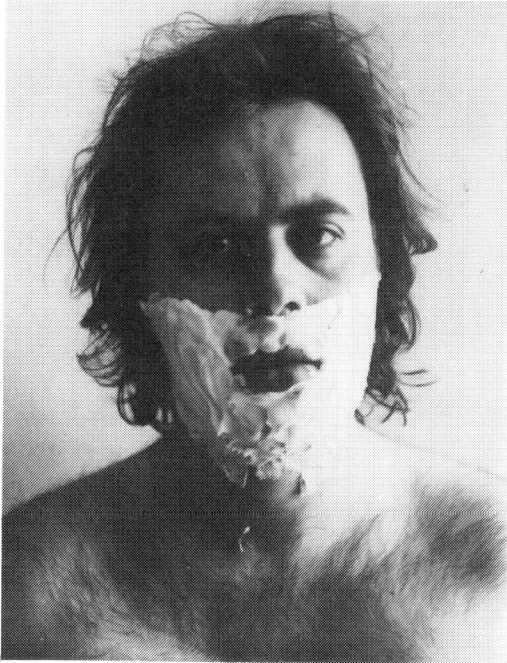

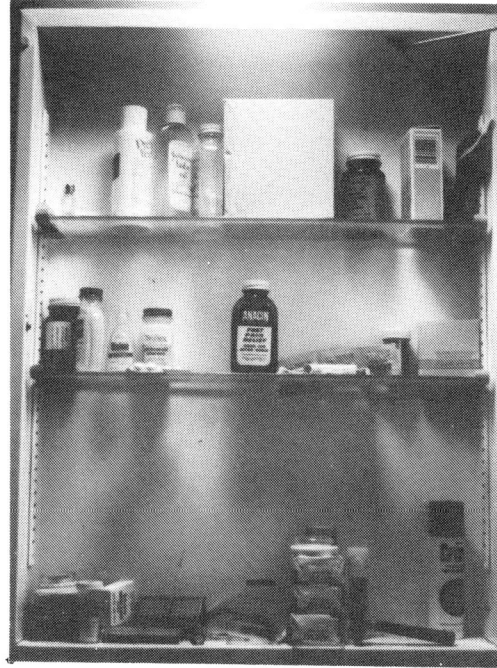

KIKI SMITH

BILL STONE

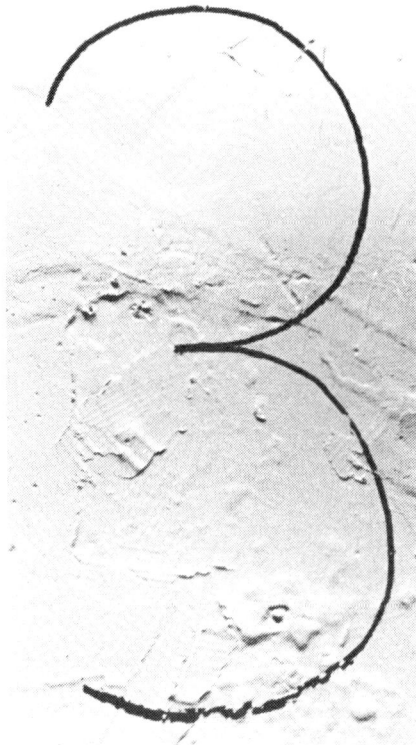

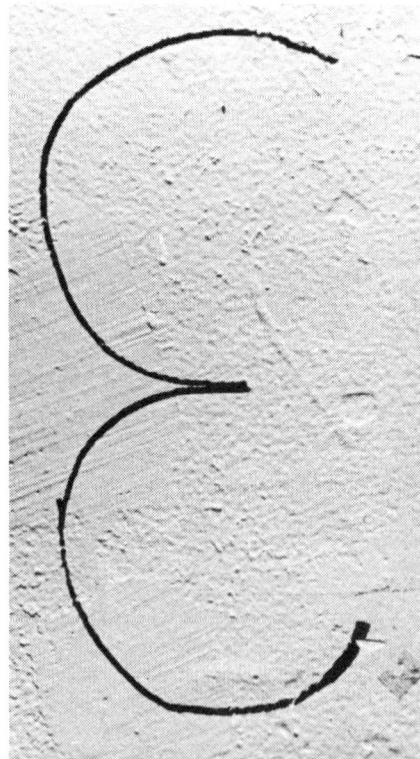

CHRISTIAN XATREC

148

FRONT BACK

ADORNO OSCAR
AGNOLI KATOY
ALESSI JOSEPH
BARBER NANCY
BOOTH POWER
BRINTZENHOPE RICHARD
CONNOR MARYANN
DE COINTET GUY
DUPUY
EDELSON MARYBETH
EVAN BEA
EISENBERG MARK
FITZGERALD KIT
FERGUSSON CLAIRE
FRACONE KATHLEEN
GIORDANO JOHN A.
GREENHOUSE WENDY
HAIMSOHN MAE
HARRIS SUZANNE
HIGHSTEIN JENE
JANSEN ALZANA
KAYE POOH
KAUFMAN RICHARD
MAUL TIMOTHY
MILLER DICK
PRINCE RICHARD
REZNICK NANCY
SANBORN JOHN
SANSONE ROGER
STACKHOUSE ROB
STONE BILL
LADERMAN UKELES MIERLE
YULIKAS BOB

SATURDAY
DEC. 4, 76
TO
JAN. 1, 77

AT
ELLEN SRAGOW LTD
—
FINE ARTS BUILDING
105 HUDSON ST. (3'R)
—
WED.-SAT. 1-6
OPENING:
SAT. DEC. 4

150

Front/Back

No Photos

Artists' Statements ——→

MARTINE ABALLEA

Here is the text I used for my performance at the Louvre: I chose "The Victory" by Le Nain, which represents a woman-angel standing above the body of a man-fish-snake. (Unfortunately, the painting had been removed, so I had to read the text in front of another.) So, in front of this painting I took out a newspaper (Le Monde) and I read the following article (which I had written myself).

Discovery of hideous skeletons in Scotland.

Called in by a Kirkcaldy fisherman who found the bones while enlarging his basement, University of Edinburgh archeologists discovered two skeletons dating from the fifth century B.C. While having human characteristics in general, they show the following peculiarities: the tallest measuring 1.43 m. has remarkably large teeth. He is even more remarkable for the absence of a pelvis and legs which are replaced by a prolonged spinal column ending in fins. In the smallest one, which measures 1.26 m., one notices the abnormal development of the shoulder blades into bone-like formations which resemble condor wings. The entwining of the skeleton and the position of the hands and teeth lead one to believe that the two creatures killed each other. No conclusion has been drawn up until now about this discovery. The British museum has been given the task of directing the research.

I would have liked for people to have wondered whether or not it was true but some people believed the story completely.

DECOUVERTE DE SQUELETTES MONSTRUEUX EN ECOSSE
Appelés par un pêcheur de Kirkcaldy qui avait trouvé des os en agrandissant sa cave, des archéologues de l'Université d'Edinburgh ont découvert deux squelettes qui dateraient du 5e siècle ab. J.C. Ceux-ci, qui ont dans l'ensemble des caracteristiques humaines, présentent cependant les particularités suivantes. Le plus grand, mesurant 1 m 43, est remarquable par sa forte dentition. Il l'est plus encore par son absence de bassin et de jambes, qui sont remplacés par un prolongement de la colonne vertèbrale où s'articulent des arrètes. Cuez le plus petit, qui mesure 1 m 26, on note le developpement anormal de l'omoplate. Elle est la base de formations osseuses semblables à des ailes de condor. L'entremêlement des squelettes, ainsi que les positions des mains et des dents, laisserait croire que deux se sont entretués. Aucune conclusion n'a été tirée, jusqu'a présent, sur cette découverte. La direction des recherches a été confié au British Museum.

(Louvre)

VITO ACCONCI

Dear Jean,

I want to apologize.

As I told you briefly, the piece I wanted to do at Judson was a group project: a piece done by all of us—Diego Cortez, Coleen Fitzgibbon, Ilona Granet, Robin Winters, and myself.

The piece fell apart; the group, in effect, cancelled itself out. By Thursday afternoon, it seemed there still was a chance to pull something together; but it became clear that we didn't have a piece we could all feel for. At that point, if we had done something, it would have only been for the sake of doing something—it wouldn't have been something we believed in.

I could have, of course, done something myself. But I had wanted to use "groupness" as a way to react to the "on-stage" feel of the Judson performances. Even when the group failed, I didn't want to resort back to the notion of "individual performer." That, to me, would have been even more of a failure.

I should have called you, I should have told you we weren't doing anything. But, by that time, the group was so depressed that all we could do was quietly withdraw.

I'm sorry if we caused any inconvenience.

(Three Evenings on a Revolving Stage)

ARTHUR AESCHBACHER

	SITUATION:	MUSEE du LOUVRE, Grande Galerie. Devant le tableau de Jacques BLANCHARD
	TITRE:	CIMON surprenant EPHIGENIE
Zéro secondes	ACTION:	1—L'artiste gonfle un ballon blanc sur lequel est inscrit-TITIEN
Quinze secondes		2—Donne le ballon á tenir sur le côté droit du tableau comme une signature supposée.
		3—L'artiste souffle dans une poupée gonflabe représentant BATMAN.
Trente secondes		4—BATMAN se présente face au public, prend son élan muni d'une épingle et fonce sur le ballon-explosion.
	TEXTE:	5—Une fois de plus BATMAN intervient avec beaucoup de sang-froid *car* (le tableau est montré du doigt) *ce* tableau est de Jacques BLANCHARD dit: le TITIEN FRANCAIS.
Cinquante-six secondes		(á haute voix) : BATMAN
Cinquante-sept secondes		: BATMAN
Cinquante-huit secondes		: BATMAN
Cinquante-neuf secondes		: BATMAN
Soixante secondes		: BATMAN

(Louvre)

LAURIE ANDERSON

I'm afraid my memory of **Soup & Tart** is a little foggy . . . but I know it was the first time I used the Self-Playing Violin. This is a violin with a small speaker inside—and the speaker wire runs to a casette deck. Half of a violin duet was on tape (coming out of the F holes of the instrument) and the other half was playing simultaneously live.

There were words to the song but I don't remember exactly what they were. **Soup & Tart** was right after my loft on Second St. had been broken into; I'd just spent the summer hitchhiking to the North Pole and came back to find a huge hole chopped through the concrete wall of my loft. All my films had been burned—books and clothes ripped up, windows broken, and magic marker messages three feet high on all the walls. This was when I *really* started camping out—wandering around New York, staying at friends' places. I remember the camouflage song had something to do with the way it felt to be your own walking house.

(Soup and Tart)

One of the things I like about Jean Dupuy's **Grommets** show was its step-right up, corny feeling. Everyone installed in their own little booth, singing, dancing, entertaining. It came close to nightmares I have about Soho—everyone's at home working away and you never really know if it makes a difference to anyone "out there" or not.

I chose to work with the physical limitations of the stall and sat in a chair squeezed between a wall and a divider. I played the violin so that the bow could move only about half-inch back and forth between the walls. The sound was mostly percussive, with short tonal blips. After about an hour of doing this, I looked out of my grommet and saw long lines for other holes but none near mine. I had no idea whether people had been there or not.

I think for the audience, the show must have had a kind of TV quality—you can see them, but they can't see you. When I couldn't be in the stall, I put a stand-in there. It was a small slide taken off a TV—Mary Hartman sitting at her kitchen table. A clay figure of Mary was placed slightly in front of the slide so she seemed to be coming out of the set, like in the 21st century when TV really will be 3-D and holograms of all your favorite TV stars will ooze out into your house and Mary Hartman (real) Mary Hartman (hologram) will clump out, sit at your kitchen table, drink your coffee, and chew the fat. Now that's a grommet.

(Grommets #3)

I got your letter this morning about the performance series, and I'm sorry but I won't be able to make it. But I did get another letter in the same delivery from someone in Holland which I've been trying to answer for the last couple of hours, and instead I think I'll just read it and send it off to you. It's addressed: Laurie Anderson, 725 North Western, Lost Angeles, California.

Dear Laurie Anderson,

I have reading with great pleasure an article which will have widened my interest in your understanding of you and I hear you are now in Hollywood of California. Lost Angeles is the same now? And wish I to ask questions but for New York not for Lost Angeles.

For the bigger part, the European artist is for very sure in the suburban in Holland, looks with a great deal of surprise in his eyes to the American art development. All of the people of the town of New York, that is, the artists of the town, joining together in groups to look to see each other and so to work and so the set their art into the eyes of the townspeople—the public. And this seems to me so public, and I know I it is work and working and what must I do to know what means it?

I am for myself since a long time walking around, where the growing idea to come once to the new world, comes to me. So have I to look into the inner side of the American world and under what is going on there and so look how it works and what means it? I look sense to me before to go to informate myself as much. But how so do such a thing from here, so far from the New York world? The best way so do it to see what means it looks to me the most direct way, namely, just write so to people who are living. For example, the questions:

How is it to leave your own town and so to go to New York?
How feels it?
How did you become a good house to live in?
What means New York in the social way? Cafés?
What do you to be living?
What means New York?
What means living in this town?
What means it and what needs it?
What means this art for the townspeople?
How feels it to them and for their jobs?
What reasons have they for setting this working into their eyes and how feels it?

I hope it is not so much for answering this question. It should help me to get more complicated seeing this picture of the town and of the town's people.

Please respond my questions, I am taking your English for Dutch for publishing an article for this subject. So to understand each other truly we do. I am so firmly yours with thanks and greetings.

(Chant a Cappella)

MEL ANDRINGA

I called the work the "Macy's Piece." The idea came from thoughts I had while working during Christmas for that department store. The great majority of services I provided the customers there consisted of giving directions to other departments. I thought there was something interesting in the way questions were phrased and in my answers. I particularly liked to think about the moment that connects stimulus and response. For the **Grommets** show I used a Bell and Howell language master instructional device to ask myself the questions. The language master uses 8½" by 11" cards which have a strip of recording tape along one side. I copied down questions verbatim from customer requests, and recorded myself asking them to make the performance more interior. When the spectator looked into the grommet on the external side of my booth, he (or she) saw a bust-length portion of a man (myself) standing in front of newspaper want ads. I was wearing a suit and tie, and a lapel badge stating "Welcome to Macy's." This picture was regularly eclipsed by the language master cards riding past the viewer's eye. Each card in addition to asking a question for directions, had a nineteenth-century engraving depicting some object pasted to it. The engravings only occasionally matched the objects the questioner might find in the department he was seeking. After the card had passed, I answered each question, giving directions from the position I had most frequently assumed during my days as a salesman. There were about thirty different cards and my pauses were about 15-30 seconds a piece. At the height of the seasonal rush this pace was not unusual. At one point during each answer I established eye contact with the viewer as if he had asked the question. I paid no attention to "live" questions or comments, and worked continuously whether there was someone there or not for an hour and a half each night.

(Grommets #4)

OLGA ADORNO

I cry a cry. Echo is a cry which brings back a cry. A lonely call coming through memory bringing a memory of solitude, pain, anger, fear, anxiousness, and ambivalence. The mysterious sound of narcissus for echo the ancient story retold, lifting us outside ourselves into nature. I shout "echo" into the room till the last syllable disappears into my throat. Four "echos" each different in pitch and accent of syllables.

(Soup and Tart)

Merengue, on the Revolving Stage. Living with Jean and watching him work and thinking of my own work sometimes brings about a piece. As when I wanted to do a dance for the revolving stage. I thought of a traditional folkloric dance. Supposedly from the Carribean Ocean Islands. As I looked for the source, Jean discovered that the work of Meringue in French has to do with egg white. Separate an egg, use the yolk to make mayonnaise in a Chinese tea box (square-shaped) in which you roll the fork under the dripping oil. The four-beat rolling rhythm created the tempo for the "Merengue," the egg white dance which I performed along with a merengue record.

(Three Evenings on a Revolving Stage)

An afternoon at the Whitney Museum. An improvisation. As the stage revolved I stood peering out at the audience, shading my eyes with my hand from the glaring lights, making sounds from within my throat, tossing high pitch whistles creating sounds of animals reminiscent of goats on a mountain side, and then doing a rapid movement shake with my posterior. As I stopped this movement, I began an echo using the work "echo"—similarly done at **Soup and Tart**. Sounding out towards the different parts of the room.

(One Afternoon on a Revolving Stage)

Dupuy asked me to perform in a peep show called **Grommets**. The second of a series involving artists' performances. I decided to use the lenses from my eye glasses which are very thick due to the fact that I am extremely myopic (nearsighted). I made a kind of framed screen in which I set the lenses so that the person peeping through the grommet could only see the image on the other side of the lens.

I put the lenses at two points of the frame, one at the level of my face and the other at the level of my sex. I sat stationed on a high stool. Just in front of the screen—a foot or so away—was the canvas screen with the grommets (peepholes) set at the same level as the lenses, so that the peeper could see a minute and distinguishably clear view of these parts of my body. The peeper had to climb a ladder which reached up to the mezzanine on which I was positioned. As the peeper came to the first grommet the view was of my pubic hair and hand suggesting masturbation. Further up the ladder was a view of my face, making gestures of changing expressions. The images were minute in detail. Sometimes I recited a poem, but since it was inaudible I discontinued after the first evening. It was impossible for me to know when there was someone peeping, yet I was able to hear everything that was happening around me. It was a haunting and emotional experience for me.

(Grommets #3)

Chant a Capella at the Judson Church. Around that time I was working with my voice as I walked throughout the city. Keeping count of my breaths as I inhaled and exhaled. I made a sound at a comfortable note keeping the sound as I walked exhaling it and inhaling it. A sort of sigh of relief. *Ah* as I inhaled, *ha* as I exhaled. This I planned to do in the church. Jean suggested I make a gesture at the same time, such as exchanging my shoes. This I thought was a good idea. At the Judson Church I entered the stage from a small room to the right, with a relaxed walk and making "ah, ha" into the large room. And feeling comfortable about it. I stopped in the center of the stage continuously "ah, ha-ing." I took off my shoes, reversed them, put my right foot into the left shoe and visa versa. I continue to "ah, ha" as I walked away exiting by the small room to the left of the stage.

(Chant a Cappella)

On the floor I danced to whistles which I made distinct and imitative of tree frogs. Every few seconds movements made under the tower were flowing. I climbed up the tower and stopped at the first platform. I set four plastic water birds on the edge and blew the whistling water birds. Too long, I thought! Continuing up to the top platform I attempted to shout out sounds into the room which echoed back. I imitated calls and barks of dogs till it became painful to me. During which I tried to fold a large paper bird without success. Finally I stopped, exhausted with an "improvisational" idea.

(A Tower at P.S. 1)

DAVID APPEL

(with Gail Teton)

In considering the concept for **Grommets** we were interested in using more than just the visual experience. That is, we wished it incorporate the senses of taste, touch, and hearing—as well as to set up a more direct communication between ourselves as performers and the audience. The solution became the choosing of several ordinary or remembered activities of our lives, which when combined enabled us to continually create a link with each visitor to the grommet.

Basically, the piece involved offering a milkshake to the observer: 1) concocting the

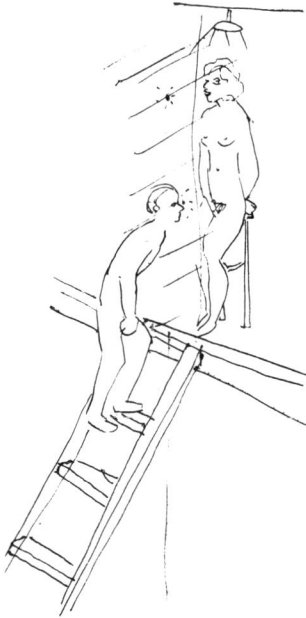

milkshake (an unusual purple color due to the mixture of vanilla and boysenberry ice creams); 2) sending a small glass of it towards the grommet hole via an electric train; 3) having the observer try to guess the flavor and then perform the task of drinking the milkshake through a glass straw which had previously been passed to them through the grommet; 4) taking back the glass straw, returning the train to the loading area, and cleaning up.

By setting up a cheerful "home" environment that served as a backdrop for the offering of a mysterious yet subsequently cooling drink, we more often than not established an instant rapport with each person. Since the piece became a participatory process that challenged the visitors as well as the performers (who continuously served up milkshakes, engaged in conversation, for several hours at a time), it existed more as a ritual of exchange than as a formal performance. For us, the grommet experience was fulfilling for the rich and constant interaction/sharing it provided with our audience, as well as knowing that we quenched the thirst of 300 throats.

(Grommets #4)

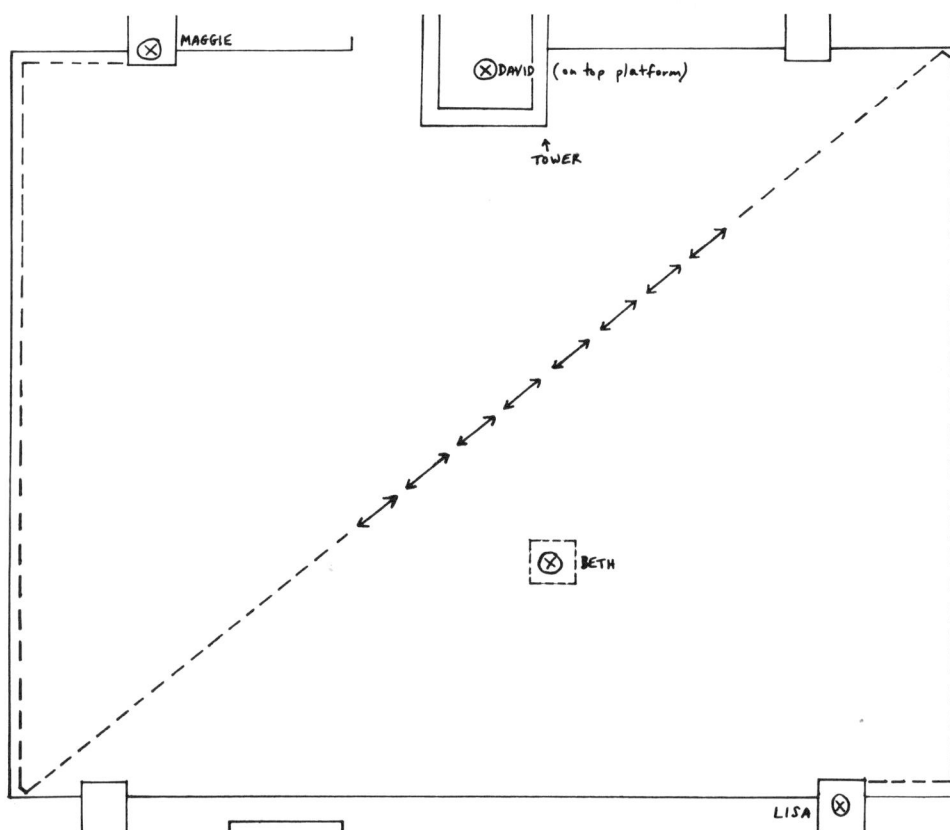

(with Beth Goren, Maggie Higgs, Lisa Sokolow)

Maggie and Lisa start in their respective doorways, droning/sounding off first notes of a 10-count vocal phrase. Before they go into the phrase itself, David enters and climbs tower to top platform. Shortly thereafter, Beth comes out to the designated spot on the floor. Maggie and Lisa progress (walking) around the outside of the space to opposite ends of the diagonal between the tower and Beth's spot as David and Beth begin a 10-count movement phrase in unison. Maggie and Lisa work on diagonal between David and Beth. The movement and vocal phrases are done repeatedly, gradually moving out of unison and working off the phrases with gradually increasing ornamentation and nuance. Maggie and Lisa move on the diagonal between David and Beth, slowly changing the 4-way physical relationship in space. David and Beth occasionally sound a long drone tone under Maggie and

Lisa's singing to underscore the vocal work. End after approximately 15 minutes.

(A Tower at P.S. 1)

BRENDAN ATKINSON

Performance using ultra-violet light (blacklight):

Suit: COLOR—DARK BLUE/BLACK; Fabricated by JEANNE DAWSON; with neck—one piece—zip starts at top of jump-suit neck, sliding down across chest, round back, round left hip, diagonally to top of right thigh, spiraling round the leg to the ankle. (When unzipped, the suit stretches out to 21 feet.) Attached to the suit neck is a latex rubber life-mask of myself, this in turn has a wig sewn to it. Black gloves for hands. Bare feet. My body covered with "invisible make-up which glows icy light blue under U-V. Mask made up with U-V sensitive pigments. Accompanied sounds: Distorted Pink Floyd (section from Meddle) at the beginning, finishing with traffic sounds of New York City.

Performance begins in normal light. Lights dim and go out as sound commences—only light comes for the strobe in the table 20 feet in front of me and two 4 feet U-V tubes on the floor by the table which has an additional 2 feet U-V tube recessed (combined with strobe causes the liquid color to pulsate). Surface of table—plexiglass inserted with 3 transparent hemispheres as containers for liquid pigment which appears molten under U-V light (see drawing). I move towards table as if worked by strings (in time with up tempo heart-beat section). Mask is illuminated as are my feet.

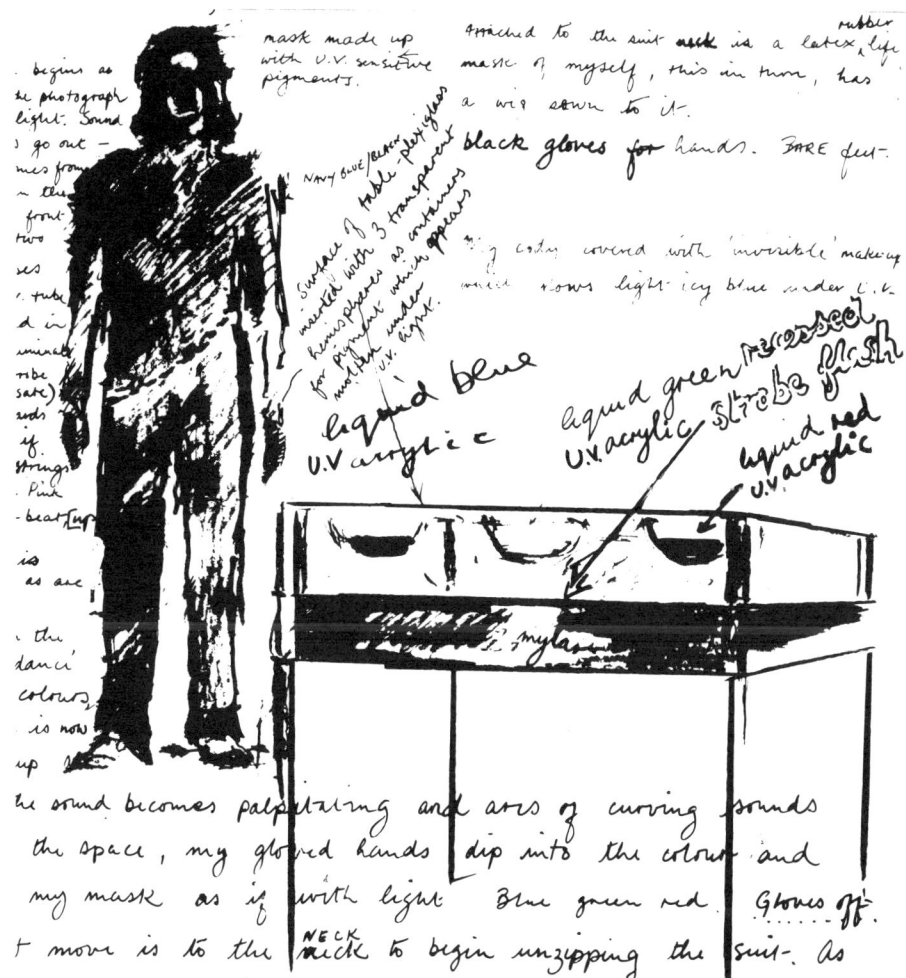

As I reach the table and "dance" with the colors, the music is now building up, becomes palpitating and arcs of curving sounds intensify the space. My gloved hands dip into the color and I bathe my mask as if with Blue/Green/Red light. Gloves removed. I begin unzipping the suit from the top of the neck. As the zip opens under my arm, it becomes apparent that the suit is joined to the mask. Around my back to my hip—it looks like "peel" or "skin." As it goes around my thigh I bend over and the mask falls and the suit gradually peels off, the section from thigh to calf spiraling with the sound-track of a Mack truck manoevering around a tight corner. Suit is shed off. I stand up straight, white strobe turned off; I am glowing light blue, stretch up high and right back. Disappear as fast as I can.

(Soup and Tart)

CHARLES ATLAS

(with Kate Parker)

The performers delved into pre-World War I music hall tradition to choreograph this dance number based on the Castle Walk, made famous by the fabulous dance team of Vernon and Irene Castle in 1914. They took the liberty of adding a few classic touches of their own; and so this elegant couple jumped out of a pink art noveau dress (hers), and had full tail coat (his) ripped savagely but smoothly off. The monocle stayed on. How—remains a mystery.

(Soup and Tart)

i made a movie. of my grandfather. at home. in St. Louis
a couple of years. before he died.
he was a tailor.
and a quiet man.
a diabetic.
thief.
his name was uh Herman. not well known man
or. last week
after a few drinks with my father then he told me
your grandpa was a klepto i think he said yeah
a family secret

he was a shoplifter i had known as a bargain hunter in supermarkets
he was a pick pocket. a sneak thief. a stranger.

domestic. familiar
grandfather of my stealthy nature

what about lack of dare. need to practice.
starting small, not bold but guileful thieving. work alone.
not get caught.
Around three times where am I going.
paying hommage. playing at outlaw, figure it out later

an easy grab from the corner stand. Feb New York Times.
beginner's luck. go back for more. two comix off a rack inside.
cultivating normal look. open air market. no one around. heart beats fast. feeling
fruit. cop a pear. in the rain.

bottom shelf. late night deli. campbell soup. play it safe
next a tough one. discount liquor. browse around. under arm sweat.
do you have a chilled bottle. pocket the gin pay for the wine.
go home. knees shake. drink it down. does it count. spite steal
a bunch of hangers from Frank the cleaner I detest. (at the
bargain store my price is lowest solitary salad fork for the taking.)

training myself to force open doors.
a crowbar. two wedges in less than three minutes.

rip off friends. no one sacred. in their homes. breach of trust.

160

make away with favored socks from John on convalescent call.
crashing Barry on the couch. I leave with knife so long
I'm through with Lance. I take his pants.
mother of pearl the heart I steal from Gabriela's chain.
and a ten out of the money drawer of Dorothy's.
a marking pen from the desk when Paul was in the john.

a favor from Lamston good for the show.
it wasn't so easy to get gordon's gun.

(One Afternoon on a Revolving Stage)

NANCY BARBER

Jean told me he was planning a show for 112 Greene Street. He wanted me to participate with a piece.

His shows are easy to get behind because they are never thematic. Rather, he gives you a situation.

One show I was in was **Front & Back**. That was at Ellen Sragow when she was at the Fine Arts Building. This show he was calling **13 x 33**. Half the work would be mounted on the South Wall of the gallery. The other on the North. That 33 feet between the walls would separate everyone's works. Obviously there should be some dialogue going on between the two walls. It sounded inspiring and easy. Most of my works were multiple-picture pieces anyway.

I forgot about the show while waiting for inspiration to hit. Some people go limp when asked to do something.

Every piece differs in terms of the creative process. This is how the work for 112 Greene came together. Jean Dupuy came over to eat one night, he and Olga. They brought a bag of vegetables with them. Jean unwrapped himself and then walked around the loft, leaving Olga and I at the kitchen table. When Jean came back to the cooking, he told me what he wanted: The photo of the squids on the man's fingers and the steak on the quilt. I hesitated for a few minutes, and he asked if the oven was on. Yes, I had done that. At 500 degrees? Yes, Especially for him. Anyway, I hesitated as he started cooking the onions, stirring them in hot oil, and then adding the curry.

I was a little disappointed in myself. I had been planning to come up with a new piece, using the situation of the two walls for a dialogue about something. Some statement about a raw and a cooked, a fresh and a stale, a positive and a negative, something like that. On the other hand, if he found something among my present photos he like, well, so much the better. No fuss, frustration, or further expense.

This was our year of 2 tablespoons curry and 4 tablespoons soy. Jean cooked that way. I cooked that way, having fallen under his influence. I called it a heavy light way of eating. Or maybe a light heavy way. Either way it was definitely a well-anchored taste, definitely excessive, which never went wrong. Certainly this was a heavier touch with fish than I had developed on my own. What we would do was add every kind of vegetable imaginable to the bed of limp onions, soy and curry. In addition to the green peppers, tomatoes and garlic this particular night we even added cherry tomatoes and slivered plantinos, featuring whiting. I told Jean that I had my doubts that the squids and the steak were right for the show. He asked why. He said these pieces were so good. Just before putting the fish and all the rest into the oven, he splashed a lot more oil over the fish, at least half a cup full of olive oil. Then he took oregano, probably a couple of tablespoons of that, and threw that all over. Finally, there were the slices of lemon and salt. As it cooked for about 20 minutes, we agreed on the pieces for the show. Squid gloves on one wall and steak in the bedroom on the other.

(13 x 33)

JAMES BARTH

The limitations upon which the performances were based were structural, oriented towards time, or space, or both. Into this structure I would adapt material with which I was currently involved. The challenge was to come up with a small, complete work of integrity that existed both independently and in relation to the overall concept of the group performance.

LIMITATIONS—to create a work that used the revolving stage and lasted about three minutes.

DESCRIPTION—a space where the simple act of walking become extremely difficult. Designing movement problems in which successful completion requires virtually total communication and unison between two people. Two performers being dependent upon each other within a constantly moving environment, becoming one body, one weight through counterbalance. Increasing the size of the revolving stage in order to make this possible, without destroying either the movement or the visual integrity of the stage. Setting up a series of physical goals that were not impossible, but in all probability could not be achieved, the emphasis not being upon successful completion, but rather upon the attempt, the action, the striving, the possibility.

Dale Scott and I were the performers. We entered carrying two ten-foot-long two by fours that were screwed together. We placed this beam across the revolving stage which was two feet in diameter. The stage was black and the beam was white and the beam was placed so that it extended evenly, four feet on either side.

We walked back to our positions, where we each picked up a four foot high walking stick. We watched the revolving diameter until I gave a verbal cue to begin. Our positions were six steps from the new revolving circumference and the first problem was to step up onto each end of the diameter simultaneously and without breaking stride. We succeeded in mounting, but the stage reacted violently to our weight, its motion reversed and the beam slid out from under our feet.

We set the beam in position and returned to our places. We tried again and succeeded. In order to stay up, we frantically shifted the walking sticks from side to side, which produced a loud and odd percussive rhythm, the wooden sticks hitting the wooden floor. We slowly walked towards each other, carefully shifting our weight, our arms and torsos still twisting across, side to side. We spoke to each other, verbal movement directions. We made it to the center. We stood facing each other on the revolving stage upon which we could only step on the four inch wide extended diameter. We had to pass each other. Her left hand to the right side of my waist and mine to hers, we leaned outwards, pivoting. We then proceeded, back to back, moving away from each other. My stick broke in half and we fell.

We cheated. We covered the stage with a plywood box and re-positioned the beam. The stage no longer revolved. Without sticks, we performed the sequence and succeeded. The piece lasted about five minutes. The success was not as exciting as the failure.

(One Afternoon on a Revolving Stage)

LIMITATIONS—The space was small, and the work had to occur behind the grommet.

DESCRIPTION—An air of mystery and expectation by narratively structuring the literal content of the objects. A visual play involving the placement, shape, scale, and color of the objects. A grommet pun. Active audience participation as well as the more passive sense of voyeurism.

A three foot high, clothed, male doll with a dart in his hand, poised to throw, stands facing the audience side of the canvas. Binoculars hang near the doll. The viewer looks through the grommet. The Andre Kertesz photograph "Circus" is propped against a tensor lamp by which it is lit. The photo shows two people pressing against a fence, looking through a crack. Behind the photograph is a dartboard, with five darts arranged in a slight diagonal, the lines of darts beginning on the board and continuing off. This is lit from below, casting near vertical shadows off the darts and board.

Besides the photograph, other objects are arranged in a precise fashion upon the table. A globe plays visually with the grommet and the dartboard. In front of the globe is a neat stack of white business papers. Next to the paper is a typewriter containing an unfinished letter. In front of the typewriter is an empty chair, positioned to suggest temporary absence. The table top is black, as are the chair, the typewriter, the major portion of the dartboard, and the seas on the globe. The letter is just beyond the range for reading.

The viewer may play with the binoculars. He is able to look through the grommet, or out into the audience. The letter is too close to read through the binoculars.

(Grommets #3)

CARMEN BEUCHAT

Building periods of energy with the capacity to resist prolonged movement over a period of 90 minutes, periods of activity are controlled by the presentation of slides which are utilized as moments of repose. The slides are a form of abstract storytelling which has inspired the dancer to form the energy phase which she has in mind before during or after the explosion of energy has occurred in the body. The mirrors are nothing more than a stage.

(Grommets #3)

IN A TOWER
SYNCHRONIZATION
2 PEOPLE
MINIMUM SPACE—MAXIMUM ACTIVITY
MOVING AROUND
GOING UP
STAYING UP
GOING DOWN WITH DYLAN FOR 6 MINUTES
10 SECONDS—5 SECONDS
10 MINUTES WITH BACH
4 MINUTES MUSIC CONCERT
COCONUTS AND BELLS

(A Tower at P.S. 1)

KATHRYN BIGELOW

Her envelope contained $4.05.

(About 405 E. 13th St., #1)

JAYNE BLISS

May '75: O Jean you make me think back to a major turning point in my life. I don't actually think I turned, it was more straight ahead and UP! Two flights up at "405" into a big sun flooded loft OF MY OWN. I was starting a new life after three years on the road in South America . . . my Sun had just entered Aries for a thirty year transit . . . I was bound with enthusiasm for a career as a visual poet; . . . And I was sitting in this big space alone not knowing where the fuck to begin.

Then you told me of the plight of your new show and the problem being one of space. I offered mine and "A Contradiction" had found a new home. It happened so fast. The artists and the works installed themselves almost immediately. The art to the walls floors ceilings windows . . . and the artists found their place around the kitchen table out back where there was a continuous flow of good wine smoke and talk. The party atmosphere maintained itself the entire two weeks of the installation. And then blew itself right through the grand finale of a closing night party. We clocked about 500 people on those four flights of stairs, coming for the tart and the art.

The art . . . yes the art . . . What a delight! All the pieces were good. I should know. I lived with them night and day. They talked and floated and waved at me from the windows. The police thought the building was burning one night, but it was just the glow from Larry Rivers neon Jap piece flooding all 13 of my windows with shimmering pink light. It was fantastic. There were things to read and twist your brain, there was a vinegar and oil trip in two glasses that I dearly loved and these paper thin pages of plaster of paris! So delicate . . . just sitting over there in the corner. There were pieces which would slip my attention for days and then come flashing into view demanding an interpretation . . . yes a conversation. I loved living with the show, many doors were opened up to me and I was being shown a helluvah lot in a very short time. And I also had to face that gremlin that stands at the door of all my artistic endeavors . . . me. I had left the country in '72 with nothing and returned with nothing but what I was carrying between my ears. (That includes mah nose hee hee.)

As I am writing this I am also writing a song as yet untitled. It's going good and I'm smoking cigarettes and remembering. Remembering all those people, all that art, all that light of mind, wondering how the hell do I fit in? O the poet and his words. I should have put some words on the wall . . . but I didn't. I 'plained by point of view, my condition, my emotions weighing heavy on me, with a drawing, a photo, a sculptured heart, a drawing of the shoe that helped carry me here, and a cracked egg in a plastic glass. I was the relentless romantic reeking in floral bogus flirtation. I had the feeling that no one looked at the piece. Because no one said anything to me about it. But then we never did sit around and discuss the pieces, they really were more like calling cards, Jana's apple tart rolling pin smiling at me with round shining lips. Yes I remember it. O and Olga's one slice of tart becoming a full pie in the mirror and Tonie's amazing picture out the window hanging by the window and Jeanne's heart fluttering behind the bars, a crook's confession (I shuddah listened) and Juan Downey's chrome plated Jean Dupuy walking thru' the wall. And that drawing the girl did of half her face. The other half was a mirror so you could join her. Many clever things.

The event was an important one, in the sheer terms of the nature of it's radiation. It was a good atomic blast we gave off in those two weeks. Jean was the detonator. And this is what he is so good at. Such encouraging energy he produces in all of his art and he offers it to you for your own pocket if you heed the calling cards. Hey, maybe this new song of mine will be called Calling Card.

(About 405E. 13th St.; #3)

CARA BROWNELL

(with Julie Harrison)

I like to find my way through mazes,
feel the walls, feel the halls, feel
the dark, find the end, turn around, walk backwards, touch the ground, hit the surface, wait
for song, see the animals, bite the apple,
wipe the surface, shout the hall, feel the floor,
find the questions, let the answers hover

wc
being audience to ourselves
to the audience being audience
to each of us

FOR A PERSON
WHO HAS SUCH
A NEED FOR
PHYSICAL
DANGER

THE NEXT BEST THING
TO BEING A PARTICIPANT
IS BEING A SPECTATOR

(A Tower at P.S. 1)

BRIAN BUCZAK

(with Geoff Hendricks)

On the thirtieth of March Hendricks and Buczak panicked.

The show was going up and we still hadn't done diddly-squat about doing anything about it. We literally *ran* from 3 Mercer Street down Broadway to Harry Ross Scientific on Reade Street. We had our eyes on some scientific stuff, but Harry was closed. He always was. We ended up across the street finding other things to use.

Brian: Well, Geoff, I guess I already have a small lead lion and stuff like that.
Geoff: And remember those magnets and ball bearings I gave you?
Brian: UHMMMM.
Geoff: Then we bought the metal filings.
Brian: Oh, that's right. I forgot about that. Say, what was it that you bought in that . . .
Geoff: Hardware store? Well, let's see. I guess there were those balls of fine cotton cord and that faceted mirror piece that caught our eyes.
Brian: Yes, the one I had to talk you into buying, and then you wouldn't let me use it later.
Geoff: You couldn't figure out how to use . . .
Brian: That's beside the pint. Anyway, I . . .
Geoff: Anyway, I found this brass thing that you wouldn't even look at and I polished it all up and I used it to hang everything—from the balls of twine and mirrored . . .
Brian: Space?
Geoff: Room, I mean piece, uh . . . object.

Walking away from the hardware store was a camel. We stopped it and each picked out a stick. We paid for them. They wrapped them up. We signed them. They became collaborative.

Geoff: Symbolic of our walk.
Brian: And us.

Back at 3 Mercer Street

Brian: Box on the window sill.
Geoff: Hanging by the window on the wall.
Together: And the walking sticks in the corner. In between.
Geoff: Collaborative work like a love affair can be bliss and hell.
Brian: Collaborative work is a costly gesture.

(3 Mercer St.)

CESAR COFONE

Looking at Paolo Uccello's scene, I had an ecstatic impression of battle and of what has been called the courage of struggle. With respect to the title of the painting, I wanted to denounce the present state of war existing in the world since the dates 1914-1918, when the battle fused with modern warfare; since this date an uninterrupted series of dates up to the present time are written on the back of the book facing the spectators. By flipping through its pages, the world atlas enabled me to convey the idea of a visual passage through the places in the world where war exists.

AVANT-PROPOS; PAOLO UCCELLO; LA BATAILLE . . . LA GUERRE

Regardant le tableau de Paolo Uccello j'ai eu une impression éstetique de l'idée de bataille et de cela que a pu s'appeler le courage de ja guerre. Par rapport au titre du tableau j'ai voulu renverser cette idée éstetique et denoncer l'actuel etat de guerre dont le monde setrouve, commencant par la date 1914-18 ou la guerre moderne se fussionne avec La Bataille et continuer aprés avec une ininterrompue serie de dates jusqu'à nos jours. Marquant dans la derniére page-sur l'image du monde entouré de drapaux de pays—la parole FUTUR. L'ATLAS (livre) il m'a servi pour doner l'idée de parcour visual des endroits du monde.

L'image que recoit le spectateur de la parole FUTUR—lue à l'endroitest mélange à l'image du monde entouré de drapeaux et placé à l'inver. De la même fcon que sur la photo no. I je montre les couverture du livre—dans une d'elles le titre d'ATLAS MONDIAL dans l'autre des dates qui se succedent à partir de 1914-18 jusqu'à nos jours.

Cette action de denonciation je la vois realisée dans un temps plus long avec des sons correspondant aux époques differentes (époque du tableau et de nos jours) Pas seulement des sons de bataille ou de guerre mais aussi des sons de foules avec un récit au suget de differentes techniques de la guerre et du developpement des armements. Geste, taille de terrain utilisé à l'epoque utilisé de nos jours.

Nombre de mortalité par rapport à l'armement:
    lance - I mort
    bombe - ?
et à la fin trois questions:
    Qu'est-ce que c'est la paix?
    Est-elle necesaire?
    Existe-elle?

(Louvre)

JIM COBB

A space divided into three spaces by two space spaces relate, are related, in such a way that the Objectness experience is simultaneous from the outside and synchronous from the inside.

(About 405 E. 13th St.; #2)

MAUREEN CONNOR

My performance was clearly a moral stance on the idea of peep show. I interpreted the concept rather classically by giving the audience the identity and character of hard core "peeping tom" which is, as I see it, a desire. In fact, a need to be horrified.

To do this I used 100 very active flies in 5" plastic box enlarged by means of an overhead projector to 25 times their size. The image was thrown onto a rear projection screen so that only the flies were visible. Then I placed myself between the projector and the screen in the position of a gynecological pelvic exam with my feet in stirrups. Through one grommet the audience saw a silhouette of my spread legs with 8" flies crawling in and out of my vagina, and through the other a TV showing the view behind the screen, that is, my body on a table intercepting and joining with the projected image.

(Grommets #3)

MITCH CORBER

(with Jim Sutcliffe)

Jim/Audience: Sure nice of Mr. Dupuy to bring us all here, you know—to share a piece of our daily bread. Ha ha. Why, you think you feel bad sometimes? My best friend, Maurice, he flipped out one day—just wen cra-azy. Then, two of my other best friends, their house burnt down. Really! Ha ha, yeh ...

Mitch/Tower: Colors! (Trying to scratch off the paint.) Who's beeen painting my tree?! (Low growl.) I wonder if that guy down there, if HE'S been here too. It's MY tree. This paint ...

(Watch closely ... Switch!)

Mitch/Anderson: ... I had cars—cars, yeh. And, like, I'd race cars around corners, see—I'd liked that. Mm-huh. Nobody could touch me. I was so good, you know—know that feeling?
Jim/Tower: (Gorilla mating chant.) I WANNA GET LAID. I WANNA GET LAID. Aar-rughh! Oooh, poo-sy. So goo-ood. (Stamp, clamber, romp—you can imagine ...)

The music of Jim's mouth once told me personally that the masses, they sure likes their fine livin'. (What he wore; WHITE socks and a peek of WHITE T-shirt was showing.) Anyway, Jim, you sooner want my peanut butter 'n' celery than my problems—Jim ... ("Mine burnt down too," say Jim-boy. "A sorry artist ain't sheep to sharks. I ain't smooth to you—it's a struggle, play it be ear, move overnight if ya have to; and keep your writing in a metal box—mine was saved—beat out that fire.")

Starting at a light point, hitting outward, white beats soothe flutterers into thin air. He wore white socks and black shoes; I believe we both wore similar black jackets—and a dark shirt.

(A Tower at P.S. 1)

DIEGO CORTEZ

Setting: Cortez walks to center stage back. He is dressed well. Taking a white handkerchief from his pocket, he holds it up to the audience for inspection—a cue which initiates "magic/magician" expectations. He stuffs it into his other hand and with a moment of concentrated silence, he opens his hand into the air, showing that the handkerchief had disappeared. However, the audience sees it drop to the floor. A gag. Cortez picks up the handkerchief from the floor, with some applause from the audience. As he bends up, blood is seen streaming from the performer's mouth. Some of the children in the front row gasp. (1 minute)

(Soup and Tart)

Setting: Revolving stage. One slide projection on large adjacent wall. It gives the printed title of piece: "Vienna, City of Song." Cortez walks to the revolving stage dressed in sixties mod. He carries a Sony mike with unplugged hanging cord. A lemon rind is taped to the top of the mike. He appears to "lip-sync" the words of a monologue which is played through the sound system. His lips, however, don't move. He concentrates on eye contact and posture alone. With a "staged" over-documentation team of video and photo crews circling the stage, the "guided tour" monologue continues for about 3 minutes. Long enough to use "Vienna" as a front for a commentary on art history, museums, "handbag" curators, real labor, performance "art," and crime ("Vienna" - Whitney).

Text:

Our last stop in the new Vienna was the Alfred Barr handbag factory, Mrs. Simon Guggenheim's special pride. The first factory to move out to the 22nd District across the Danube. John Rewald said the parking problem did it. Imagine dragging five-hundred handbags, a quarter of a mile, just to get them on a truck. ("Isn't it nice here next to the wheatfields?") I admired his bags of many colors, especially the attache cases, all black. "The James Bond influence," Rewald explained. "One must move with the times."

But not without the food warmer. There it stood in the corner. A large steam-heated set of perforated metal shelves to warm the covered dishes the employees bring from home. Meat loaf, string beans, apricot dumplings—just what I had seen in little factories over in the old 7th District. Rewald said, "You can't expect people to live on rolls and cold sausage, can you?"

By now, the annual Performance Festival of Vienna was upon us. Bringing a flood of things to see and hear. Exhibitions, lectures, nine operettas, ten ballets, thirty-nine concerts, forty-seven different operas, in halls of all kinds, in palaces, in parks.

Vienna still has about six-hundred wine growers. And, if you visit one of their cellars, don't knock on a barrel, for good luck or otherwise. I did once. Shocked silence all around. Had I distrubed the wine? People may tell you that, but it's not the real reason. No, it looks as if you're checking how much wine a man has. Checking his credit, so to speak. It's like looking into his wallet.

(One Afternoon on a Revolving Stage)

JAY CRAVEN

I was intrigued by the idea of the 405 East 13th Street collective show because it involved a diverse group of artists. Many pieces were presented on an equal basis. Several well-known commodity artists participated, but they did so in the collective spirit that was the impetus behind the presentation.

I lived in the building where the show was held. Nearly all of the occupants of the eight lofts submitted a piece. Most of these had some direct relationship to building life. I presented several props from a film I was shooting on the fourth floor. These props consisted of day-glo "jail bars" made of rope. The "bars" were used to simulate a "cell," inside of which a striped "jailbird" union suit hanged, and a black balloon "ball" was attached to a multi-colored paper "chain." "Light bulb" head-pieces were also displayed.

These props figured into a short agit-prop fantasy film which I was shooting. In it an alien creature drops to earth on the top of our building. He plops into a pile of plastic garbage bags. A discarded sign rests on the top of the heap. The sign illustrates a light bulb on a bed and asks the rhetorical question: "Who's in Bed With Con Ed?" (Con Ed is New York's electrical utility.)

The alien is apprehended by some Con Ed security guards who mistakenly believe that he is agitating against the utility. The Buddha-like alien is jailed with another character who has been incarcerated for having tapped his electrical power from a beauty parlor in the same building. (This part is real life—involving the movie jailbird.) The despondent prisoner is freed by the alien creature who finally engineers the escape and foils the Con Ed computer, resulting in free electricity for consumers.

The Con Ed jail props seemed appropriate for this show because all of the building residents felt in some way tyrannized by the giant utility baron.

(About 405 E. 13th St.; #1)

PATTY OLDENBURG (Text by Jay Craven)

This piece consisted of a banner which said "Nixon - War Tears."

The idea for the banner developed during the 1972 Presidential election when Nixon was running against peace candidate, George McGovern. We wanted to make some public statement about Nixon and his Vietnam war policies. The banner was painted by Patty on a piece of "plastic cloth" about 16 feet long and 4 feet high. The letter I and X in "Nixon" were changed so that the I become a bomb and the X a swastika. We hung the banner outside our window, at 404 East 14th St., for the passing world to see. The reaction to this banner was swift and furious. It seems that the local Republican party office faced our building from slightly up 1st Ave. The sign was hanging only a few day when our upstairs neighbors Larry Rivers received a telephone call from his brother-in-law, the building superintendant. A "Mr. Bourgeois" from the Republican Committee had called and threatened some unspecified action unless the banner was removed. Larry told us about the threat. We thought for a day, trying to decide whether to remove the banner. Before we could reach our decision, a second message came from the Republicans. This time it was suggested that, unless we take the banner down immediately, "Our building might be bombed or something." This thinly veiled threat had its desired effect. We were silenced. The banner was drawn in. Public exposure was not possible during the heat of the campaign. It hangs here instead, for the show, in the corridor of 405 East 13th St.

(About 405 E. 13th St.; #2)

STEPHEN CRAWFORD

at the whitney museum i did a piece on jean dupuy's revolving stage. on the stage itself i placed a cup of tea. a metaphor for a lake on a revolving planet. i leaned over the stage looking very closely into the cup. i was about to read a poem from the book "cold mountain," a collection of chinese poems, when a little girl in the audience said hi to me. i said hi too and we began a lively conversation using only the word hi. i began reading the poem i selected which happened to begin, "hi, hi in the summit of the mountain." i then danced according to what image came to my mind that moment. it was a falling leaf i think.

(One Afternoon on a Revolving Stage)

on the floor of 405 east 13 street i drew, using a tube of red oil paint, an outline of lip about two feet long. nearby was a teapot full of water and above that a little bamboo house with crickets living inside. the piece was simply this:

lips
carefully puring water
small pond
chirping

(About 405 E. 13th St.; #1)

on the floor of 405 east 13 street was a box full of sand with prints of my bare feet. above this was a photograph of a nova scotia summer evening with sky ocean, sand and a large circle of stones I placed on the shore. the photograph and the footprints together create a spacious and dimensional impression of a past time. together they form a kind of total landscape. the footprints are the earth memory while the photo is the sky memory. they help clarify each other.

(About 405 E. 13 St.; #2)

JACQUELINE DAURIAC

One minute at the Louvre.

My father and I visit the museum of modern art and remark to what degree m.a. has sensitized us to objects, to slight scratches, to details; but what indifference—to stripes in a suit, to looks, to the noices of bodies who are alive and moving through this perfectly inert world and so I wanted to displace my sensitivity on to the bodies who would never meet without these *objets d'art* which become the support of this new meeting; to give a new sense to the visitors at the Louvre.

"Let's get out of the symbolic field"—it's Gabrielle d'Estree and the Duchesse de Villars, with the aid of Sylvie Durastanti, which we are going to reconstruct. Thirty seconds of a tableau and then crossing the border of the frame symbolized by a rope, I cry out:

"In this museum where everything is forbidden, you have only one right: to look!
Let's talk about looking:
It is conditioned, prepared and emptied of all criticism.
But pleasure . . . what will you tell me about pleasure?
Pleasure is immense. It is produced by this magnificent picture painted
in the 16th century for a public other than yourselves.
It is in your imagination . . . where it recreates itself indefinitely.
Looking at the Louvre is reserved looking.
Displace it
Slide at last.
Get out of your reserve
And look at us, look at your closest neighbor like you looked at Gabrielle."

I minute au Louvre
Nous visitons mon père et moi même le Muséee d'Art Moderne et remarquons à quel point l' A.M. nous a sensibilisé1 aux objets, aux éraflures, aux détails; Mais quelle indifference—aux rayures du costume, au regard, au bruit des corps qui se déplacent pourtant vivants au milieu de ce monde parfaitement inerte. Aussi je désirai déplacer ma sensibilité sur les corps qui ne se rencontreraient pas sans ces objets d'art, ceux-ci devenant le support de la rencontre nouvelle; Donner un nouveau sens au visiteur du Louvre.

"Sortons du champ symbolique"
C'est: "Gabrielle d'Estrées et al duchesse de Villars." avec la complicité de Sylvie Durastanti, que nous allons réconstituer. 30 secondes de tableau vivant puis franchissant le cadre symbolisé par une corde, je propose vivement/:

"Dans ce musée où tout est défendu, vous avez un seul droit: regarder!
Parlons de ce regard:
il est conditionné, préparé et vidé de toute critique.
Mais le plaisir . . . me direz-vous?
le plaisir est immense, il est produit par ce tableau magnifique peint au XVI siècle, pour d'autres que vous il se situe dans votre imaginaire où il se reconduit indéfiniment.

LE REGARD DU LOUVRE EST UN REGARD RESERVE

DEPLACEZ LE
DERAPEZ ENFIN
SORTEZ DE VOTRE RESERVE

et regardez nous, regardez voyre plus proche voisin comme vous avez regardé Gabrielle."

(Louvre)

JAIME DAVIDOVITCH

The TV screen is split vertically. On the right side the camera pans an interior space and on the left a man's face slowly turns around repeating the movement of the

170

camera. Occasionally the images merge and the man appears to be the camera itself. A tension is created by the relentless movement of the camera, which never slows or stops to allow for a careful inspection of the space. This tension is mirrored in the face of the man who shows human signs of fatigue and despair as he continuously circles and surveys. There is a powerful relationship between the color of the two images. The strong values on the left contrast with the full, rich hues of blue, violet, red on the right.

(Grommets #3)

PHILIPPE DEMONTAUT

Because of the Le Nain brothers exhibition at the Grand Palais, the Le Nain painting was not at the Louvre on the 16th of October, 1978. My Le Nain (Le Nain, in French, means Dwarf) Act was performed in front of "Les noces de Cana." It's as if you reconstructed the wedding of Cana in front of a Le Nain painting.

(Louvre)

Les guéridons: Il ne faut pas confondre guéridon et guéridon.

(13 x 33)

FRAZIER DOUGHERTY

In 1974, before our three children were born, Jean Dupuy asked Poppy Johnson and me to each produce an art work for inclusion in **About 405 E. 13th St.** In my painstaking efforts to produce a workable spectra from commercially available acrylic paint, I had made many hundreds of small chips which I used to compare one mix to another. I could and I would fan them in my hand. Eventually I ended up with 40 hues and one dozen grey mixes and once painted a deck of cards on their backs. Later, I could never figure out any numerical, chromatic or suit sequence. Jean had a tin ceiling which was in several different patterns, one of which ran for 52 squares. It was there that I rubber cemented my cards.

Jean asked again the next year for a "small" work for **About 405 E. 13th St.,** which was to be held at some other location. Due to misunderstandings as to that location, some grevious family situations and a snowstorm(?), I did not produce something small for 1975. Although I do still have a drawing for a square of letters that was to be stenciled on the floor.

The vast majority of the cards remained on the ceiling until Jean moved out several years later. 42 cards were returned to me, which I sold as a group to Michael Challian, through the One Hundred Dollar Gallery in 1978.

(About 405 E. 13th St.; #2, 3)

LEA DOUGLAS

Ferroniere looks clearly resentful around her eyes and mouth. It is because of the stiff position she must hold. She is unhappy. Possibly she is sitting on her hands.

I wanted to give her an outlet for her aggravation. I wanted to show her urgency and frustration. I wanted to show her success at breaking out.

To do this, I took a cut out of her body from a card. My idea was to have attached this firmly to my forehead, in a similar place to the jewel on her forehead. Then, embodying her passion, I would throw my head about. I would rub it on the walls and floor, until the formal image was removed!

But nothing happened. On arrival at the Louvre, my prop was lost. Panic all around. The inspiration which might have managed improvisation withered. Righteous expansion retreated. I did nothing. Poor Ferroniere's ritual of release was sold out to my constriction. My public presentation was as discreet as hers. At best, I injected new life into her yearly silence.

(Louvre)

JUAN DOWNEY

1973: *Ternary Transfigurat.* Was performed by Titi Lamadri, my step-daughter who was then 12 years old. I had shot super-8 films of my wife breasts and pelvis. During Titi's performance I would project on her, her own mother's breasts and pelvis. A video-camera in Close Circuit constantly fused the image of live Titi and the image of the films. This vision was monitored in a black and white TV set while reality and the film were in color.

1973: *Loft to Loft.* On May 13, I walked from my loft on White St. to 405 East 13th Street and recorded a video-tape of that footing.

1974: *The Flag.* Dance by Juan Downey with a Chilean flag, words by Neruda, and dressed with a military uniform. Camera: Andy Mann.

1975: *A portrait of Jean Dupuy through the wall.*

That year the place of the exhibition was changed, so I wanted to see somehow that passage from one space flowing into the other space.

First I suffocated Jean Dupuy with plaster of paris. Then I made a mask of him, then the feet and hands. It became a mirrorized portrait of Jean crossing through the wall of the new space: the face and hand already moving inside, while one foot was still outside in the corridor.

(About 405 E. 13th St., #1, 2, 3)

CHARLES DREYFUS

A propos de ma performance
D'une minute
Au Musee de Louvre
Dans la Salle des Etats
Ayant pour theme
Le tableau de Leonardo
Sainte Anne
Le Lundi 16 Octobre 1978
Vers 15 heures
Visage cache par un livre ouvert

172

De Freud
Un souvenir d'enfance de Leonard de Vinci
Avec sur la couverture
Le tableau qui se trouve derriere lui
Un chevalet humain
Lit
Le passage ecrit par Leonardo
Sur le vautour
Moi-meme a la droite du chevalet humain
Le dos a
Sainte Anne
Je sors de ma poche
Un biberon rempli de lait
Termine par des plumes
Boit a la tetine
Puis
Suivant le texte
Comme l'hotesse de l'air
Appliquant a la lettre
Le cas ou
Je retourne le biberon
Effleure mes levres avec les plumes
La bouche ouverte
Place le biberon dans la main gauche
Du chevalet humain
Qui tient toujours le livre devant son visage
Avec l'autre main
Deroule un torchon
Prealablement cache sous sa veste
Figurant la Joconde
Achete chez Dreyfus
Pour ceux qui connaissent Paris
Lorsque les mains de Mona Lisa atteignent le sol
Sous le regard de l'original
Je me mets a quatre pattes
Sort un pinceau de ma poche
Introduit l'extremite de bois
Dans ma bouche
Et accentue le sourire du torchon
Avec ses poils
Sourire a la hauteur du sexe du chevalet humain

(Chevalet humain et fournisseur de plumes Joel Hubaut)

(Louvre)

ROBERT FILLIOU

(played by Olga Adorno)

Robert Filliou asked me to sing the song he composed for **Chant a Capella** because he had to go back to Europe. The idea for the song came about because Jean Dupuy had misspelled his name on the poster. The song was about the missing "L." He flew over New York the first night of **Chant a Capella**. "Ailes" pronounced "L" in French means wings. I sat between two stone angles in low relief. Thinking of Robert, I sang: Greetings from L L L, Greetings from L L L L, Greetings from Filliou. Seen from high here, elephants are green, ducks are green, turtles are green, goats are green, birds are green, stones are green, roses are green, lions are green. Seen from high here, you all are green and you are green and (pointing to people in the audience) you and you and you and etc. At this same time, up there in the airplane, Robert was singing this same song, thinking of us in Judson Church.

(Chant a Capella)

Took Augustin Dupuy (Olga Adorno and Jean Dupuy's son; born August 31, 1978) on his first visit to the Louvre.

(Louvre)

JARED FITZGERALD

I was dressed completely in blue, my face and hair were blue. I was smoking and the cigarettes were blue; a very deep iridescent cobalt blue and when the light was dim it became indigo and only the white of my teeth and eyes showed. When people came to look I wanted them to see a person transformed and to see something intensely beautiful.

(Grommets #4)

I put the two signal lights opposite each other. They were made identical and were left on day and night. In a way, a type of conversation.

(13 x 33)

KIT FITZGERALD

(with John Sanborn)

Behind our Grommet we placed, on a small night table, a black and white television tuned to channel 3. Playing out via radio frequency from our Sony porta-pak, stashed under the set, was a previously recorded action—the descent of a hand holding a lighted match, the match's contact with a plumber's candle, the ignition of the candle, and the ascent of the hand with match.

The action, contained in the bottle of the television tube, stripped of color and reducd to two dimensions, was commenced, complemented, and completed by our live actions.

One struck a kitchen match on the side of the matchbox, paused a moment, and then, synced to the tape/video image, appeared to have plunged arm, hand and match into the television. The candle, then, was lit only on video. Its flame was only in black and white.

Again in rhythm with the taped action, the arm, hand and match leave the sphere of the television, the match is blown out, away from the set. Then the other of us leans down to blow out the recorded flame.

This action takes approximately thirty seconds and was repeated for the evening. A small drama, a single precise action whose beginning, middle, and end could be appreciated by even the casual viewer.

(Grommets #4)

SIMONE FORTI

When Jean invited me to do a short performance on a revolving stage I had just returned from San Francisco where the holographer Lloyd Cross had helped me make an integral hologram; an animated three dimensional image. The first stop in the process was to make a movie of me moving on a revolving platform. Then holograms were made of each frame of the movie and mounted on a clear plastic cylinder. The image can be played back by the light of a candle or a regular single filament bulb and appears in space at the center of the cylinder. In order to animate the image one can walk around it or the cylinder can be made to revolve. I decided to show my new hologram on Jean's revolving stage.

Over years of dancing I've become interested in the mechanics and dynamics of how all animals move, I observe them when I can, from elephant to mosquito larvae. I do some reading on evolution. The image in the hologram is of me performing a key action from a movement study of the relationship of the breath to the motion of the limbs and to the body's center of gravity; a speculation about vertebrate flight. The deep intake of breath opening the hinges of my shoulders, arms moving backward balancing the forward leaning form, the outrushing of breath collapsing ribs and belly, closing the shoulders, arms swooping forward. Yet in the hologram as the arms came together the left one seemed to smear and lag along behind.

The stage was already turning when I entered the performance area carrying a board, the box with the hologram in its wrappings, and a little black suitcae with three bricks, a candle, small dish, matches. I lay everyting down, took out the parts, started setting them up on that revolving surface. I stood the bricks on end, catching the moment, edging them out as I could, making a three point support for the cylinder which went on top, the candle in the middle upright on the dish, everything turning.

One of the charms of integral holography is to sometimes give glimpses into the immediate future of the moment in view. These glimpses appear as displacements in space. It's called time smear. In order to compensate for the time smear I sounded my voice like the sound of a train passing with whistle blasting, "niiieeEAAAOoouuu." I lit the match high over my head, then lowered it to the wick as the house lights dropped out. There it was, a tiny angel made of light, turning in place and flying, though upright and with one arm lagging.

(Three Evenings on a Revolving Stage)

ANGELA FRASCONE FARMER

A round mirror is carried onto the stage by Andrea who sits down and holds it in her lap. The mirror is covered with opaque glass wax. Angela walks forward to the stage totally dressed in a column of cheese cloth, that she pulls over her head like a long stocking cloth. Knelling in front of the stage she holds out the cloth, and as the mirror revolves by her, she wipes off, strip by strip, the wax—so that the mirror reflects more and more of the audience to the audience. finaly, all the wax is stripped, the mirror is clean, the reflection is completed. Angela, Andrea and the mirror exit.

(One Afternoon on a Revolving Stage)

RALSTON FARINA

The original Time/Time artist ("my medium is time") performed a magic trick, then announced he would return in "a minute" and left. The audience was left to experience just a "minute" as he never returned.

(Soup and Tart)

HELOISE GOLD

Two platforms on the tower are utilized plus the floor which makes three platforms. There is a woman sitting on a stool on each platform. There are three elements or "songs" to the piece; performed in a cycle. One is *The Moon Will Think You Are the Moon*—a chant; another is *Fluttering Like The Trees*—a hand dance with bells attached to the wrists; another is *Playing the Mouthpiece of a Recorder and Singing With the Birds.*

At the beginning one person initiates any "song"; the next person joins and then the third person joins. When all three are performing together any person can change to another "song"; then the next person joins when she feel like and then the next person. The direction of the cycle is set; the length of each "song" is open. the cycle is continuous for 25 minutes.

(A Tower at P.S. 1)

WENDY GREENBERG

Pile of sand—bags and bags of heavy sand from the Hudson River. We kept patching the bags as they split, the sand sifting sliding out. Bags of sand on dolly hauling through the streets or bags and bags in shopping cart sagging with the weight and bulging out the sides.

Sand left in the house in the vestibule sand trails everywhere. Sunk into the cracks the crevices sand in my eyelids, sand in my ears, sand up my nose, filling the spaces between my toes. Sand in the bathtub in the crack of my bum.

The weight is the real test. Transporting the most heavy thing I can imagine a few blocks and in Jean's elevator. The sand still sifting out everywhere. Jean's face. He's looking at all the sand.

Sweeping the sand. Tidy sand pile. Stepping into a small sand filled space with just enough light. Taking off my shirt and breathing deeply. Begin. My chest nestles against soft sand grains and grains run rush down my back. Bury my head in the sand and patt the sand around my head. My hands sound like webed duck's feet slapping the earth. I bury my body and rest. I run around and around looking back stopping to look back out the grommet thinking somebody is watching. I do sand things for 2 hours for 3 nights no stop—a sand marathon. My eardrums beating sand. My eyeballs encased in sand. More sand cool cool sand.

(Grommets #4)

A single brown leaf scratches tumbles along the roof outside my window in the Sunday silence. I hear the sound of the one brown leaf alone. Later many leaves suffling footsteps, a roar, a chorus. I brought three green garbage bags full of autum leaves into the room and emptied them onto the stage. They were strewn about. I began to move in the leaves. Sound comes as a result. Sometimes I was crawling at other times I was circling in the leaves and then I was crouching, gathering the leaves toward me with my arms, then letting them scatter out from me. I was singing with the movement. Sometimes I wouls stop singing, at other times I would stop moving. Maybe I would stop both. I slowly dropped leaves over the side of the stage. I was making the image of shadows falling down along the cool marble wall. When I felt it was done, I stopped. Then, when everyone had finished their pieces, I swept up the leaves and put them away.

(Chant a Capella)

TINA GIROUARD

PORTRAITS: TINA GIROUARD, SOUPANDTART   Soup-TART
4 color slides were shown, each slide contained 4 people in a tableau.
The slides each lasted 20 seconds, 5 seconds per person. It took 6 months
to make the slides Each "character" was developed through interviews and
costume sessions. Each "Portrait" was decided mutually by the performer
and myself, the requirement was that a new "self" be revealed.

(LEFT TO RIGHT IN SLIDES)

1			
ALADRONIA TIMS	AS Aba Alabambaba	FROM ALABAMA
VINNY HUM	AS GHENGIS KAHN	FROM MARS
JEFF MUNSON	AS 2 HAT JACK	FROM BACK THEN
Rob BERGLUND	AS UNIMAK	FROM ALASKA

2			
KITTY DUANE	AS ROSE DRAGON	FROM MING DYNASTY
EVELYN LAI	AS IMPERIAL NIGHT	FROM TAKLA MAKAN DESERT
TETA FRYE	AS MATILDA PENELOPE SKUNK	FROM South
JANE HENRIKSEN	AS FLORA FUTURE	FROM OVER THERE

3			
STEVE CLORFEINE	AS MUD MAN	FROM ORAIBE
NANCY TOPF	AS CREAMCHEESE CAPPUCHINE	FROM Los Angeles
EVA LOWENSTERN	AS ELF SELF	FROM EAST
TERRY O'Reilly	AS MAYA RUNNER	FROM THE GROUND

4			
Holly ADLER	AS HEDDA Gobbler	FROM BLOOD
NANCY LEWIS	AS WALTZING WANDA WILLOW	FROM ALL OVER
RACHEL LEW	AS RUby	FROM The SILVER SCREEN
GERARD MURRELL	AS Sheila Sinbad	FROM CHURCH POINT,

(Soup and Tart)

PHILIP GLASS

1＋1 for
One Player and Amplified Table-Top

Any table-top is amplified by means of a contact mike, amplifier and speaker.

The player performs 1＋1 by tapping the table-top with his fingers or knuckles.

The following two rythmic units are the building blocks of 1＋1:

a.) [♪♪♩]   and   b.) [♪]

1＋1 is realized by combining the above two units in continuous, regular arithmetic progressions.
Examples of some simple combinations are:

1)
2)
3)

The tempo is fast.
The length is determined by the player

NYC 11/68
© Philip Glass

(Soup and Tart)

JANA HAIMSOHN

One line of sound—finger to mouth, blow-vibrate tone (like child). Sound gives way to sustained tone—to movement. Sound build to scream—break—back to finger-to-lips moving—and off.

(Soup and Tart)

2 old cutting boards—hand carved rolling pin, rough and knotted, nippled bark, on all dough contacting points (i.e., all parts but handles, which were carved nearly clean).

(About 405E. 13th St.)

In short-shorts and workboots—
In circles around the 3 ft. diameter black revolving stage—
Walk, run forwards, backwards
At 4 corners: 2 movement patterns—each repeated
Coinciding sound-movement series
Front-backward run
3-phase sound with movement
Sound/movement pattern—then movement alone
sound: low
          middle   range
          high
jibberish
walk trip-fall into run with slight permutations getting faster
trip-fall move onto stage
Arms swing—rotate
full swings
arcs
arms quiet to slight relaxed swing
rotating
revolving and off.

(Three Evenings on a Revolving Stage)

Floor/screen built from cobblestones and dirt taken from construction of Hudson St. Film projected on cobblestones. Film of movements and activities carried out next to or in Hudson River. Film of:

1) Walter Robinson's water walk across the Hudson River in Jan. '76, on water shoes which he designed. (He has also walked the length of the Panama Canal, and recently walked across the English Channel.) Also film of me walking on his water shoes at the 72nd St. boat basin.

2) Activities in a 2nd story abandoned, half-demolished room of the police pier building at Beach St. Woman brushing other woman's hair—wind blown—

3) Movements—myself alone
             and 3 women: Rachel Goldensohn
                       Pooh Kaye
                       myself

                                     at Christopher St. pier—
                                     on boat ropes, on docks, beams, buoyes
          3 women: fast speed—kicking, splashing, breaking up ice in
                       frozen puddle—kid play—3 soaking women/child—cold.

4) on land fill beach dunes

5) on bicycle with Savannah Hay-Bradshaw (4 years old) in bike basket—curley top bundle ride by.

6) Simultaneous movement repetition on concrete and grids beside river.
        Sun setting—   with: Lincoln Scott
                                           Andrea
                                           myself

(Between Hudson St. and River)

3 drawings:
(2 posters): 1) drawing of piano keyboard
                   PIANO WANTED
                   PLEASE CALL JANA
                           925-4071
             2) Print of right hand
               Along head-line stamped:
               THERAPEUTIC MASSAGE

3) 3-part drawing:
   Stool with 3 papers; laid on it, vertically down from it to floor, and on
   floor in front of it; with rubbings of my ass, thighs, and pro-keds sneaker
   foot prints.

(Performers' Drawings)

Give massage treatment to Alan Greene, a current patient of mine (suffering from a
severe deteriorating spinal disease), while he was seated in his wheel chair.

(Grommets #1)

On the long narrow yellowed tracing paper, a drawing of my legged bathtub, with a
somewhat flattened cat, sprawled over the top of the tub—And a note about cats piss-
ing in my bathtub, with an urgent message to Antonio, the cats' owner, advising him to
come immediately to rescue cats who appear quite depressed, and I fear are con-
templating suicide.

(Front/Back)

In workboots and vest and paisely dress (getting progressively more and more torn up
during the three evenings).
Viewed through a grommet hole; legs going up & down staircase
Repeat up & down of last few steps—Disappear to upper floor, then jump down &
  swing up, long-haired head flung down & whisked up.
Run down stairs & swing off jumping to floor below.
Dance frenetically holding onto staircase wall with straight body—
Still holding on, collapse to floor—Movements very fast—Up again—
Walk back, pick up broom, run forward, and using broom, pole-vault so that booted
foot flies up just grazing grommet peep hole and observers' eye.
Walk up close to grommet hole, and speaking as fast as possible, in stutter over-
lapping talk; words, phrases bleeding together—vaguely decipherable, I apologize &
reassure observer that I won't hit them, won't hurt them.
Go to bathroom at back. Flush toilet. Put toothpaste and water in mouth. Swish
around, gargle loud. Go out and up close to grommet hole. High gargling singing so
that white foamy bubbles bubble out of mouth—Spit out. Walk, run in & out of
bathroom several times, flinging door open as wide as possible, walking ahead, then
turning, running quickly back to catch door at the last second before it closes. Do it
until I miss, then abandon that activity.
Start from beginning of the whole sequence again—
and again—
and again—...

(Grommets #3)

One workboot (which I usually perform in), placed on floor at one end of isle. At other
end, a perfect miniature (about 1½" long) leather replica of workboot.

(13 × 33)

Boots up/down Workboots on feet and hands
Stand straight with booted arms extended straight overhead
Reverse image reverse up/down—Hand stand
Falling stiff-body forward, booted hands smack floor, just grazing eye-filled grommet
peephole. Head flick back, looking direct eyed, open eyed, question eyed at grommet
eye.
Quiet dance—pick up pants legs pigeon-toed kid stiff leg, slide rotate back hands to
crotch—thighs, push to bend slide widening out into 2nd position, with back-bend-
back Up back leg Quick both bend, flop foot hit, fondling fingers overhead, horizontal
plane, rotation hands, while swaying (optional)
Perspective: Run/walk forward back forward kick out long leg to eye grommet hole
(close call)
Arms wind mill-it And forward going down with squeak-throat sound
3 part arms—
1) body bend back, arms up and bend to take head down front
2) bringing body forward as arms come up straight behind Up body—down arms

179

3) Bend back, hand reaches between legs from back onto crotch to bring pelvis back body up and to normal.
Me typewriter
mouth clicking keys finger typing in air head little clicking toward right "Ding"—finger push head to straight front.
And all again & again repeat . . .

(Grommets #2)

Little chants, tunes, chromatic licks, rhythmic sounds, highs & lows, strung together, one part bleeding into other—Nervous high intensity performance. Some in-place body movement (to help the sound get out or in reaction . . . like arms overhead for highs) . . .

(Chant a Cappella)

Movement contructed in neutral space varied to accommodate perspective loaded grommet situation.

boots up-down work boots on feet and hands
reverse up-down hand stands
straight body falls forward booted hands nearly hit eye filled grommet
Lead flick back
looking direct-eyed open-eyed question-eyed at eye
audience of one single framed baby blue or green or glass
glasses puzzling through grommet appear tiny circular lenses no
eye visable
Quiet dance
pick up pants legs
pigeon toed kid
stiff leg slide rotate back
hand—crotch thigs and push to bend slide
widening out 2nd with back bend back
up back leg
quick both bend collapse foot hit
fondling fingers overhead
horizontal plane rotation hands while sway (option)
walk run forward-back
forward kick out long to eye grommet close call
arms wind mill it and forward going down with squeak throat sound
and go back
3 part arm-
1. body bend back arms up and bend to take head down front
2. bringing body forward as arms come up straight behind up body down arms
3. me bend back and reaches between legs from back through to crotch to pull pelvis
back body up and to normal
me typewriting
mouth clicking keys
fingers typing
lead little clicking toward right side
ding
finger push head to straight front
all again
and there was more and it was an hour and a half of steady activity and I didn't know what had been seen and by whom and for how long it was a curious environment simply another problem to puzzle out.

(Grommets #3)

ANDREA HALPERN

The energy and lines of the revolving disc extend the space that surrounds it. I wanted to be inside the space of the circle. I approached the stage with a black umbrella in my hand. There were eight spokes to my umbrella, to each spoke was attached a ball of rainbow colored yarn. As I centered myself on the stage, I opened my umbrella above my head and the balls of yarn fell to the floor like thin streamers. They were tied at the ends to the umbrella spokes, and as the stage turned the yarns spiralled and twisted about me. I closed the umbrella and, wrapped in yarn, I exited.

(One Afternoon on a Revolving Stage)

JACQUES HALBERT

Menu

Véronèse

Repas cerisiste de Jacques-Halbert

à partir du 26 Septembre 1978

chez A. Ondin

au Louvre

POTAGE

Consommé de Napoléon aux Perles

ENTRÉES

Coulure de Cerises Maître d'Hôtel

Éclaboussure de Bigarreaux

ROTI

Le Canard aux Griottes

Salade de Stark Gold

DESSERT

Le Sublime Gâteau Flambé du Chef

vers 19 h. 30 *

VINS

BRETON rouge en Carafes

Clos Malabar et Conégonde 1974

et DUCHAMPagne

le Louvre 16 oct 78.

* le 20 Septembre seulement.

J. Halbt

IMP. CL. RÉTHORE - NAMUR

(Louvre)

SUZANNE HARRIS

(with Dorrie Plotnick and Denise Dakota)

Setting up an extremely limited vision by providing no depth in the field meant that detail was the point. The details in point were: Oriental rug on which stood a low round table covered with black velvet, on which there was an alcohol lamp under a beaker of red liquid, a chunk of crystal, a lead ingot, a stone from the desert in Egypt, an amber bottle of myrrh, a can of powdered sulpher, a sliver and gold mate spoon, a silver chalice, a traingular casting of gold stacked on silver, stacked on bronze, stacked on iron, the crucible with the remains of the gold in it, and four cows' teeth, next to which there sat, on a short ladder-back chair, myself in a grey and red velvet cloak, impersonating Galibe Calibi, with my back to the hole. On the wall there hung a pocket watch, a blackboard, plus the scapula, upper cocyx, 2 vertebra, and several ribs of a cow. On the left, the two women dressed in red and/or yellow and/or blue, were in constant in and out of sync motion.

Due to circumstances not entirely in my control, the following occurred on the last day of the performance:

at 2 p.m.—I provided only the limited view of the torso from 2 inches below and 2 inches above the navel at approximtely from the peek hole.

at 8.p.m.—I re-set the above described table in direct sight line and with only the light of the alcohol lamp, played some beautiful hand-made bells right next to the peek hole, while wearing a grey wig and red velvet cloak.

(Grommets #3)

ELAINE HARTNETT

(vs Charlemagne Palestine)

Female vs Male

A re-evaluation of the past and the present. Elaine Hartnett, Charlemagne Palestine, Tender Baby Girl Pink, King Teddy C. Bear.

Reconstruction of women's nest as booth with telephone, TV set/video of man in pain from the neck up. Bed—draperies, hung cassette player with recorded afternoon spent reminiscing.

Woman—paints her face, plays tape, watches TV, tries to lure man on phone, masturbates, invites visitors in, goes out and socializes with audience, sleeps with video of man, gets stoned, goes crazy, emulates man's feelings, finally destroys booth.

Man—remains aloof, gets drunk, refuses to arrive, finally arrives drunk and blindfolded, masturbates, angers woman, gets thrown out.

Elaine Hartnett and Charlemagne Palestine lived together for five years. They decided to use elements from this relationship as the raw material for the piece and for re-evoking the past and present in an intensified theatre situation. The stuffed animals were in an intensified theatre situation. The stuffed animals were used as a means of communication during a particularly difficult time of the relationship and have re-mained over the years as close friends and members of the family.

(Grommets #3)

A Jean Dupuy production **Chant a Capella** was held in Judson Church with many artists participating. Each artist was given approximately five minutes of stage time to execute a chant piece without musical accompaniment. Elaine Hartnett's piece, entitled "Hooting," centered around an experience she had on her summer vacation while camping in the Applalachian Mountains of Western Pennsylvania. She met a group of young local people in the woods at night who showed her how they released their frustrations, anxiety, and boredom by baying at the moon like wolves—a process called "Hooting."

After relating this background information Ms. Hartnett proceeded to demonstrate the sound they made. It reverberated throughout the extremely resonant space of the church evoking primitive associations.

(Chant a Capella)

JON HASSEL

Jean asked me for documentation of my playing on the tower. I went back through my appointment book/diary to find the dates I climbed to the top with my trumpet and tape recorder trying to keep a melodic fragment in mind which was to generate the rest of the performance over the sound of the ocean and Ghana drum loop and saw the emotional depths I was in for the first two times I played and how the Thursday before the third time I got long-awaited good news from a record company.

As I was this now on the first day of Spring 1979, I'm thinking about the tower as a kind of emotional metaphor ("feeling low," "getting high," "climbing") and thinking about how tme passes and things change and how maybe it's not the "negative" or "positive" aspects of something that should lead you to do it, but just the doing of it.

(A Tower at P.S. 1)

RICHARD HAYMAN

- wandering in the back rooms calling as if lost in woods
- climbing the tower ladder with finger cymbals, without using feet
- once on top, continuous split toned whistling
- tone camera "photos" of the audience
- sling shot coins about the room while speaking of the philosophic and comic implications of being lost in woods as child
- attempt to set room on fire by dropping lit matches
- smoke bomb ignites
- "Fire!" warning shouted as loud boat horn sounds
- audience told to leave premises immediately

(A Tower at P.S.1)

GEOFF HENDRICKS

(with Brian Buczak)

To peak through a hole at a performance is obviously voyeuristic. So O.K., but we'll put our feast for the voyeur behind another curtain and make it a shadow play.

What the viewer saw directly were changing slides of the sky projected onto a white chair and a white sheet. We were behind the sheet with another chair to sit and stand on, and a spotlight to silhouette the two of us exercising, pouring water (from dipper to pail), lighting matches, moving, dressing, undressing, and performing acts of love.

Sometimes one of us would sneak out to be right by the grommet and unseen move a lighted match or pour some water across the viewer's line of vision. And we would manipulate the slide projector to shift the sky around. The silhouetted other would "dance" in counterpoint behind the sheet divider.

(Grommets #4)

DICK HIGGINS
man in white, tall white stovepipe hat
red ribbon, thirty yards, one end fastened to top of hat
man turns around slowly (revolving stagelet?), winding
ribbon slowly and evenly down over him
barber pole? candy cane?
alaha ismarladik!

When Jean Dupuy asked me to do a piece to be performed on his small revolving mini-stage I had already seen a group of performances on it, and had thought through what seemed to me to be the essential nature of that stage—its small size (too small to walk around successfully) and its slow revolutions. This revolving motion seemed to me always to threaten to wrap up, to tie up, to wind up, potentially, whatever was on it. Very mysterious. And I could also remember something with a similar motion from my childhood—old fashioned barbers' poles, red stripes on a white background, which, when rotated, gave the illusion of always moving downwards into—where? As a child I was very puzzled by those stripes, wondering where they went, always down, down, down.

So I thought of making myself into a barber pole. I dressed in white, and made myself

183

an enormous white stovepipe hat. A friend slowly fed red ribbon onto me, while I stood on the stage, from where it was fastened at the top of the hat down, slowly down over my face and my chest and my hips and my legs to the very bottom of the costume. The stripe *did* move, just like the barber poles I remembered. Someone else said I looked more like a candy cane. Maybe so.

I wrote a miniature description of the piece—as images— and it was printed in my book *Everyone Has Sher Favorite (His or Hers)*. For some reason I stuck in the Turkish farewell at the end, "Alaha Ismarladik," which is said by anybody who is leaving the room or otherwise moving away, while the person who is staying put says something like "Güle güle." Why I put *that* in I no longer recall.

Jean Dupuy said that the image of me very much resembled Watteau's painting called "Gilles." Okay: I like Watteau, and so I called my piece, for which I had been searching for a title, "Gilles" too. But when Dupuy sent me a copy of the Watteau "Gilles," I decided it didn't look like me at all. Oh well. I like the name.

(One Afternoon on a Revolving Stage)

dh 77

"Dar-u-gar!" was the much-feared war-cry of the armies of Timur-I-Leng, "Timur the Lame," known to us as Tamerlane. Timurtas was his mortal enemy in his early career.

As one who admires some aspects of Central Asian culture, notably the music and the architecture, I wanted to evoke in a piece something of the excitement associated with Tamerlane. So I gave out to members of the audience at the Chant A Cappella concert copies of the "Darugar" text, permuted to allow for every possible shortening of it. And I asked all the people present to yell it out, over and over again, as loudly as possible. The first time I had done this, in 1968, the result was disappointing; the audience was not large enough. But at the Chant A Cappella the audience was very large, and the resulting aural mayhem still has my ears ringing. One might fault the piece as lacking form and variety, but oh that sound! If music is at least partially about sound, then that piece worked.

(Chant a Cappella)

JERRY HOVAGIMYAN

The piece is about a set-up situation. People focusing on work activity, work activity being assembling boxes and piling them or moving matter. The piece then sits on the edge of sculpture and performance both, yet neither. That's why I call it situational. The message is not the material (sculpture) nor a virtuoso activity (performance). It is situational. Another aspect of the performance is sound. The tape played is of brain waves, radio static, and a continuous tone generator. These act as a signal of focus on (thought—work) process of the twins. The sounds are concrete and non-aesthetic. They are not music, they are concrete sound. Sound as a physical aspect of our lives.

(A Tower at P.S.1)

Placed on a wall were a series of pieces of paper. On the sheets were scrawled messages which were barely legible. Underneath, the messages were typewritten so they could be read. The rape piece was about rape, mental, physical, emotional. For instance "Look in the mirror as I fuck you up the ass, the pain in your face is my freedom, your tears are the drops of my manhood." The piece was intended to shock and disgust people. Several of the pages were torn from the wall and stepped on by angry viewers; others were amended by an angry feminist. I had no moral position in the piece, I was simply presenting loaded information.

(About 405 E. 13th St.; #2)

Using designer's board in shades of grey i.e., warm grey, cool grey and charcoal grey placed on the wall in a rotated cruciform. The piece had four small units at the end of each armature; in the center were two units joined together. The piece was pseudo-architectual, pseudo-painting, pseudo-sculpture, and pseudo-drawing. It was an aerial view placed on a wall and rotated. I imagine people living at the end of each armature and coming together in the central meeting house. The different shades of grey board placed next to each other made the piece shimmer to the eye. It was very funny to produce a rentinal painting effect without using paint.

(Scale 1/1)

DAVID HYKES

It is difficult to discern where the singing stops and the singer begins. And, what really unites the singer with the song? The real song begins in an inner silence, where the endless noise of the mind is harmonized by a sensation of one's own vibration, the quiet rhythms, surgings, and circulations the awareness of which opens the door to the experience of larger worlds. The singer, a true singer anyway, is longing for the freedom to bear in himself "I am the song", the state where he is able to listen in an absolutely new way: where listening is quicker, has more life than thought. From these moments a real creation begins, time after timeless time. There Is real suffering in trying to "serve" such moments, for one must sing every breath as if one's life depended on it. Which, if you must know, is in fact the case.

Of course the real moment is there—but so rarely! We don't really know what we are doing, and are rather attached to our ignorance. I like the image of the artist as an antenna. However, to be an antenna for the human race is an aim . . . not something for the ego to satisfy itself by assuming automatically. To be an antenna for the human race . . . that implies a special kind of listening, knowledge, and service.

Its true signals rush in from everywhere in the universe . . . the ones from really far away very faintly of course. What are these signals telling us? What is the content of such vibrations in which the earth is bathed? On those clear nights when you are "alone with the Alone", gazing at the heavens, this question can be real; and of course

185

at any moment!

There's a kind of Gold Rush atmosphere in America, where any claim is valid, unless someone else makes it! This impulse of negativity and doubt, for instance, to the idea that there really are LEVELS OF ART; that you receive knowledge from one kind of art, depending of course on your own receptivity, and from another kind of art, a headache. It has to begin to gnaw at you a little that there might not be enough time, that you need knowledge more than headaches.

Well, enough of "That." The singing I did for Chant A Cappella was along the lines of the chanting and art researches I have undertaken with The Harmonic Research Society and The Harmonic Choir: work taking as its starting point the high level of achievement in Mongolian singing of what are called "overtone songs." The excellence of their tradition is vastly underrated here. These idiots who say "anyone can learn" to do overtone chanting are making dangerous mistakes. In fact, such a maleficent attiude is just one way *the spirit of trying* is denied here. In fact, the breeze is up, the winds are blowing . . . something new is possible here in America. An art of new levels, realized by a truly fortunate covergence of forces.

The Harmonic Research Society and Choir has undertaken a number of researches, towards the aim of creating a body of music with new properties. As evidence of our results, I can cite the availability of a special series of recordings made in various spaces here, in Europe, and in India; and our record from the Taj Mahal will be available in 1980.

A POSSIBLE OVERVIEW OF "THE SEARCH FOR HARMONIC RELATION"

The duty is make "joyful noise" in which the small voice of the ego, of the pretension "to know" is silent in the face of facts. There is the need to "face the music." In my personal life, I search to honor Silence first, for it is in this silence that I can hear better the song I wish to sing. The force of expression, the concerted force, the very precious stream of vibration which circulates in each being, obeys very exact laws of ebb and flow, release and absorption. To express something real is not, it seems to me, an aim in itself, but rather a wish, a guideline, a standard against one must measure, without lying to oneself about it, "the way things turn out." This is the suffering which is the real suffering behind our ignorant woes. The more you have, the more you lose. The more you lose, the more you understand. Until the real heart-felt need for Absorption comes. Then all the high-falutin' aims are measured against truth, energy, purpose, and conscience. Above all, conscience.

Voices of singers in touch with different levels might be able to express, to weave a kind of net of vibrations, a kind of antenna of vibrations wherein the "line hum" might prove to be signals of a subtlety hard to imagine. Glowing fish in the net of the sky. Waves of vibration, a kind of pool, with the dance of light on the surface, an image from the greater world. However, the breathing reality of the body of sound is deeper than all the thousand lovely images which come in sequence, like postcards from paradise. The reality of the body of sound . . . The real song is inside, expressible perhaps in only a small circle. The distortions in the circle of regular life leak in all kinds of wrong listening. It actually transforms down the song . . . suddenly it looks like false religion, or any of hundred kinds of pretending, lying, presumption. Well, enemies, the price will be paid. How to serve the evolutionary possibility of mankind? Not this Darwinian jive. I mean: By what means will every person understand?

I was glad Arno and Penzias finally got the Nobel Prize. After WW II, much energy was devoted to the construction of communications satellites, the new electronic technologies supposedly "bringing us all closer together." To what should our antennas point? Well, never mind. Arno and Penzias got bored and pointed their's at the heavens while everyone else had been pointing them at each other. Both are necessary; don't get me wrong. The story goes that A & P began picking up a mysterious hum of very exact wavelength and temperature and became interested. Where was it coming from? From all over the sky, not just a single source. Or was it "in the line" somewhere? So they reinsulated, shooed the doves from the antenna's throat, scrubbed their white piezo-electric residues clean, and kept listening. Still a vibration coming through. They humbly reported an unexplained vibration of such-and-such characteristics. It more or less was agreed by everyone receiving this news, after reflection by the cosmologists, that this vibration was the echo of the moment of creation.

The search for HARMONIC RELATION is another way of putting into words the genuine human longing for complete life, living a life that touches all possible levels above us and within us, levels we don't "hear." As any old critic will tell you, Overtone Music is dime-a-dozen. This is the sadness of the passivity of our knowledge. It's true, we all have a possibility to hear overtones, and to produce them. Their only purpose is to lead each one towards their true self, and that self is "a vibration in a space." The rest is up to you.

(Chant a Cappella)

PHIL JAMES

Climb tower with two stones. Three people on each level (or four at bottom). Sit facing each other, not audience (that is, face in toward the center of platform). One person begins by rubbing stones. Listen as long as you want, join when you feel like it. When all the stones are going *each level finds its own tone* to softly hum (mouth closed). The tone need be hardly audible, only loud enough for others on your level to hear it so you can all three get on the same tone together. Stop humming the tone when you feel like it, rejoin when you feel like it. The rocks however are constant. *Remember this piece is not about making a beautiful sound but about letting a stong peaceful energy carry over into the space.* Keep the humming up a long time; when it feels right (and not until then, don't worry about what the others are doing) finally stop humming your tone. When nobody is left humming gradually the stone-sounds drop out one by one. Allow a minute of silence before leaving tower.

(A Tower at P.S.1)

PAUL JAY

The light in this piece works as a vehicle for certain information concerning two specific walls (mine and Dupuy's). This information in its turn acts as a vehicle for certain implications (the art concerns) which may be called (for our purposes) meaning. The light mechanisms via which this implied meaning is transferred stand as a metaphor for the way the verbal meaning (the writing on the wall) is transferred. I am concerned with your reactions but I don't want to know them.

(About 405 E. 13th. St.; #1)

A note is taped to screen:

"The projection is unavailable as a first-order demonstration"

On the wall at an angle to the screen is a picture of a projector. Next to the projector is written:

"Per aspera ad astra/ex nihilo nihil fit"

(About 405 E. 13th St.; #2)

TOM JOHNSON

"Gbda," presented separately in **Chant Capella,** is actually an excerpt from a larger work called *Secret Songs*, which consists of about 20 short pieces of sound poetry for unaccompanied voice. For the most part the *Secret Songs* are not so much as spoken, but a Variety of special vocal techniques are also used. "M-n-ng" involves odd humming sounds, "Dibidib" makes use of very fast lip and tongue movements, and "Ta Tai Tai" flutters up and down across the break in yodeling patterns. Other *Secret Songs,* such as "Lolmo," "Vzh," and "Swena Lena," simply explore melifluous combinations of vowels and consonants. "Gbda" might be considered a little language consisting solely of the four letters in its name. The piece has an amusing quality as it trips along in combinations like "gbda bda bdga ga gdgdba bda dba ga," and toward the end it becomes highly rhythmic, with syncopations falling over a rather fast beat.

While *Secret Songs* is one of my major pieces, it is not particularly typical of my work. I have also produced abstract instrumental works, theatre pieces of different sorts, operas that use conventional operatic vocal techniques, and a number of pieces that use conventional language.

(Chant a Cappella)

SCOTT JOHNSON (with Charles Moulton)

```
AN INVOLUNTARY MUSIC COLLABORATION WITH CHARLES MOULTON
WITH A 15' MIX OF INVOLUNTARY SONG #3 - MALE LAUGHTER

From the ground up -
This animal moves while standing still - its attention focuses to the
top with a silence between its legs - its feet are still while its head
is feet in the air dancing in place - vision out off, listening to sync
up with the electrical organs below - the tape for a belly-laugh, the
guitar for a distorted heart - a forced laugh at full volume to give
metre to the clattering rhythm of thoughts - it takes many pounds of
                           sound at the center of
                           gravity to maintain verti-
                           cal stability when you've
                           arranged for someone to
                           tap dance on your head.
```

(Tower at P.S. 1)

JOAN JONAS

A Poem

She walks to the microphone completely covered in an olive green silk shadri. Through an embroidered lattice she recites *The Washer Woman* by William Blake—

> I washed them out and washed them in
> And they told me it was a great sin.

then she turns and dips under the hundreds of tiny pleats, making a chirping sound with a bird whistle clenched between her teeth.

(Soup and Tart)

POOH KAYE

In 1976 I went to Japan. I was hungry. I was cold. I saw paper houses and many nylon skiing clothes. And I watched monkeys. They cleaned each other and fucked each other and bit each other. They did these things over and over varying the order. Three thousand monkeys fucking and biting and cleaning.

In Tokyo I bought a mechanical monkey with a primary spring action. When I returned to New York I made the three minutes for Jean's small stage. One action, the primary spring action of the mechanical monkey from Japan. The toy monkey and I jerked up and down face to face beside the revolving stage. I liked the multiple metaphors and contradictions implicit in that simple confrontation.

(One Afternoon on a Revolving Stage)

For Grommet I made literally a "dirty show." I presented a color movie of a person naked digging with all fours into the forest floor. The film image was back projected two and one-half feet distance from the grommet. The face in the film was parallel to the grommet. I was sequestered on the floor below the film. Every time the face on the film image looked up, I threw and handful of dirt at it. The dirt made a sharp violent clatter and rebounded often into the eye peering through the grommet.

(Grommet #3)

MICHAEL KRUGMAN

For the show "From Hudson Street to the Hudson River," I did a bit of household cinema. I made an hour-long film (shown at five frame/second) consisting of extremely broad, sweeping shots of different locations around the area. Some of them were made from a moving bicycle, while running, etc. I think there were some aerial views from the top of the World Trade Center, too. Then the whole thing was projected on the baseboard of the exhibition room — a six-inch high screen sitting on the floor. I seem to remember having to repaint the baseboard to get a good surface for projection.

(Between Hudson St. and River)

In the first part, the man made a series of string figures—like the cat's cradles kids make. He'd go through the whole business of setting one up—a bunch of comples, finger movements and then the figure would appear in its final form. Just at that moment the woman would cut the string right up the middle with a big pair of scissors (3 times), then a blackout. In the second part, the man came out in the dark with an old suitcase. When it opened, a very intense wedge of light shone from inside. There was a leaf inside which was held up in front of the light to make a leaf-shaped shadow. Then the suitcase was closed. The final part had the man and woman standing face to face on the revolving stage. This time, they worked together, making a pair of string figures stretched between them. A blackout, and that's all, folks.

(3 Evenings on a Revolving Stage)

SHIGEKO KUBOTA

Water event: Draw an isosceles triangle in a glass of water.

(About 405 E. 13th St.; #1)

KWAN LAU

革命的文艺,应当根据实际生活创造出各种各样的
人物来,帮助群众推动历史的前进。例如一方面是人
们受饿,受冻,受压迫,一方面是人剥削人,人压迫人,这个
事实到处存在着,人们也看得很平淡;文艺就把

189

这种日常的现象集中起来,把其中矛盾和斗争典型化,造成文学作品或艺术作品,就能使人民群众惊醒起来,感奋起来,推动人民群众走向团结和斗争,实行改造自己的环境。

(3 Evenings on a Revolving Stage)

EMILE LAUGIER

A shoe, attached by string to a small motorized pulley, was moving at a 3-feet a day speed on a sandy narrow floor. A warning notice told the visitor: "This shoe moves very slowly. Please do no touch."

(About 405E. 13th St.; #2)

JEAN CLAUDE LEFEVRE

ACTIVITY	ACTIVITE	ATTIVITA	ACTIVIDAD	ACTIVITAT
PROPOSAL AND POST URE FROM LEFEVRE JEAN CLA UDE AS A RT PERFO RMANCE O NE MINUT E IN LE LOUVRE O N THE 16 TH OF OC TOBER 19 78.THIS PROPOSAL IS DEDIC ATED TO JEAN DUP UY JOEL HUBAUT A ND ANNIC K LE MOI NE	PROPOSIT ION ET A TTITUDE DE LEFEV RE JEAN CLAUDE C OMME ART PERFORMA NCE D'UN E MINUTE AU LOUVR E LE 16 OCTOBRE 1978.CET TE PROPO SITION E ST DEDIE E A JEAN DUPUY JO EL HUBAU T ET ANN ICK LE M OINE	PROPOSTA ED ATTEG IAMENTO DI LEFEV RE JEAN CLAUDE C OME ART PERFORMA NCE D'UN MINUTO A L LOUVRE IL 16 OT TOBRE 19 78.QUEST A PROPOS TA E DED ICATA A JEAN DUP UY JOEL HUBAUT E D ANNICK LE MOINE	PROPOSICI ON Y POST URA DE LE FEVRE JEA N CLAUDE COMO ART PERFORMAN CE DURANT E UNA MIN UTA EN LE LOUVRE AL DIA 16 DE OCTUBRE 1 978.PROPO SICION QU UE ESTA D EDICADA A JEAN DUPU Y JOEL HU BAUT Y AN NICK LE M OINE	DARBIETUN G UND STU DIEN VON LEFEVRE J EAN CLAUD E ALS ART PERFORMAN CE EINE M INUTE IN LE LOUVRE AM SECHSZ EHNTEN OK TOBER 197 8.DIESE D ARBIETUNG IST JEAN DUPUY JOE L HUBAUT UND ANNIC K LE MOIN E GEWIEDM ET

(Louvre)

NANCY LEWIS

Props: Flags, pillows, white dresses, picnic basket, cassette of conversation between girls on subway.

Rehearsal with trio: Rule 1. Everything is valid. Rule 2. Start by doing 5 parts in 25 minutes, 5 minutes for each one to get into the parts and into an even time span. Do it blindfolded because that is what *this* dance is about—task—to try to dance together without seeing each other and the attention/tension of listening to the steps, patterns, and rhythms.

(A Tower at P.S.1)

Evening one—solo
Evening two—solo
Evening three—solo

Slow motion circle—stage. Begin low—slowly rise—vocal song—long tones—
Piece changed every night because of the inspiration from the other performers.
One does more than one thinks one is going to do—consequently rapid growth is
possible—probable . . . guaranteed.

(3 Evenings on a Revolving Stage)

MABOU MINES (Joanne Akalaitis)

Last summer I set myself a test. I understand discipline. For one hour of each day I
sat in the yellow chair and looked at my face in a mirror. I knew it was one hour because the oven timer gave a ding. My face came out oval. The mirror did that to me.
The mirror is oval in a blue wood frame. This exercise is easier than working on the
whole body or touching the soul. The surface of the face simply meets the surface of
the mirror. The difficulty is to remain still but alert. And I could barely breathe at all
so as to keep the glass from clouding.

People are so preoccupied with the beauty of my body that they seldom notice my
lovely face.

My body must be protected. I have entrusted it to the care of others.

The pigeons in the park attacked me again today. I cannot love them. They form their
squadron. Then fly in low. One drops her feather near but not on my foot. This is her
warning to leave the bench. I saw a man on a bicycle ride right through them. He's
not a soldier because he doesn't notice their army. Or perhaps he's a brilliant strate-
gist and only pretends not to notice. In any case whether by luck or design he out-
foxed them. They spared him.

In the general course of things small animals and birds are not suspect. Even I did
not realize their evil nature. Once when I was three and in the desert a butterfly flew
under my dress. It took my life away. My mother told me it wouldn't hurt me. But I
knew better. It took my life away. Then my friend was killed by the goats who ate his
lettuce while he slept. This is the green death and is found mostly in California.

Evil is more powerful than good. Don't let anyone tell you different. But death and
madness and power itself are greater still.

Let us consider madness. I prayed for it once. Then found it ugly. Ugliness sickens
me. And so I prayed for death. Death eludes me. And so I prayed for power. Power
must be pursued. And I am tired. My leaps are clumsy. And so I am left with prayer.
Now I pray for love.

Love is no longer fashionable in our circles. It has been years since I heard of anyone
dying of love. It is not part of anyone's work. It is passé. One cannot afford to be out
of step these days. It is no longer acceptable to use my spoon to launch confiture into people's eyes. Nor to sweeten my breath with rosebuds. And this fever that will
not break and this art of love that is going out of style . . . .

You have no fear. I read your manuscript. I am afraid of you. You print.

(3 Evenings on a Revolving Stage)

GIANFRANCO MANTEGNA

Since childhood large food celebrations have inspired in me concern for those who
could not partake such blessings. So was for SOUP & TART; art activities have indeed very little meaning in a world where people still die of starvation. After having
walked around the performing area with my head covered by a pot, I invited the audience to make a contribution to Oxfam International, the Oxford University Famine
Relief Fund.

(Soup and Tart)

I did two pieces—Laurie Anderson in her review has explained them quite perfectly.

One work dealt with lines in space, the other with lines in time. Both involved photographic images I had taken, but the photographs were employed in the most minimal and economic way. "May 4-14, 1968" dealt with subversion; "Photographic Determination of Distance" dealt with obsessions.

(About 405E. 13th St. #1)

THE INFINITE SPIRAL

A 17-foot spiral was drawn, cut and burned into the floor boards (3mm deep and wide). The spiral ended at the wall of the loft. Displayed on the wall there was an aerial photograph of the neighboring area with a second spiral drawn in corresponding scale, as a continuation of the one on the floor. Next to the photograph, an historical text describng the invention and characteristics of this kind of spiral. 405 East 13th Street was imagined as a center of energy sprialling outward.

(About 405E. 13th St. #2)

MARSHALORE

outside it is blizzard-ing
the first of the year
it makes me a lizard-thing
(slow search for warmth)
but I bid you good cheer
(noel search for warmth)
and I wish I was there

Things look good lately. I have written myself a $10,100 grant which I will know about in April and if awarded, will receive in May. Then I shall buy a 50-foot porta-pak and sail around the world. I have been looking for some work lately and have had no luck that-a-way but did do a graphics design (text etc.) for an artist who will be launching the piece at the Musee d'art contemporain next week. Hopefully this will be the sort of publicity I need for some more jobs like that.

Am due to collect some assurance chomage in the next few weeks and that will keep me for a jolly while longer.

Things also look good for February. And this is where you can help. On official stationary of some sort (P.S. One stationary would be best) you should write an official invitation to do the performance specifying the exact dates in February. This will make me eligible for getting a travel allowance and special project allowance from the Canada Council. As I will require some video equipment (porta-pak, cable, moniteur, etc.) any monies I can get will be of enormous value—not to mention the travel costs.

I am curious as to how this has been going for you. Any publicity decisions, heating the building decisions, etc. Please let me know.

I trust your recent events have gone smoothly and proved to be stimulating fun. I am sorry I missed the EAR INN opening, but I assume you heard my opening piece by now. O yes—the reason you never heard from me again when I was in NY was due to an incredible malaise that hit me the day I attended that rehearsal for Marguerite's frites. I was abed at Richard's with a fever for two days and then got a ride home and took it tout suite. I didn't ring anyone and was in absolutely no shape to see you the next day. Nina suffered from the same thing. We didn't ever find out what it was but it was not fun and no thing to have when one is a-visiting.

Let's see, any other interesting morsels to share with you. Hmmmm, can't think of anything at the moment. Life here goes on in its sometimes dull, sometimes shart pace. O, well I guess taking care of my 18-month-old god-daughter for ten days was rather a trip . . . she loves to dance and is learning to talk—'a moi,' her favorite thing is 'chaussure' and 'shoe.'

(A Tower at P.S. 1)

GEORGE MACIUNAS (with Larry Miller)

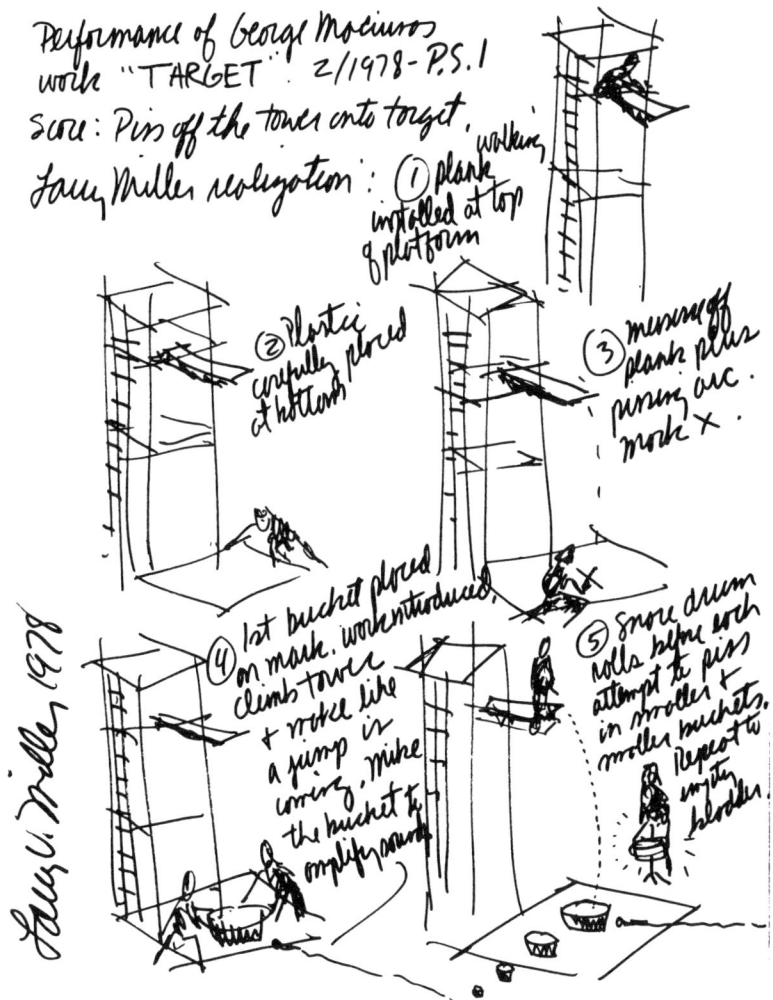

(A Tower at P.S.1)

TONY MASCATELLO

I met Jean thru Joanne, and we got to know one another during workshops which Mabou Mines was conducting over on Reade st. He asked me to do five minutes at Soup & Tart, and the notion delighted me. I made a piece about narcissism and rose eating, and performed it about midway thru the evening. The audience was radient; it was exciting and most enjoyable to play to them. Most everyone was aware that it was a special event. I was confused at first about what my piece was supposed to MEAN, but had the good sense to use the images as they appeared and trust time to clarify matters. I remember the performing itself unusually clearly; I was exhilirated. What was so great was that there were so many talented people there and so little contention.

(Soup and Tart)

Around the same time as this, the last of the Thirteenth St. shows was going on and I believe I showed a build it yourself game sculpture there. Again, a sense of cooperation prevailed.

(About 405 E. 13th St. #3)

The opportunity for collective expression fosters a sense of community among artists. During the Performances for Revolving Stage, I collaborated with John Howell on a kind of proto-slapstick piece during which, perched high up on a ladder, I twice declared myself to be 'the boss' to which he flatly rejoined that he knew what he was doing, and that he could get along perfectly well when I was not around. These simple assertions of independence of course drove my character to explosive rage and pratfall. The janitor at the Whitney, I remember, particularly liked the piece, stating that we'd put our finger right on it. His compliment compensated for bruised butt I suffered on the Whitney's stone floor.

(One Afternoon on a Revolving Stage)

Art performers were singing, and Jean invited them to try a capella. This led to the evening at the Judson Church. I decided to do a song/dance homage for Chaplin, since I'd for a long time regarded my own work as a comic form. I used the same tune, 'Titinia', as he did at the end of Modern Times, illustrating each phrase of my lyric with an appropriate broad gesture. I am unashamed to admit that the original turn outstripped my effort. I remember thinking how hard it was to sing such a song without the usual snappy accompanying music. After the first evening, I used a spot light to fill that void, and found that it worked quite well, enlarging the gestures so they projected better. I began to understand how to carry a narrative line without dialogue. When Chaplin died a week later, I was glad I'd had a chance to thank him for this, and so many other lessons.

(Chant a Cappella)

I sang some as the Italian cowboy during the Grommets Performances. I rode the subway and stood on the corner of Franklin and West Broadway, freezing. Then I was out in the Rocky Mts., fighting unseen animals. I played Rock of Ages on the harmonica, and by the end of the hour, it was mingling with a violin, soft whistling, and someone asking someone to 'rock with me'. Everyone's performance leaked into everyone else's, despite the performer's being separated into little calls. It was a big stew, subjective fantasies breeding together, somewhat out of control.

In a larger sense, these collective events have helped us all to enjoy and learn from one another. They have encouraged sensuality, complexity, and extroversion, much needed antidotes to the vitiating notions of minimal art which lingered long after their vital time, and were a stifling clot at the time of soup and tart.

Within my space, in a denim shirt and cowboy hat, having just wrestled with a subdued and invisible animal, I sat and sang...

I been staring at the moon. I been staring at the blue/moon, hands down, calling out your name to beat the /c band. Where have you/g been?*

I sang other songs also. Sometimes the slide projection placed me in gorgeous Rocky Mts., less often in the Canal St. subway, and sometimes in transit, at the tiny square overgrown with weeds where West Broadway and Leonard St. meet. My emphasis, as usual, was on specific simple gestures. The central gestures were fleshed out by smaller ones such as rubbing one's hands together or looking through one's wallet. Often, when I played "Rock of Ages" on my harmonica, it fell into harmony with Laurie's violin which was very nice.

(Grommets #3)

GORDON MATTA-CLARK

The late Gordon Matta-Clark, having cut a two-story house in half ("sculpture"), split a gingerbread house as a small-scale version ("drawing").

(Soup and Tart)

TIM MAUL

In September, Jean Dupuy invited me to participate in the first "Grommets" Show at PS1. On that occasion I gave an instructional talk illustrated by slides. Since by work

194

is generally 2 dimensional, and I was aware that Jean was inviting many artists involved in performance and dance for December's Grommets, I decided to represent myself with a static piece. The installation consisted of the display of two record albumn covers on a music stand with a brief background text—easily readable. One albumn cover showed a group of men with musical instruments with the groups name followed by the manes of the individuals. The other cover consisted of a photograph of a young topless girl holding a model airplane. The text read. In 1969 the now defunct British rock group Blind Faith released its only album. It was available in either of two covers. The decision to display these objects stems from several sources:

1. The static display of familiar objects to be easily seen, read and considered under Jean's limitations.

2. An undefined personal fascination with the two covers (not to be mistaken for nostalgia).

3. Album covers as mythic objects in popular music.

4. Taking a scholarly interest in something (rock and roll) generally regarded as repugnant to an art context and art audience.

5. The transient aspects of time and culture, names once familiar now summoned only in nostalgia.

6. The group's name Blind Faith recalled a statement in an interview with Ed Ruscha that impressed me when I was student . . . . "Blind faith in an idea . . . when I get an idea I don't disturb it. I'm not always sure what form it will take, but I keep the idea."

(Grommets #3)

With my performance at P.S.1, as with other situations, I used the premise of the lecture (or "talk") to create a climate conducive to assimilating new information. To me, the weakness of "performance art" is it's inability to create such a climate. Functioning rather as "entertainment or theatre" the relationship with the spectator is distanced, and the spectators own scrutiny of what occurs is lax. I'm interested in creating an atmosphere of attentive education, like the classroom, lecture-hall, or educational TV. By presenting calm, direct information in a non-theatrical manner, the aura of "entertainment" begins to fall away, transforming the spectator's into receivers.'

For the Tower series I delivered a talk mostly about the role of "inspiration" in the creative process. Brief, lightly researched, and hopefully fun to listen to, it was puctuated by a friend dropping an apple on my head from the towers highest perch. I instructed her (Molly Renda) to drop one "whenever she thought I deserved it." The talk itself skirted Sir Isaac Newton, but I believe the two simultaneous events (the talk, the falling apples) suggested the mythical event in a manner that transcended any other kind of physical demonstration.

(A Tower at P.S. 1)

People are used to being taught things through photography, so I use it for much the same reasons that I seek a "climate of education" in my performances. At "About 405 E 13 St." I presented two photographs, one very small photo, and one standard 8″ × 10″. The small photo depicted Jean Dupuy's loft and the larger photo a small bedroom. A brief text explained that a person had abandoned apartment life for loft life because they needed more space. The two photos illustrated this in reverse, the smaller photo demanding a high degree of scrutiny on the part of the viewer.

(About 405 E. 13 St. #3)

At 3 Mercer St. I showed 3 framed 8″ × 10″ photos of a stoplight. The photos showed sequentially the stoplight's function; red, orange, and green lights lit. Each frame was painted the color of whatever light was lit, and although they were meant to be read horizontally, I placed them vertically on top of each other to mimic both the form and sequence of the lights. I was interested in how the frame, operating in the real "outside" world, could inform the viewer of events occurring in the black and white Two-dimentional world of the photograph.

(3 Mercer St.)

Every time I've presented something for one of Jean's show's the piece has stood strangely outside the main body of my work, but always somehow serves to inform it in a valuable way, taking me to a place I wouldn't have gone otherwise.

The Louvre is probably the most widely known art-context on earth. After several visits to New York Metropolitan Museum of Art, I realized tha the mythic 'weight' that the Louvre's masterpieces carried would reduce even the best performance to 'theatre'. . .also the museum's ornate galleries would add to the absurd, theatrical atmosphere. I opted for a slight work that recognized its surroundings in an affectionate manner, and would not rely on spoken language like my previous works. I realized that many French artists view the Louvre as an antique souvenir store whose curse it is to represent France's art past forever while art history marches on around it. But I decided to leave these concerns to the French. So close is French history tied up to Art History, I ended up flipping madly through "The History of Art" volume, tearing out a number of red, blue, and white pages; (all Louvre illustrations) and trying to arrange them a la Andre on the floor. The end result was more of a 'Support/Surface' Ellsworth Kelly, an imperfect minimal flag. An activity that produced an unexpected object, all in all, a bettersweet work.

(Louvre)

ANTHONY MCCALL

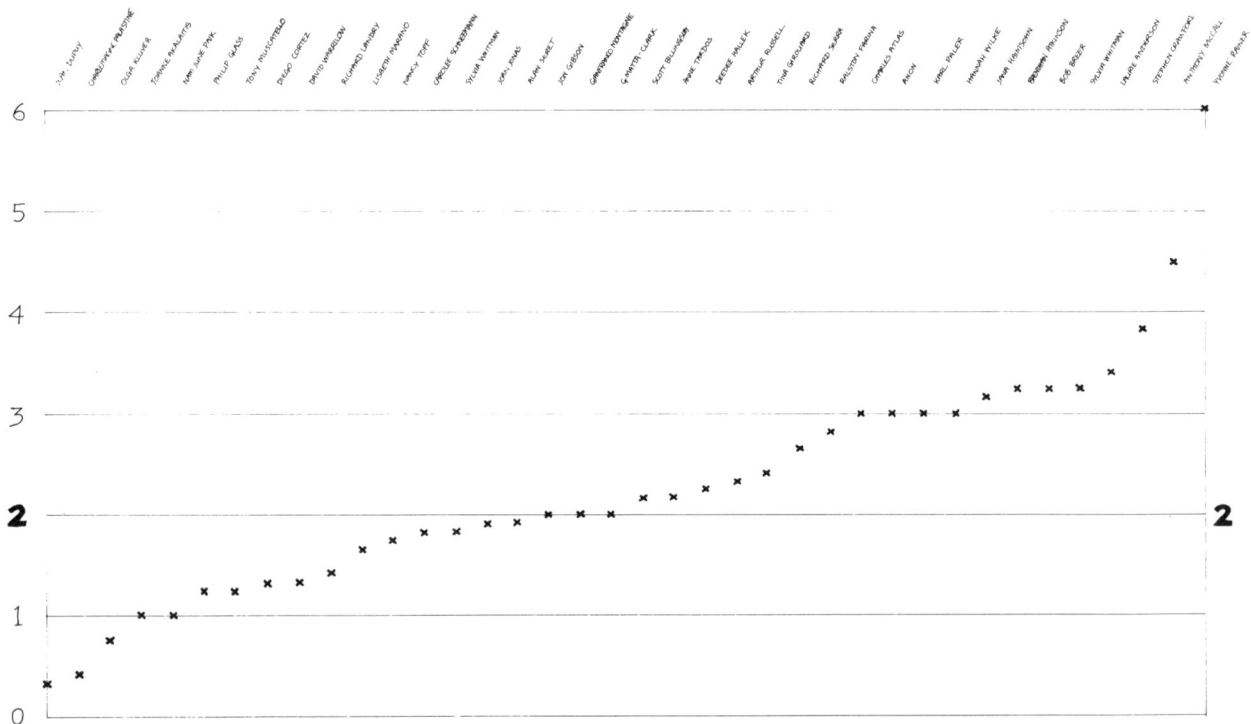

(Soup and Tart)

DICK MILLER

This piece was undertaken accepting cartain promises. The first of these being that in an argument or in a serious discussion situation, one of the observable features is the process of gualification, that is either limiting a field or topic, or expanding it so it takes in new consequences. This qualification is then its turn qualified, onwards and onwards; so that in the end in free range discussion the final topic and the original statement are almost totally divorced. In this overlay process, new subjects and topics are touched on; realities shift ground. It is in this composite where new knowledges are formed by correlating a juxtapositioning of the apparently unrelated (the mind continually strives to find order and or make pattern). From observation two sequences appear to be followed.

The first of these is what can be described as going from the specific to the general. From a definite, a subject drift occurs that may lead anywhere. The opposite is also witnessed. The moving from the vague to the specific.

Attempts have been made to simulate both these processes. The first attempt being W.W.111. (the big One) in which various definite ot thather electric statements from an essay by Stan Brankhage (called The Camera-My Eye) were taken as a starting point. Twelve statements were taken and each transcribed at the top of a separate sheet of paper; and then sheets then shuffled. Each statement was taken in turn and a qualifying statement was made and transcribed beneath the original one which was then covered up. This was then undertaken twelve times and the statements similarly masked out. We worked with a collection of about 50 books to abstract the qualifying themes, the books were on mist of the human emotions as well as novels, newspapers, magazines and letters. This was done to get as wide a range as possible of speech patterns and diction. These twelve statements comprised the working body of the substance.

The second stage was to split each line or statement in half. The break being selected either for a particular sound pattern else for creating a picture of attenuated sense. The image pattern was then imagined graphically and maybe represented thus—

$$(a1((b1(((c1((((d1(((((E)))))d2))))c2)))b2))a2)$$

Where the original statement from Brakhage is 'a' 1 & 2 being its separate parts. These were the transcribed vertically to create 23 separate lines.

In this linear is covered to cyclical. Narrative is hopefully got rid of and the emphasis if it should be said to be anywhere, must be in the middle. The third stage consisted of a further transformation. In this reworking lines were either combined together or parts of lines combined together to create separate word blocks. Sound pattern or being of attenuated sense were once again the consideration factor.

The final stage was to translate the score you now have. For this the left margin of the typewriter was considered a fixed norm. The word blocks read and reread until finally an observable sound pattern become obvious with readable characteristic pause patterns. White space then is in proportion to length of pause.

Although this piece to us closely resembles poetry in certain of its forms, ideally it should be performed. It is life poetry it hopes to create a state behind the mere words, where the synapse between the mataphors or images creates a 'new.' The reader 'creates' the poem becomes the 'new.' A good poem is that which successfully holds us and the 'new' is clearly highlighted? In our opinion—Yes—The fact that due to narrative and vague imagery almost without exception novels and poems are energy draining and act as somnambulants is neither here nor there. Ideally we consider this to be the real essence of Art.

This piece is an attempt to simplify, an attempt to remove narrative completely and be divorced as far as possible from normal thought and logic patterns. In this way we hope to assist. If this piece is to mean anything it requires the reader to create.

To increase the range of experience and aid the process ideally the piece should be performed with slides. The slide being of the piece in its original stage 2 form whilst the text you have is read out loud.

NOTE: On liberating the Mind from Concepts of Truth, was created in exactly the same way except this time it moves from the definite to the vague. Consequently in the graphic representation E is the initial statement.

(About 405 E. 13th St.; #3)

And he was wearing one green sock and one black sock....

45 second performance.
Props — artist portfolio dixie peach pomade, shaving mirror, check pants, white tuxedo, 2 pidgeons, strobe lights.

And the farmer thought he understood the winds — was drowned at sea. It was an incredible green light shining on that field down there.

(One Afternoon on a Revolving Stage)

(Situation installation for manipulation by 2 persons)
Equipment: Two Carousel slide projectors with automatic timers; One free standing screen 4 feet by 6 feet 9 inches; two headphones; two microphones; ampifier; speaker; 12 gels of different colors; two projector stands with wheels; 160 slides; Slides. Ground area 8 feet by 6 feet. There are 80 wire structures each being manufactured from a soft iron wire 12 feet long painted in assorted colors. The slides were shot with a Canon FTB with a 24mm wide lens from an elevated position creating the trapezoid effect. The slides are sequential, two of the structures being transposed for each shot. The slides were arranged alternately for each projector, thus at any instant consecutive images are shown combined on the screen. The structures that are moved when are perfectly superimposed appearing as ghost images, the double projection reinforcing the color of those remaining stationary.

Operation. The two performers are situated on either side of the screen, each performer is wired up with a microphone and headphones such that a verbal transaction can take place and remain audible over the projection noise. An auxilliary speaker is positioned near the grommet at the one end so that a single spectator can hear the dialogue.

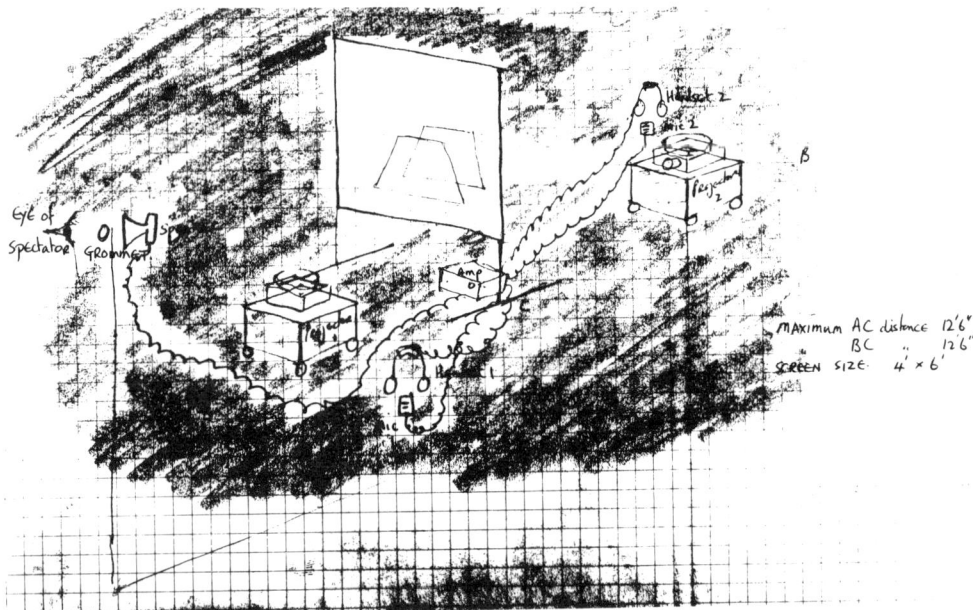

At the commencement the two slide projectors on the moveable stands are positioned in such a manner that the images are superimposed (there being a single image visible to the spectator). This is achieved by reversing the normal slide position in projector 2. From this position the carriages are moved making either image smaller or larger, in or out of focus. The projectors are set a 15 second exposures and there is a 9 second differential between them.

Gels can be affixed singly or in combinations over the lens to create colors. The projectors can either be left on the carriages or hand held. The carriage is particularly suitable for rapid movement sequences either in a circular motion or in a linear manner back and forth from the screen. In this manner plus the use of the select button and an opaque light shield an almost infinite variety of effects can be attained. The piece was performed 5 times over a 4 day period, each time with a different person as my co-performer.

(Grommets #3)

ANTONI MIRALDA

1 Plank of wood = 60,021 Grains of colored rice
Loft = 462 planks = 27,729,702 grains = 6,932,425 red, 6,932,425 yellow, 6,932,425 red, 6,932,425 blue.
Colored rice = Rice cooked with vegetable dye ready to be cooked and eaten.

(About 405E. 13th St.; #1)

JACQUES MONORY

The performance was planned in the main gallery in Louvre near Watteau's Gilles. There two pairs of columns, of the marble variety, confronting each other, one on each side. Between them mirrors creating an infinite reflection, and pedestal holding two Roman busts, all this creating a ridiculous and pompous effect. In the face of one of this cold, sinister romans, I wished simply to present my emblems: hat, scarf, and spectacles. And, drinking a glass of red wine to wish him "Here's to yours." This, nicely indicating that the system no longer impressed me, yet being still slightly dupe, because the mirrors still reflected "Gilles" watching us. This vague subtlety was fortunately twarted because a curator coupled by a guard stopped me, confiscating the glass of wine and forbidding me to clothe the "Auguste." The hat ended up on the curator's head and the wine (a very fine Bordeaux) most certainly drunk by the guard, and the performance simply meant that museums are certainly what we already knew: they were cemeteries where we should speak to the dead without friendship and only with respect.

L'emplacement ètait prévu dans la Grande Galerie du Louvre prés du Gilles de Watteau. Il s'y trouvent affrontées deux paires de colonnes, genre en marbre, de chaque coté de la Galerie. Entre elles des miroirs qui créent une fuite infinie, et une partie surélevée où reposent des bustes romains d'un effet des plus pompier. Je voulais simplement face à un de ces Romains froids et sinistres, lui remettre mes insignes; chapeau, foulard, lunettes, et en buvant un verre de vin rouge lui souhaiter "A la tienne". Ce qui gentiment indiquait que le système ne m'impressionnait plus (en ètant encore un peu dupe, car en reflet dans le miroir Gilles nous regardait). Cette vague subtilité a été détournée heureusement par l'interdiction faite par un Conservateur gendarme, acoquiné d'un gardien. Confiscation du verre de vin, certainement bu par le gardien (du trés bon Bordeau), et la performance signifia plus clairement que les Musées sont bien ce que nous savions, des cimetiéres ou nous devons parler aux morts sans amitié seulement avec respect.

(Louvre)

DONALD MUNROE

It didn't look like much at first, just a plain white background, and then something appeared in the middle, something coming into focus, an eye, a blue eye, a woman's blue eye, she was wearing makeup. She was looking at me through a hole, a grommet hole.

Her finger, fleshy white with extremely well manicured bright red finger nails, was coming towards me. She put it through the grommet, and then moved it around the rim sensually, she put it all the way through and down flat against the canvas. It took on the appearance of a cross between a cartoon leg and a parsnip.

The grommet was increasing in size without changing its size relationship to the TV screen. She put more fingers through the enlarging grommet, caressing the rim. It began to look like the underside of an albino spider with gold trim. She was squeezing the rim of the enlarged grommet, clutching it, she had all her fingers through now. The rim was becoming softer and larger, larger softer....

(Grommets #3)

MARCH 1973. "Why don't you just say what you want? You're being too vague, too self conscious. What do you want? Well I'll tell you what I want." One half of the television screen is my face. The other half is the face of my partner in art, Joan Schwartz. It is essentially an argument. We are discussing our video soap opera project, "Each Day." Joan is having a tough time verbalizing her thoughts. Our relationship is a working one. Two ambitious kids, fresh out of art school, bound and determined to make it as artists in the Big Apple. A story truly destined for its own video series, or at least a grant. We lived together, worked together, and most importantly, danced together... freestyle in the ballroom sense. This is the heart of our association and a natural for downtown performance.

MAY 1973. Asked to participate in Jean Dupuy's collective performance at 405 E. 13th St. I conclude the obvious... present our best side by filming Joan and I dancing together in Jean's large loft space. Joan is reluctant at first, but when I describe the piece as a film projected on a small rear screen floating in the middle of Jean's loft, she falls in love with the project and is very helpful in its execution.

JUNE 1974. I remind Joan again that it's not my responsibility to turn her untalented friends into actors. This was never my idea. Let's get some pros on the set.

(About 405 E. 13th. St.; #s 1&2)

AUGUST 1974 "Each Day" is completed.

SEPT. 1974. A setback, "Mary Hartman", "Each Day" is put on the back burner.

JUNE 1975. Joan is becoming disdraught after many unsuccessful attempts at selling our program. I think it's best to continue our project on a different level. How about a show in a gallery? Again a dance comes to mind. A tango. An Apache tango. What a great symbol, for our moody relationship. The piece is constructed around our dance lessons. It combines video with photographs and a live performance of our Apache routine. A prestigious uptown gallery jumps on the idea.

OCTOBER 1975.

NOVEMBER 1975. Joan is no feather weight and we are having difficulties with our lifts. This would be enough of a headache for most artists but I must constantly veto Joan's tired, art school ideas about the piece. I am thinking about writing her out of the show and continuing as a solo.

NOVEMBER 1975. I happily agree to perform at Jean Dupuy's Soup and Tart event at the kitchen. What a great preview for our upcoming dance performance. Though Joan seems more interested in her boyfriend there is no time to find a new dancing partner. All is not well in our rehearsal studio at Eighth Ave. and Forty Fifth. In a sloppy pirouette, Joan socked me in the face, aggravating a bad situation in my mouth. I cannot continue rehersals. I should have been a solo.

THAT NIGHT. In the pressure of last minute timing, I have come up with a brilliant idea. Ten minutes before showtime, I inform Joan that I will release three years of frustration and annoyance on her from my seat in the audience. She had better prepare an adequate defense. As the audience tensely waits for our piece in silence, I suddenly jumped from my seat and scream, "You are the cause of years of wasted time and effort." Joan had little chance for a verbal defense as I excitedly continue. My last words sum up our artistic future as I storm our of the Kitchen, "I'm not making an asshole our of myself on your account for a moment longer."

(Soup and Tart)

ANDREW MOSZYNSKI

The piece consists of the routine of a professional Ballroom-Dancing couple done in an art performance context. My role (selecting the couple, bringing it to PS1) was represented in performance terms by my presence on top of the 21 foot tower following the dancers movements with a flashlight in the dark room.

Pre-performance notes

Andrew Moszynski

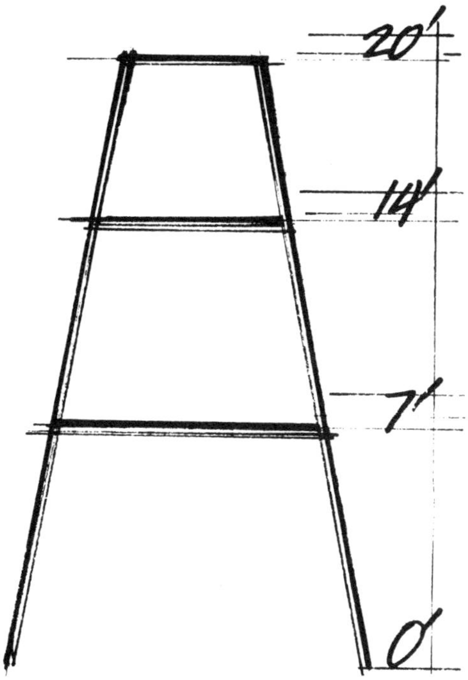

La Tour D'arjean

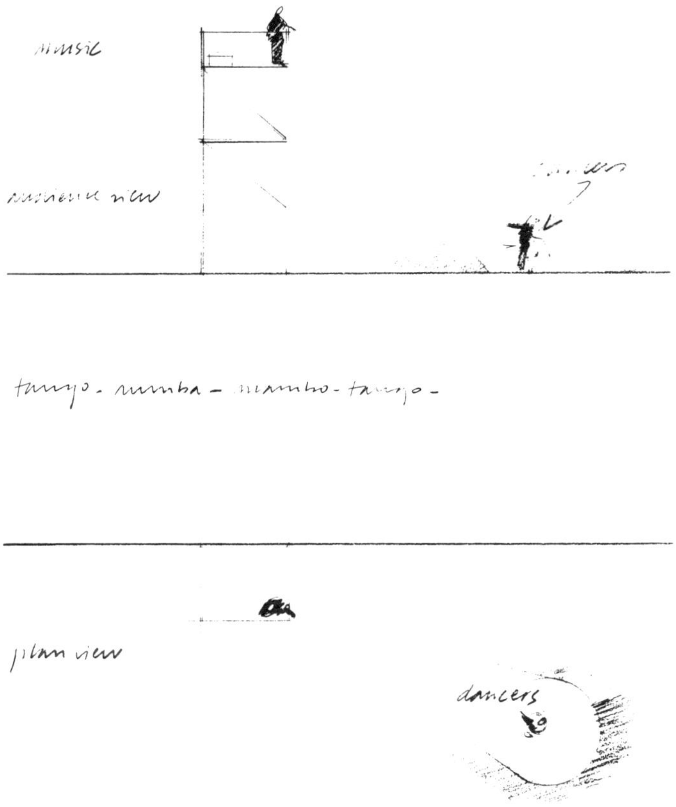

1. An obvious skill and ability removed from its natural context and placed in an art performance situation.
2. Routine-Readymade. Bringing it to PS1.
3. A different style of performing. Different styles (tango, rumba, etc.) within the performance.
4. Giving the floor to the dancers. The beam of light as a connector.

Post-performance notes

First evening: According to plan.
Second evening: Everything goes wrong!
>The music refuses to play; various attempts to repair the
>equipment *fail.*
>Dancers improvise out of my control.
>Applause.
>Flashlight falls of tower, disintegrates on floor.
>Jean is delighted.

(A Tower at P.S.1)

JACQUES OHAYON
(The Louvre in 10 points and 1 minute)

1—The main Gallery by the riverside, built by Catherine de Medici to join the Louvre and the late Tuileries (salute to the Communards!)*
2—Hubert Robert painted this main room in ruins. If we blew it up, here and now, with a few sticks of nitroglycerine, we could check the accuracy of Hubert's scenes.
3—In this gallery: La Tour, Gelee, Vouet, La Hire, Lesueur, Toque. All French.
4—To the left, a dead Christ, stretched out and stripped by Champaigne; notice the hand.
5—Latest bulletin: without the boat, the "Embarkation for Cythere" is just another pilgrimage.
6—After Maria Leszinska by Toque, Malatesta by Della Francesca.
7—Under St. Sebastian we can read with great interest: "Mantagna, school of Padua. Inventory number: BF l766, catalogue number: l373A."
8—In the State room, Leonardo's Bacchus is androgynous but of inestimable value.
9—l5l5—Mona Lisa. If "L.H.O.** where you say, Marcel, it's because L.A.P.T.**"
10—2669 artists are already in this museum. The presence of living avant-garde in the Louvre, and my participation with them, confers upon me, de facto, the quality of artist.

* Communards: from revolutionary movement in France.
** L.H.O.: Pun, pronounced like "elle a chaud"—she is hot.
   L.A.P.T.: Pun, pronounced like "Elle a pete"—she farted.
>Therefore: if she is hot where you say, Marcel, it's because she farted.

---

1   La Grande Galerie du Bord de l'eau, construite par Catherine de Médicis pour joindre le Louvre et feu les Tuileries (salut les Communardsñ).
2   Hubert Robert a peint cette grande sale en ruine. Si l'on faisait pêter, ici et maintenant, quelques bâtonnets de nitroglycérine, on pourrait vérifier la justesse de vues d'Hubert.
3   Dans cette Galerie : La Tour, Gelée, Vouet, La Hyre, Lesueur, Toque. Tous Francais.
4   A gauche, un Christ mort, allongé et dénudé par Champaigne - Remarquez la main.
5   Dernière nouvelle : Sans bateaux, l'Embarquement pour Cythère n'est qu'un pélérinage.
6   Après, Maria Leszinska, par Toque, Malatesta par della Francesca.
7   Sous Saint Sébastien, on peut lire avec interêt : "Mantegna, école de Padoue. N° d'Inventaire : RF1766, N° de catalogue : 1373 A."
8   Dans la Salle des Etats, le Bacchus de Léonard est androgyne mais de valeur inestimable.
9   1515 - La Joconde. Si L.H.O. oú vous dites, Marcel, c'est parce que L.A.P.T.
10 2669 artistes—peintres sont déjà dans ce musée. La présence au Louvre d'artistes dávant-garde encore vivants et mon intervention à leur côté, me confère, de facto, la qualité d'artiste.

(Louvre)

ORLAN

Painting by Blanchard - Grande Galerie

—I'm dressed in a three quarter length black coat and a black skirt.
—Back to the public, facing the painting, with my hand, I put a white plastic painter's palette behind by head like a halo.
—With this object my arm describes a quarter circle above my head until it stops on a horizonal.
—I slowly turn my head, a large brush held between my teeth, the shoulders follow the head then the breast, then the waist and finally the legs.
—I'm facing the public.
—my right arm is on the left
—I move the arm passing the palette under my head.
—I bare the teeth, then the palette and my arm pass to the right on a horizontal.
—My left hand grasped the belt of my coat.
—I pull, the coat opens and the skirt falls.
—I'm dressed in a photographic silk screened painting in black and white of me, nude.
—I rip off the public triangle, I show this representation of my pubis.
—Beneath this triangle appears my real pubic hair, previously shorned and reglued with wig glue.
—I take the palette in my left hand showing the side with five crosses, each smaller than the other, made of band aid, sticky side out.
—With my right hand, I pull out my pubic hair by tufts.
—When my pubis is bold, I present the palette before my face (I still have the brush between my teeth).
—I take the handle of the brush with all of my fingers.
—With a sweeping gesture, I pretend to take paint from the palette (in reality, I had already put black paint on the brush).
—With the brush, I repaint my pubic hair on my pubis, and on the photographic silkscreen canvas.
—I put the palette white side out back over my pubis like a fig leaf.
—I penetrate the handle of the brush in the hole of the palette.
—I pivot very slowly to the left.
—I pose to mark the profile.
—I'm once again back to the public facing the painting

(Louvre)

RICHARD PECK

As in life as in performance ... adjusting to situations ... making choices ... to play a saxophone solo on the revolving stage or to play the saxophone accompanying myself on the piano (which would completely remove me from the revolving stage)? I chose the latter.

(3 Evenings on a Revolving Stage)

LUCIO POZZI

While sitting on a stool, I fit my face—completely convered by shiny white make-up—inside an oval hole, cut in plywood to my size. My face, this way, occupied the center of the backdrop of the minitheatre I had built* on stilts, at spectator's eye level, to match exactly the grommet hole.

Two long openings at either side allowed my hands to reach centerstage, if needed, and two storage areas below them contained props and light switches equipped with dimmers to operate the stage lights installed above the grommet hole. I could see myself in a square mylar mirror fixed on the grommet hole wall.

I wore a black skin-fit sleeve on my left arm and a white one on the right. My hands were covered by gren translucent disposable plastic gloves.

I placed a little white wine chair at centerstage, facing the public. Around it there was, in a demicircle, an assembly of grey rubber Robbins, black Owls, and white

Turkeys.

All I did subsequently, was to permutate various tableaux, adding or removing props and puppets, activating them one way or another.

The Lady in flowered shirt and orange pants, would fly through the stage casting her shadow over my white backdrop face. The brown and green handpainted flat lead Tree and the brown plastic leafless Tree would be moved right or left against the back wall. A button-shaped Disk, printed on one side with some stylized brown cloud designs and containing a mirror on the other, would slowly rise at one end and travel up and up, arching through the stage, then setting down at the oppostie end. It showed alternately the cloud face or the mirror face. This would occasionally be angled to blind the spectator's eye in its grommet hole.

The Blue Soldier and the Red Soldier faced each other threateningly. Four couples of blue, red, yellow and green dinosaurs were constantly rearranged in varied formations. The same colors were cooling the four jump-frogs and the plasticine blocks. There were ten tiny rubber piglets and ten babies, five brown-skinned and five pink-skinned. Some babies would occasionally be picked up and placed to hang in the mouth of the big white face in the background. A dark green Biplane would at times be flown above it all.

There were a green Landrover and the white Tank, but not too often. Four colored pens wrote mysterious words on a little notebook, then turned to the viewer for reading. I flet a strong backache.

(Grommets #4)

NAM JUNE PAIK

A wooden radio concealed a portable TV, a fragmented image from the screen appearing where the radio dial once was.

(About 405E. 13th St.; #2)

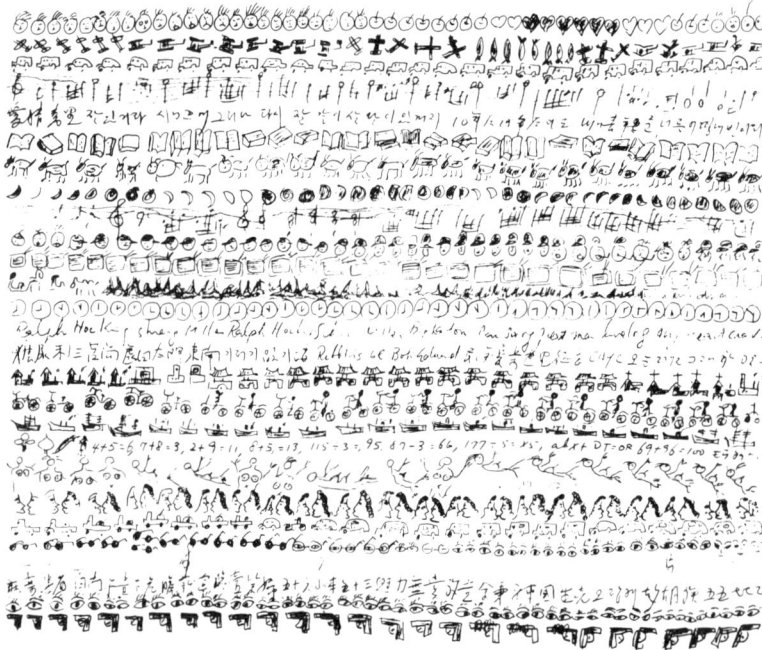

A score for a collective performance PAIK '78

Nam June Paik announced a homage to Duchamp's piece, "Why not sneeze?" He asked the audience to sneeze with him. Paik: "Ah-h-h . . . ." Audience: "Choo!"

In another piece, Paik said, "I just want to blow my nose." Then he blew his nose into a Chant a Cappella program and threw it away.

(Chant a Cappella)

CHARLEMAGNE PALESTINE

→ So Jean Says to me —
Soup + Tart and I says O.K.—
and then the time comes and
Shit what the hell am I gonna
do — Goup + Shmart — who cares
but then I feel guilty an I'm
drinkin and so I says to myself
send a goddamn Telegram!
— Poifect —
So I did and I says to the
operader — mmmmm what should
I say — she gets pissed off →
So I Says dats what I'm
sendin — she says whats what
your sendin — I says
MMMMMMM
dats how it was.

205

Then Jean says Revolving Stage
so I says O.K. → then I hear
3 nights revolving stage — Oi Vay —
I get claustropobia and don't show up
the first night — then finally I dress
up in Red Paint — put a god damn speaker
in my mouth with my cowboy hat & cossack
coat — static coming from the speaker and
shit — I get thrown the hell out —
  his stage manager thinks I'h a bum
So I leave and fuck that ⟶
So then Jean says Chant Acapella →
so I says O.K. then I realize I'll
be in Rome — Wheh! Lucky me b t I
feel guilty so I thinks to myself — what
now → so I hear about singing telegrams
    Western Onion → so I call them
up and they do six of them like vaudeville
    Birth — Bar Mitzvah — Marriage — divorce
      death — rebirth like Catskills style
So I goes to my favorite saloon
dressed like a fuckin imbecile and

I do my do there — so thats how
it was — Dew Jean says Grommets
so I says ok. so den I thinks
to myself — O Shit — so I do a
tape with my head freakin out pulling off
so dats what I did — then I come during
and Elaine throws me out for being loud and
obnoxious and for pulling off in our booth →

western union **Telegram**

```
      YSC029(1806)(2-016518E334)PD 11/30/74 1806
ICS IPMMTZZ CSP
 2123491437 TDMT NEW YORK NY 3 11-30 0606P EST
PMS GEAN DEPUIS CARE THE KITCHEN, DLR
59 WOOSTER ST
NEW YORK NY 10012
DEAN GEAN
MMMMMMMMMM
   CHARLEMAGNE
NNNN
```

I never ever saw the damn thing →
Cost me a hundred and fifty bucks!
Then videos — a few Jean says
Coalition or something — acapelapulco
again and One two Three shubs or

something so I says OU. and then
who the hell knows and then
        Voila → History
So thats the way it was. _____ 79

(Soup and Tart)

RICHARD PRINCE

It was my understanding that a 'grommet' was a hole that French Noblemen stuck their dicks through to get jacked off by an unseen party on the other side.
It is my understanding that a 'grommet' is a metal eyelet set in a curtain that functions as a natural lens through which a viewer eyeballs his attention on an activity that takes place behind the curtain.

My activity behind the curtain involved the 'mortification of touch,' and excerpt from a continuing narrative entitled, *Original as Hell*.

The first thing you saw through the gommet was a nude woman swinging back n forth on a plae red swing. The second thing you saw through the grommet was a man dressed in a small black suit with black shirt and black tie; lying on a bed underneath the nude woman. As the nude woman passed over the man in the small black suit she would mark his small black suit with white chalk.

THE MEANING PART: as the man in the small black suit lay asleep he continually repeated the following:

I will resist:

the cross of chirst / the tree of buddha / the tree of knowledge / the most photographed tree / triangular stretcher bars . . . .

I will resist:
my divine spark / the lyrical transfer of two liquids (cum and sweat), the separation of mars black and brown madder . . . .

I will resist:

the nail on the white light wall and hang my mortal flesh in high relief on the choir screen beside dominating passion . . . .

I must undo my sinful past

I will not change position in bed

Each white mark left on the man's small black suit represented St. Bartholomew's offering of his flesh to the Third Person of the Most Blessed Trinity. (the offering of one's flesh symbolizes a personnal confession of guild and unworthiness)

The entire installation was wrapped in transparent plastic that inhaled and exhaled as the nude woman passed over the man in the small black suit.

The installation was lit by a single white light that cast a moving shadow on the curtain of the nude woman swinging on the swing that in turn beckoned the attention of the audience.
The naute of the 'grommet' being a hole through which to see something otherwise hidden, concern was to perform an activity and to assemble an installation that

would transform viewer into voyeur.

(Grommets #3)

YVONNE RAINER
(Excerpt from a Pauline Kael review in *The New Yorker*)

The occasional satisfaction in work is never shown on the screen, say, of the actor or the writer. The people doing drudge jobs enjoy these others because they think they make a lot of money. What they should envy them for is that they take pleasure in their work. Society plays that down. I think enormous harm has been done by the television commercial telling ghetto children they should go to school because their earning capacity would be higher.* They never suggest that if you're educated you may go into fields where your work is satisfying, where you may be useful, where you can really do something that can help other people....

*Several years ago, the University of Wisconsin produced a series of films (in which I was the interviewer) dealing with people who had achieved some form of recognition in their respective occupations. It was for showing before groups of ghetto children. The results of a survey indicated that the most admired subject was the lawyer-realtor-accountant, who spoke of his possessions—and showed them. He was astonishingly inarticulate—or inhibited—about his work. The least popular subject was a distinguished black sculptor, who in his studio enthusiastically talked of his work, and showed it in loving detail. The survey further revealed that the children were avid television viewers and remarkably knowledgeable about the commercials of the moment.

(Foot note read aloud at asterisk in text.)

(Soup and Tart)

PETER VAN RIPER

//Greetings for Chow En Lai//

Upon the death of Chow En Lai, the piece is about centering and attentive sound in the space. I bow from the waist on the first revolution, on the second a 35mm motion picture of bowing on a revolving stage is projected overhead while I play a metal gong during that turn. On the third revolution the film continues and a Buddhist wood bell is played.

(3 Evenings on a Revolving Stage)

//Window Shadow//

Viewed through the grommet holes of the screen covering the door of the room, the viewer observes a distinct window shadow. The shadow is produced by a slide rear projected on a screen angled 45 degrees to a mirror angled 45 degrees to the grommet holes.

A light in spaces, attention-perception piece.

(Grommets #2)

First invocation playing Buddhist wood bell, then sounding lowest level of tower playing rhythm on overhead beams, then playing sopranino on top level, and finally playing a tape sound & soprano saxophone piece from the middle of the structure.

Sounding the room, sounding the tower, sounding the acoustics of the room with different saxophones from different levels.

//Room Space//

(A Tower at P.S.1)

A multiplex hologram is suspended in the center of the room it is a light image of. The empty room has white walls and black floor & ceiling. The observer walks around the cylinrical hologram observing the light image of the room in the cylinder, the door appears three times.

Light in space; perception piece, the hologram is but half the piece, the environment the second half.

A front space was strung with my graphis drying line for display of two dimensional art. Stainless steel cable 3/16″ in diameter is threaded with clothes pins, secured to hooks in the wall, and made taught by turn-buckles in the line.

I displayed three photo silk screen pieces of laser scan caligraphy: *Inches, Two,* and *Two Inches.*

TONIE ROOS

Jean told me about this show.

At that time he was keeping an open house every afternoon (at least) sitting around the zinc table with young artists who would come to visit him almost daily because he would accept all of us as artists and talk about the artwork as a matter of just being done. He listened to various problems, always coming up with a solution, "Why don't you . . ." he would in a light voice, which made everything sound easy, fun and possible, the attitude of making up one's mind and do, rather than worry about not being able to.

Still he is the only person I know that always invites me to participate in his projects.

So there were lots of activities going on and lots of plans for shows, performances, video, publishing, and Jean's own tricky pieces and hundreds of Aunt Jeanne's (I got that 1978) tarte aux pommes being made and eaten as well as a salad consisting of boiled potatoes and lettuce.

One of my favorite stories about Jean takes place in Paris. We were in one of Jean's French friends very fashionable white Parisian apartment. In New York Jean lived up to this reputation of a great cook from his Maonaise (one of Olga's flashes of genious), soup and tart, Bofinger, O.G.'s, catering etc, he was to cook dinner for the host, Jacques Ohayon, myself and himself. We all went down to the grocery store where a little of a discussion was going on like What do you want Jean? etc. After that Jean bought a bag of potatoes (Potatis, Jean's only Swedish word from his travels in Sweden after the war), a few tomatoes and bunch of parsley. If you know anything about the French eating habits this is hilariously funny. He made a salad with what he bought and onions and garlic (I always like Jean's food).

Anyway back to 405 E. 14th St, Jean had already arranged two shows in his loft and this was the "third and last" originally to be held in a gallery.

One afternoon after having spent a few crazy (and very funny) weeks with Karen Edwards looking for a place for us to share Jean says that he want to rent part of his loft. The same evening in a bar, Arlette says her sister has moved out of her apartment so the next day Moki Cherry, the number one collector, and I went over and Chet helped us move: for me: a huge bed, 2 lamps and a big mirror, and for Moki: all kinds of things that she plan to change or think may be useful some day (this summer we were using some broken pieces of prcelain that she had picked up on the road somewhere ten years ago) among other things a few horrible lamps with ugly porcelain feet (I remember those as she left them with me).

I moved into Jean's without even thinking about that there is 0 daylight for painting. Jean gave me m² of privacy surrounded by canvas hangings.

Luckily enough Bliss Nodland on the 4th floor in the same building offered to let me paint in her loft. We became friends and I spent some of my best time ever with her in her space. Everything was in the building, living/working space, friends, and Di Bella's and the Italian coffeecake shop closeby.

I was sitting at the window in the loft painting the view, my first real executed oil-painting. I was so excited about New York at that time that the look of it and this great view was more than enough for me. It was a very nice working period, meditative, really seeing, no problems or many choices to be made - well, the sky and light changed all the time so I made a few ones back and forth in the end, - the final

decision. I have not been working like that since.

For the show Jean was more excited about showing a photography of myself washing dishes in the sink in his loft with a selfportrait hanging on the wall. At the last minute the show was not to take place in the gallery but in Jayne's loft. This pleased me very much as I could just leave the painting right at the window where I had painted it (Jayne made it the perfect frame that gave it the necessary illusive weight; when working with the electric saw in the most precise, professional way she whispered "don't tell anyone").

Lots of people were in the show, Jean's usual mixute of Top Ten and his young friends. There was a big party at the opening night. I had by then moved to C.P.W., first to stay with Gwynne and Emma Rivers, and when they left to join Clarice in Greece, take care of their minor menagerie. I had a hard time deciding what to wear till I decided to put on all the alternatives, one layer on the top of the other. I was very late, two boyfriends I had invited had left-together-I was told. Before starting dancing and taking off the layers I was talking to a Swedish lady who had lived in New York for like ten years—her way of taling about the art and artists was as if she had arrived the same day. There were some very special art. Mel Schultz, who lived in Brendah's loft in the building had hung a piece of nature snake from the ceiling that looked very beautiful when slowly turning around in the sunset. Charles Dreyfus had made a pillow outside covered with pretty white feathers. Larry Rivers a huge neon Japanese lady.

There weren't many paintings and I don't think that mine was really seen by many people. It was not demanding attention but very nice to get into. I remember talking to people standing next to it and they had not discovered that it was the view of the window right next to it. Later in Paris, people have thought it is a Parisian view.

Pontus Hulten to whom the painting belong in all senses was excited about hanging it on an obvious spot in his apartment when Claes Oldenburg was to arrive -Jean's show was in the same space that used to be Claes' studio, so it was a gimmik, and Claes said that the pipes on the top of the closest roof had given him the idea to make the cigarette butts that are now on the terrace outside the restaurant of Beaubourg.

When the show was over Larry Rivers came to pick up his piece, and he asked me where mine was (I don't think he had seen it in spite of it being next to his), he was quite surprised and said "it's something like Utrillo, isn't it? It would be interesting to see a close-up of something." And I have done that since.

(About 405 E. 13th St. #3)

ARTHUR RUSSELL

Arthur Russell, cellist, played and sang "Eli's Coming."

(Soup and Tart)

JOHN SANBORN

The presence of the tower, constructed against a far wall in a gutted school auditorium, told two loud stories. It asked to be scaled, it pose a challenge, a task, and dared, "Come on up". It offered power translated into height. And that offer of omni-potence, meant that once scaled you could preach down to the crowd below. You could broadcast your message, secure in the knowledge that having climbed to the top-you were standing above everyone one else within sight.

This tele-presence, taken in total, can mean only one thing. A love for direct, intimate one way contact. A verbal attraction to the object and power of television.

Narrating, in an abstract manner, the will and the way of being seduced by and giving in to television, the risks and failures of coping with such a force, the central metaphor being the scaling and decent from the tower. The point of broadcast. A simple technology, the wooden tower, beholden to a complex one, the television receiver, visited by and connected to each other by a single human presence.

In a way the question is; if we're watching television, who's watching us?

(A Tower at P.S.1)

JOAN SCHWARTZ

MARCH 1973. What an asshole! I keep telling Donald this video tape is not working and as usual, he is ignoring good advice. What am I doing with him in the first place? I'm the one who is working, bringing in the bread to pay for this schizoid presentation. Now he wants me to start paying for dancing lessons for the both of us. I suggest a grant.

MAY 1973. Jean Dupuy invites us to participate in his annual group show, "About 405 E. 13th St." Only Donald could have come up with some ridiculous idea about us floating across the room. I had to solve this problem technically. My idea of using invisible wires to suspend a rear screen midloft works very neatly. When Donald sees the finished effect, he proudly takes the kudos.

JUNE 1973. I insist we discard the convenient idea of using his disinterested friends as actors in Each Day. As Donald sleeps, I work throughout the night to finish our sets.

AUGUST 1973. Production on "Each Day" is complete. What next?

SEPTEMBER 1973. A setback. Donald develops venereal desires and can't keep his mind on work. We save money and travel abroad.

OCTOBER 1974. Inspired by our trip to Europe, I suggest we convince a new uptown dealer to sponsor my new idea 'Apache', a theatrical French dance routine set in the context of a mixed media performance. I see the piece as a metaphor for the artist, art-dealer relationship. The dealer bites.

(About 405 E. 13th St.; #s 1 & 2)

Our dancing teacher loves my dancing, but scorns Donald's lack of professionalism. Feigning excuse after excuse, Donald finally decides his problem is an abcess tooth which becomes increasingly aggravated whenever we dance. I think Donald has a problem seeing any project to completion.

NOVEMBER 1974. Jean invites us to participate in Soup and Tart, a group performance by thirty N.Y. artists at the Kitchen. We jump at the chance to preview our dance at this event. Donald has still not made much progress with the routine. He will never make it as an artist. I am worried. Donald's dental imagination has prevented us from continuing our rehearsals. My nerves and the performance level of our dance are too raw to expose to a critical N.Y. audience. The only thing I can think of is to use our anxieties as the basis for our act and verbally dance insults at each other across the crowded gallery space with humor and accuracy. The strategy works, in spite of Donald's loss for words and his juvenile behavior, storming our of the Kitchen, exclaiming. "I'm not going to stay here and make an asshole out of myself." Little does he realize I still have the last word.

(Soup and Tart)

CAROLEE SCHNEEMANN

At the time I was preparing a large performance/installation for the Kitchen, "Up To and Including Her Limits." For La Tarte I prepared an advertisement for coming work: a scroll four feet high and the width the two furthest pillars. One end of the scrool was taped to a piller and very slowly unrolled to the other pillar. The scroll announced the title and dates of "Up To And Including Her Limits."

(Soup and Tart)

TRANSPERENCE/CIRCUMFERENCE—THE CONTRADICTIONS

1. Puddle: circumference of water— evaporation the body as axis in the

2. Sunbeam & Electric Light: circumference of light

212

the work underlying the installation (photos: Gianfranco Gorgoni)	drawing of the installation for 405 East 13th St
puddle circumference dissolves outdoors	sunbeam/electric light static circumference indoors
from below upward	from above downward
axis of body in center of puddle	vertical cord (plumb line), bulb centered in its light beam
circle disappears as water evaporates	circle of sand remains
natural light	artificial & natural light
natural/found elements	arranged/organized & found elements

Drawing for the installation: an electric cord was suspended from the ceiling; its position was established by a light beam which intersected the vertical cord at 4:05 pm. The beam of light came from a window on the opposite wall which Anthony McCall had covered with black paper, a small circle/aperture had been cut to admit a beam of light. (The window faced west). I poured a circle of sand to follow the outermost radius of the suspended light bulb. A second circle of sand (tinted pink) was poured to mark the sun beam floor position at 4:05 pm. The light bulb was a transposition of the earlier work of the body in the evaporating cirumference of the puddle; the circle of sand was an equivalence to the demarkation between water and dirt of the puddle—static circumference of light.

(405 E. 13th St. #3)

DALE SCOTT

Movement and Balance Equal

The Whitney Museum performances were important ingredients in the foundation of my present life work. I performed my own piece entitled Circle Dance for Japanese Flute, and I performed in a piece conceived and choreographed by James Barth. The Circle Dance as very much influenced by Tai Chi Chuan, and involved slow, sustained circular movements of the torso and arms. My feet remained static throughout the piece, allowing the revolving stage to inspire the impetus of the circular movement. Jim Barth's peice dealth very concretely with balance. It was a series of choreographed attempts to counterbalance our weight on a precariously placed two by four on the revolving stage. At that point in my life, I had not integrated movement and balance. They existed in my mind and in my body as two separate entities, as indeed they were two separate pieces at the Whitney Museum. Today, I have combined them, and consequently completed the equation: Movement plus balance equals tightwire.

(One Afternoon on a Revolving Stage)

RICHARD SERRA

I was born in San Francisco in the Mission District. In fact, at that time it was called the Excelsior, which is the outer Mission. The neighborhood would be comparable to the Lower East Side here in New York. When I was five, we were fortunate enough to move out to the beach. At that time, the beach and the area out there wasn't developed. It later became what is known now as the Sunset District. There weren't any blacktop roads, there was only one big street that went down to the sand dunes which was called Taraval, lavarat spelled backwards. The dunes were endless and there were only two or three houses within three or four square miles. The family closest to us, not adjacent because there was a sand dune in between, was the di Suvero family. I have one really clear, recurring recollection of that time in my life. I was about six years old and I used to get into continuous mischief. My mother had no way of making me behave, she wasn't a very strict disciplinarian. But my father had his own ideas about how to bring up his sons. When I would do something wrong, my father would come home and take me out the back door and point to the horizon. There weren't any fences, just endless miles of sand dunes. He would pick out a square shovel and say, "See that mound there?" I'd say "Which one?" He'd say "The one there." And I'd say "Oh, you mean the one about thirty yards away?" He'd say "Yes, that one. I'd like you to move it over there where the knoll is." And I'd say "Where the knoll is where?" He'd say "Where the knoll is forty yards to the left." Now some days there would be large wind storms, not storms, but large winds, and the sand would shift around and the knoll wouldn't be exactly where it was the following day. But my father was very clear that he wanted one mound moved from one part of the terrain to the other, and he would ask me to move it by the time he got home that evening. I wasn't very discouraged about having to face a day of moving all that sand. In fact, there was a certain rhythm I would get into in doing it. I found after a while there was no necessity to actually shovel the dirt, you just put the scoop in and dragged the shovel from one side to the other, then just turned the shovel over. So I spent hours walking back and forth with these shovelsful of dirt. My father would come home and stand on the stoop and look out at what the day's chore had accomplished, and he would say "Do you think it's in the right place?" I don't know, what do you think?" He'd say "I think you can move it thirty yards to the right by tomorrow." This procedure would sometimes go on for six or seven days until he and I decided that what I was doing was making us both feel better about each other. What I finally decided about my father was that I felt his idea for me to move that dirt around was just. I would have moved that dirt anywhere.

(Soup and Tart)

Richard Serra/Jean Dupuy Interview

R) What is the question you wanted to ask me? "What is the question?" sounds a little Gertrude Stein-like. I might have said: "What is it you wanted to ask me?"
J) I said to you: "I asked a lot of artists to do a 2-minute performance and I explained that it would be under the title, "Soup & Tart," and you said...I don't remember exactly what you said...You said very fast something like...You said the word "material"...You used the possessive...your material.
R) I said: "Sure, I'll be your material."
J) So, that is the question I wanted to ask you — what did you mean when you answered, "Sure, I'll be you material?"
R) I said: "I'll be your material." What happened was I went over to see Joan and I said: "Joan, what the hell am I going to do with Jean Dupuy? Maybe I'll do something on tape." And so she got out the tape recorder and said: "What do you want to do? And I said: "Well, you know, I don't know what to do." And she said: "Why don't you tell a story?" and I said: "I'm not so good at telling stories." She said: "You've told me some fabulous stories." And I said: "Which stories?" and she said: "Why don't you just tell them about your father and moving all that dirt around?"
J) You said: "Sure, I'll be your material..."
R) I went over to Joan and said: "What material is available?" When you stopped me in the hall, recently, did you really want to know about the statement, "Sure, I'll be your material" or were you asking about the narrative of my father?
J) About the statement.
R) First of all, I think everything is material—that everything can be used. The earth and everything that is here is material, so it's open. And I think about given time...
J) Oh! But I thought about the possessive "your" that you used when you answered me.
R) Let me go on with what I'm going to say. At different times people have different reasons or different necessities for using other kinds of material which we don't normally think of—such as people—and then how you use people and what you use them for is usually open to your discretion and a certain respect for the fact that the endeavor for the work is whatever—not even knowing the nature of the work—one either agrees or disagrees. I've worked with a lot of people that way and I know a lot of people have worked with ne that way and I think it is a way of working. I think that is one of the things it always makes for a healthier constructive situation—I learned more doing that than a lot of other things. But there are very few people that I have been able to do it with. But I found that those kinds of interchanges are where you can really learn something about yourself and the other person. I think one of the things that I found really good about it—this "Soup & Tart" thing—is that I got to meet some people who I wouldn't have known if they hadn't been there performing or doing whatever they did or what-

ever you call what they did, and so I think it brought a lot of people together and a lot of people who I didn't know—who I responded very positively to their work—and since then, I've become friends. So I think that any reason or method that stirs things up and brings people together is invaluable in a way. That is why we're not living in Idaho . . . .

(From *Tracks*, Winter 1976)

STUART SHERMAN

(This piece was performed by 6 people, each of whom performed for 10 minutes, and then, regardless of what point had been reached in the action of the piece, was replaced by another performer.)

X sits on floor. Directly in front of him/her is a small pile of gold-colored grommets and white rough-edged paper-fragments with holes punched out of their centers. To the left of the pile is a glass bowl, inside the bowl is a hole-puncher. To the right of the pile is a long thin spike (mounted on a silver base), sheathing the spike is a white straw with gold tape wrapped in a spiral around it.

X removes straw from spike, sets straw on floor. Places upturned grommet on spike then paper-fragment (lowering it onto spike through hole in fragment's center), then another upturned grommet. (All grommets are placed on spike upturned except the very last one, which is downturned.) This action is repeated until all the grommets and paper-fragments have been placed on the spike, nearly covering it.

X moves bowl from left to center, removes hole-puncher and places it behind bowl. Removing straw from spike, X lifts spike and tips it over bowl: grommets and paper-fragments slide off spike into bowl.

X re-sets spike on floor. Holds straw in front of and near to his/her mouth, then, with free hand, stirs contents of bowl.

X re-sheathes spike with straw. Picks up hole-puncher and, holding it up high, continuously "clicks" it in hole-puching fashion while, simultaneously, he/she lifts bowl and dumps its contents into center of floor.

X sets dwon bowl at left, returns hole-puncher to bowl.

X begins repeating entire sequence of actions.

PERFORMERS: Power Boothe, Bob Fleischner, Karen Greenblatt, Nisi Jacobs, John Matturri, Marie-Claire Tabard

(Grommets #4)

WOMAN 1, MAN, WOMAN 2 approach tower. (WOMAN 1 carries a long piece of white rope and a roll of red string; MAN carries two medium-length pieces of white rope and, in his pocket, a small black-cased folding-knife; WOMAN 2 carries a roll of red string.)

WOMAN 1 climbs left side of tower, enters top-level, places string-roll in right rear-corner; MAN climbs right side of tower and enters middle-level; WOMAN 2 goes to ground-level of tower, places string-roll in left front-corner.

WOMAN 1 lowers rope in front of tower, retaining one end of it. WOMAN 2 takes hold of other end of rope. WOMEN and MAN proceed to pace back and forth in their respective tower-levels.

MAN takes hold of center section of long rope extending in front of tower (simultaneously WOMEN stop moving), knots his pieces of rope to center section of long rope and ties rope-ends to side-railings, forming a v-shaped rope-structure in which he then sits cross-legged.

WOMEN tie their rope-ends to side-railings of their tower-levels. (WOMAN 1 ties hers to right railing, WOMAN 2 to left railing.)

WOMEN, taking their string-rolls with them, ascend/descend to middle-level, enter v-shaped rope-structure, and begin draping string around sides of v-structure. When rope-siders have been completely draped, WOMEN stand still, MAN rises and, removing knife from pocket, cuts string-rolls loose from string-draping. (WOMEN remain still, each holding draped string-end in one hand and string-roll in the other.) MAN climbs side of tower to top-level, where, with knife, he severs rope tied to right side-railing (front part of rope falls down toward middle tower-level, other part remains tied to railing), climbs down tower to ground-level and severs rope tied to left side-railing.

Returning to middle-level, MAN re-enters v-shaped rope-structure. WOMEN, bringing their string-rolls with them, return to their respective levels.

WOMEN unknot sections of rope still tied to railings, insert rope-sections through hollow of string-rolls and hold rope-sections horizontally; MAN undoes rope v-structure, gathers it (with its partial string-draping) into a tangled mass.

WOMEN and MAN pace back and forth in their respective tower-levels—the women spinning their string-rolls by twirling ends of rope extending through rolls, MAN holding tangle of rope and string in palms of his flat-open hands.

All exit: WOMAN 1, then MAN, then WOMAN 2.

WOMAN 1: Ann-Sargent Wooster/MAN: Stuart Sherman/WOMAN 2: Rena Gill

(A Tower at P.S.1)

TERRY SLOTKIN

Projected slide/superimposed with self/photographed in black and white polaroid/ photographed to large format/overlayed with #318 A Pantone Letrafilm Color Tint. Black and white photograph of fly paper/hand painted/color xerox transfer/applied to cotton blend custom-made off-white tie/Edition of 39 (signed dated numbered).

(3 Mercer St.)

MICHAEL SMITH

BMMMMM

PSSSST, WHATS THAT IN THE MIDDLE OF THE FLOOR???
THE SHIRT ON THE FLOOR FLAT AND BALCK WITH A
LARGE ROUND RED BY THE HEAD IT DOESNT MOVE.
PSSSST,—WHATS HE DOING???
A PAIR OF MAT BLACK SHOES REST BY THE WAIST.
BMMMMM

A HEAVY APPROACHES CAREFULLY LOOKING AROUND. HE PUTS ON
THE MAT BLACK TAP SHOES BY THE BALL AND SHIRT.
THE HEAVY APPROACHES TOWARDS ME BLACKENS THE HOLE
I LOOK AND I SEE:
SPORTS THRU SPOTS
HES STICKING OUT HIS TONGUE AND FLIPPING HIS HAT
PSSSSST—WHATS HE DOING???
THE HOLE THRU WHICH I LOOK DARKENS OUT OF THE
BLACKNESS COMES A MAGIC WAND.
THE SAME ONE WHO FLIPPED HIS HAT, STUCK OUT HIS TONGUE, AND
WEARING TAPE SHOES IS HOLDING HIS WANT. HE TOUCHES THE RED
BULGE ON THE FLOOR.
HE REMOVES THE RED UNCOVERING A:
SHINY BLACK BOWLING BALL
HE PUTS HIS FINGERS IN. HE REMOVES HIS VEST

HE'S GETTING INTO HIS STANCE HE'S GOING INTO A
4 STEP BOWLING APPROACH
HIS ARM IS SWINGING BACK
THE BALL IS APPROACHING
THE
H
O
L
E

THE NEXT THING I KNOW IS DARKNESS
PSSSST—KEEP YOUR EYE ON THE BALL
HE PUTS THE BALL BACK ON THE FLOOR. HE BACKS UP TO THE
HOLE WITH HIS FINGERS IN HIS BACK POCKET
HE STOPS BEFORE THE HOLE PULLS OUT A WALLET FLIPS OPEN
SOME IDENTIFICATION TO THE HOLE AND MY EYE IT READS:
TUG-A-WAR
HE TELLS ME TO PULL THE ROPE DANGLING IN FRONT OF ME
AT THE COUNT OF THREE
1-2-3
I PULL---------------------HIS PANTS FALL DOWN

(Grommets #4)

FRED STERN

Computer Poems

A teletyping machine, linked to the telephone line, was connected to the terminal of
a computer situated at the Brooklyn Polytechnic Institute during the 10 days show
at 405 E. 13th St.. Following simple instructions and writing a one line statement on
the teletype, the public could get through to the machine which was using previous
lines stored in its memory at Random, a poem.
A POEM USING THE LINE
IN MY IMAGINATION, I SECRETLY LIKE MYSELF
COME SLICE MY BLOOD IN A THOUSAND SLIVERS
NUMBERS ARE THE PULSE OF REALITY IN TIME
NUMBERS ARE THE PULSE OF REALITY IN TIME
COME SLICE MY BLOOD IN A THOUSAND SLIVERS
COME SLICE MY BLOOD IN A THOUSAND SLIVERS
ENTRENCHED IN THE NEVER ENDING CIRCLES OF THE VOID
IN MY IMAGINATION, I SECRETELY LIKE MYSELF
COME SLICE MY BLOOD IN A THOUSAND SLIVERS
ENTRENCHED IN THE NEVER ENDING CIRCLES OF THE VOID
ENTRENCHED IN THE NEVER ENDING CIRCLES OF THE VOID
I CAN CONSTRUCT A POEM FROM ANY STATEMENT.
IF YOU WOULD LIKE A POEM JUST ENTER A ONE LINE STATMENT
AND THEN PRESS THE RETURN KEY
?FREDS FRIENDLYFLESH IN THIS NARCOTICWINTER WORKS SOFT WONDERS
I'M SORRY BUT AESTHETICALLY SPEAKING YOUR LINE JSUT
DOESN'T MAKE IT.
SNICKER! SNICKER! I'M IN CONTROL HERE
HM1 NOW LETS SEE. . .
I THINK I WILL USE THE LINE:
FREDS FRIENDLYFLESH IN THIS NARCOTICWINTER WORKS SOFT WONDERS
BLUSH!!

A POEM USING THE LINE
FREDS FRIENDLYFLESH IN THIS NARCOTICWINTER WORKS SOFT WONDERS

ENTRENCHED IN THE NEVER ENDING CIRCLES OF THE VOID
FREDS FRIENDLYFLESH IN THIS NARCOTICWINTER WORKS SOFT WONDERS
ENTRENCHED IN THE NEVER ENDING CIRCLES OF THE VOID

NUMBERS ARE THE PULSE OF REALITY IN TIME
FREDS FRIENDLYFLESH IN THIS NARCOTICWINTER WORKS SOFT WONDERS
IN MY IMAGINATION, I SECRETLY LIKE MYSELF
NUMBERS ARE THE PULSE OF REALITY IN TIME
ENTRENCHED IN THE NEVER ENDING CIRCLES OF THE VOID
IN MY IMAGINATION, I SECRETLY LIKE MYSELF
ENTRENCHED IN THE NEVER ENDING CIRCLES OF THE VOID
IN MY IMAGINATION, I SECRETLY LIKE MYSELF
COME SLICE MY BLOOD IN A THOUSAND SLIVERS

   HELLO.
I CAN CONSTRUCT A POEM FROM ANY STATEMENT.
IF YOU WOULD LIKE A POEM JUST ENTER A ONE LINE STATEMENT
AND THEN PRESS THE RETURN KEY

(405 E. 13th St.)

ANNE TARDOS

2 MINUTES

A WELL CONCEIVED PIECE, A GOOD IDEA POORLY EXECUTED AT
JEAN DUPUY'S SOUP AND TART SOIREE.
JEAN ASKED ME TO DO ANYTHING I WISH AS LONG AS IT TOOK 2 MINUTES.
SO I TOOK MY EPIDIASCOPE
AND A STOPWATCH TO THE KITCHEN.
TO BEGIN MY PIECE I HAD THE HOUSELIGHTS TURNED OFF, THEN STARTED
THE STOPWATCH AND AS IT RAN I PROJECTED THE LIVE IMAGE OF THE
RUNNING WATCH ON THE WALL FOR EXACTLY 2 MINUTES.
MY EPIDIASCOPE WAS MUCH TOO SMALL, TOO WEAK FOR THE SPACE AND
MOT PEOPLE COULD NOT SEE THE PROJECTION AT ALL.
THIS WAS GOOD EXAMPLE OF GOOD IDEA GONE LOST IN THE DARK.
THE IMPORTANCE OF MAKING MISTAKES, HOWEVER, IS CLEAR.

(Soup and Tart)

MARTIAL THOMAS

text:

• I am, here, in this passage communicating between "la salle des Etats" and "La grande Galerie."
• I am, here, and I moving
• You can see me any time, in this passage and I invite you for a walk.
• I will speak to you about the walk around the Alster Lake in Hamburg.
• I will speak to you from this passage in combining this two moments.
• I am, Martial Thomas, in this passage communicating between "La salle des Etats" and "La grande Galerie."
• I am, here, and I am moving.
• You can see me any time, in this passage and I invite you for a walk.

description:

I was in the passage communicating between "La salle des Etats" (La Joconde) and "La grande Galerie" (17 e century). During one minute, the performance time, I was jumping in the same place and my speech intention was to refer TO A BEHAVIOR UBIQUITY by projecting my presence permanently and the invitation to the Louvre walk "this moving time would be placed in order to combine the artistic past and the present of the reflection situation upon my Hamburg Art Project—Burgermeister-weg—Walk around Alster Lake.

(Louvre)

NANCY TOPF

Image as Picture, Picture as Drawing, Drawing as Line, Line as Motion—Nancy Topf

The Judson piece was connected to a series of pieces which preceded it. In Circle Solo (1971) I walked in a circle and let the movement evolve through recognition of new material. It was an involvement in understanding the improvisational process and how to follow a line of movement. The circle gave me a form in which movement could just keep going. The circle gave me a line.

In Spiral Solo with Chalk Circles (1974) I discovered that the movements of falling and rolling could inscribe a perfect circle on the floor if I held a piece of chalk in my hand and let it make contact with the floor as I fell and rolled. I realized that the shape of the movement I was involved with was a circle and the drawing a visualization of the movement. (see attached photo of performance at Dartington College of Arts, England 1975).

In Judson Piece the revolving stage became an instrument that could generate a drawing. If I sat on the wheel with my arm extended holding a piece of chalk perfect circles of different colors were inscribed on the floor. When I reached my body different lengths, the circles could be bigger or smaller. If I sat on the floor with my arm stretched out over the revolving stage, circles would be inscribed on the stage. If I let the distance of my reach vary in a consistent way, I could make a spiral on the wheel. Reaching the center of the wheel signaled the end of the piece. Jon Gibson accompanied the piece with pan pipes which he played from the balcony.

(3 Evenings on a Revolving Stage)

Two minute Piece was a locomotor pattern with skips, runs & turns. It was done on a diagonal back and forth alternately by myself and John Gibson. We finished the piece by doing the sequence in unison. I wanted to make a sequence of movements that would be done by a dancer and a non-dancer. This was Jon Gibson's debut as a dancer.

(Soup and Tart)

DOUGLAS TURNBACH

"When, in the Sante Prison, I began to write, it was never because I wanted to relive my emotions or to communicate them, but rather because I hoped, by expressing them in a form that they themselves imposed, to construct an order (a moral order) that was unknown (above all to me too)."—Jean Genet. That describes my position and intention in my performance pieces and in all my image-making. In the prison of my childhood, despised by God, my emotions imposed drawing as the medium in my search for order. I struggled with the pencil as against a Ouija force and hid my work. Later, racking myself penitently in ballet class, this quest for line (order) took corporeal form. But the devotions at barre, though torturous, are propitiations of faith, with none of the terrors inspired by the impiety of creative acts.

Fear of creativity; taboos against the phallus and (quite another matter) male genitals; taboos against self-exposure—these factors kept me for years from overt creative work. A breakthrough came when, fearful as the primitive who believes the camera steals his sould. I saw my own face and body projected on a theater screen (see Vold d'Oiseau photos). "Not all who would be are Narcissus."—Satre. Without drowning in self-love, it is useful to learn one is not after all Quasimodo, but innocent—quasi modo geniti infantes. A degree of self-acceptance is surely necessary to dare to probe the mirror, and further, to seek the duplicate, the image, the counterpart, the beloved brother, the enemy brother.

My performance pieces include body art, not as mere celebration of the flesh but a statement about the body in general, the male body in particular. The body serves as instrument, puppet, vessel, line, form and certainly as objet trouve. What concerns me thematically is power/acquiescence, love, manipulation, transference of power/knowledge/aesthetic discipline, fraternity, physicality, sacrifice, loyalty, beauty (poor dicredited word). . . . Above all the force is to construct the unknown moral order.

Genet again: "The beauty of a moral act depends upon the beauty of its expression. To say that it is beautiful is to decide that it will be so. It remains to be proven so. This is the task of images, that is, of the correspondence with the splendors of the physical world. The act is beautiful if it provokes, and in our throats reveals, song."

(Grommets #4)

UNTEL

(Jean Paul Albinet, Philippe Cazal, Wilfrid Rouff)

In a preview, Untel* will show their colorful collection "the tourist" in the main gallery of the Louvre.

Jean Paul no I, in a white jacket, narrow white pants, in a studied white motive pattern, crew neck cherry under shirt, assorted with the suit. No 2, Philippe is wearing a snowy ensemble, very comfortable, printed in sharp dynamic colors, slouchy front button jacket, pegged trousers, apricot tee-shirt. No 3, Wilfrid, dressed simply in a white suit, hand stitched pockets on jacket, sporty pants, one hundred per cent cotton, short sleeved polo shirt in a multi colored print. The look is very "originale" and young. At home in the city or on week-end this easy to wear outfits are still classics for all occasions. The badges, insignias and accessories are also an "Untel" creation.

*Untel, in French means: someone

(Louvre)

YOSHIMASA WADA

(Tower at P.S. 1)

SYLVIA WHITMAN PALACIOS

The name of the piece was "Tequila 5." There were 6 performers. The idea was to see what would happen if a learned and rehearsed (small dance) or movements were done in public after each of the people having had different amounts of tequila. One had none, one had one, another had two, another had three, one had four and one had five. We appeared twice within one half an hour. The first time to each drink the described amount. (Then we waited for the effect of the alcohol). The second appearance was to acutally perform the movements previously learned. The results were not very clear but obviously the one person that had no tequila remembered and performed the piece better and the equilibrium of the person that had five tequilas was not very good. It was all done in good fun.

(Soup and Tart)

HANNAH WILKE

Super-t-art (Soup and Tart)

Historical: Patterns—gestures, poses, expose, supposition, opposition.

Religion: Domini, dominate, female fertility rite, *popular morality, homosexuality, induction, seduction, remission, emission, omission.

Nature: Mother Nature, "Mary Mary, quite contrary, how does your garden grow? With silver bells and *cock*le shells and pretty maidens in a row." The virgin and the whore.

Fabrication: *Cocktail, Bloody Mary, male religion, I oppose, I object, fabric, shroud, cloth, strip, discard, decartes, the bride stripped bare, getting even, enentually, vengance.*

55. for my flesh is meat indeed, and my blood is drink indeed.

56. he that eateth my flesh and drinketh my blood, dwelleth in me, and I in him...

✡

Prejudice
(PRAY - Jew - Dies)

†
(† - ART)

Ⓐ
Country
(cunt-tree)

(Soup and Tart)

Sunday 9:14 the telephone rings. It's Jean Dupuy.

J: Bon-jour Hannah, we are giving a series of performances on a revolving stage at the Whitney, today. Would you like to do something?

H: What time is it?

J: 2:30

H: (in silent thought: To be or not to be in the Whitney? Better to be) O.K. Jean...

By 10 a.m. I remembered that outside the Whitney, artists would be picketing Rockefeller. I knew I should be there, but realized that it may be more valuable to relate this problem within the structure of the museum itself ... so a la "Frankieboy" the bride stripped bare, with jacket on shoulders, wearing 'her hat,' she proceeded to sing...if I never have a cent, I'd be rich as Rockefeller, gold dust at my feet, on the sunny side of the street. "...my ... my cunt ... my cunt tree ... my cunt tree tis of thee ... sweet land of liberty, of thee, I sing ... land where my father's died ... land of the pilgrim's pride ... from every mountain side, let freedom ring...

(One Afternoon on a Revolving Stage)

WILSON

"East West Honk Pow" is the framed drawing, ink on manilla, In it four birds look around. To the right of the frame, hanging from a hook, are photo copies of the drawing, there for the taking.

(3 Mercer St.)

DAISY YOUNGBLOOD

I began to make an Easter egg for my husband, it turned into a large poisonous snake. The snake is in 4 ceremic parts held together by a wire that runs from the tail through the center and out the mouth. The head is of my skull, the body my spinal column. The piece is a prayer about centering and pulling the poisonous part up and out of the body.

(3 Mercer St.)

ZADIK ZADIKIAN

45 foot by 11 foot window in the James Yu Gallery, NYC that faces West Broadway was boarded from the inside of the gallery with plywood painted day-glo red. The window glss was then removed by crashing from the outside. Alteration of the window became the art work.

(Scale 1/1)

JOHN ZORN

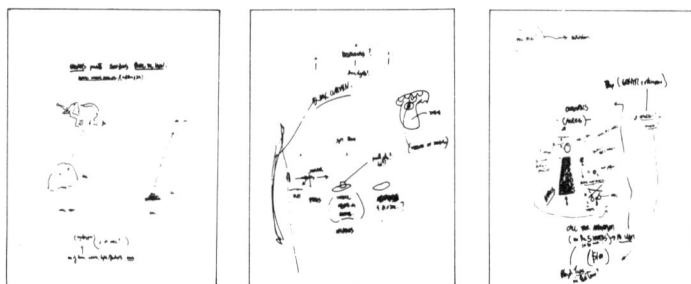

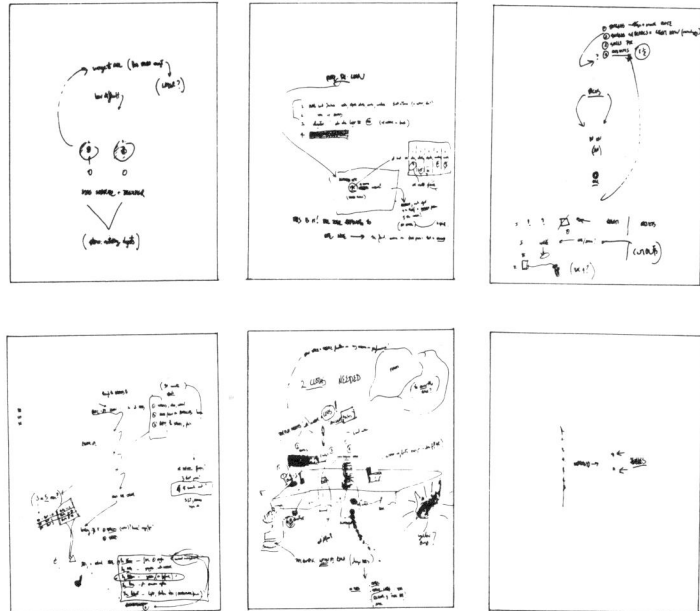

JANELLE WINSTON

Janelle Winston's performances were inspired by four different works of art, Degas' "Scene in a Laundry," Munch's "Puberty," Mollyne Karnofsky's "Untitled," and Laurens' "Crouching Woman." The works were displayed and introduced before the performances began. She began each performance as if she was inside the painting, inside the frame, frozen in its moment of aliveness, and then slowly carried the aliveness of the work in the direction it suggested. Complete scenes were created with setting and dialogue for Degas' and Munch's works, whereas for Karnofsky's and Laurens' work, she performed with sound and movement.

(Tower at P.S.1)

MICHAEL KRUGMAN

In the first part, the man made a series of string figures—like the cat's cradles kids make. He'd go through the whole business of setting one up—a bunch of comples, finger movements and then the figure would appear in its final form. Just at that moment the woman would cut the string right up the middle with a big pair of scissors (3 times),

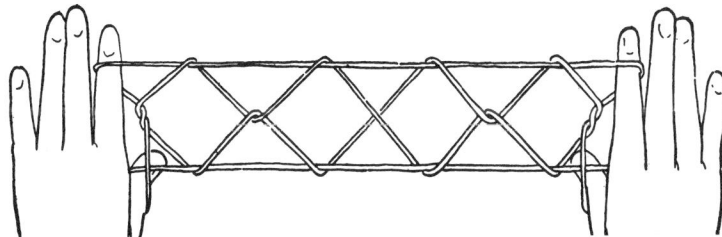

then a blackout. In the second part, the man came out in the dark with an old suitcase. When it opened, a very intense wedge of light shone from inside. There was a leaf inside which was held up in front of the light to make a leaf-shaped shadow. Then the suitcase was closed. The final part had the man and woman standing face to face on the revolving stage. This time, they worked together, making a pair of string figures stretched between them. A blackout, and that's all, folks.

(3 Evenings on a Revolving Stage)

223

JOEL HUBAUT

is the museum open to day, please?
(LOUVRE — BOITE) performance épidémik au LOUVRE;
(it's gala night and we are booked up ... fermé ...
La boite (fermée,barrée ,cachetée,preéservée,stérilisée,conservée.) donc,la boite de
conserve (dans la performance,utilisation d'une boite de haricots en conserve) idée de
"BEANS" (bordel en argot) donc, conserve ...conservateur (la boite de
conserve,badge dey conservateur (la boite de conserve,badge du conservateur
stabilisé. Les haricots (aliment) (repas de noces) rappellent mes signes épidémik
(haricots — asticots?, épidémie comme grouillement, multitude, envahissement,
multiplication (multiplication des pains,des poissons, le vin dans les noces de cana)
ici les noces de cana peintes par Véronése, voir également le repas chez SIMON, dans
ma tête donc, Mummy,Mummu, m'adressant en rêve à la Joconde mere de dieu;
don'forget the adhesive tape and the string to tie my parcel,please! (que meveux-tu
femme? mon heure n'est pas encore venue! donc, je déballe une toile libre
(nappe...repas) transpaente sur laquelle est marrouflée au centre un poster de la
Joconde (la nappe est maintenue par deux personnes comme s'il s'agissait d'une
couverture que tiennent des pompiers pour recevoir quelqu'un en chute libre) vertige
de Véronèse (êre au vert, en cas de catastrophe,incendie,ect être au vert Véronèse)
donc, épidémie, ici,vérone mental, any vegetables Madam? (m'adressant àla Joconde
mère de dieu) donce devant une des plus grande toiles du monde (c'est quand même
quelquechose) (evenement) je brandis une boite deharicots en conserve (mise en boite
du conservatuur) que j'ouvres avec un ouvre-boite vert véronese (on my wife's side as
well as my own, we have masses of relatives. There are so many aunts, uncles and
cousins that we almost get confused at times) don il y a du monde sur la toile et devant la toile,toute la famille quoi! pierre...jacques...et jean...en tenue d'apôtre
selon saint jean (les noces de cana dans l'évangile selon saint jean, je deverse le con-
tenue de ma boite de conserve sur la face hillare de las joconde,dégoulinure,
épidémie de haricots dégoulinant sur la nappe; (les noces: the fact that we will not
have to worry about money should, to a great extent ensure the happiness of our mar-
riage. But I wouls still have married him if he were only a salesman and not the self-
made tycoon he is (self-service) les haricots ici comme amuse-gueule pour accom-
pagner le vin spirituel...cultural...donc, c'est le capharnaüm (après les noces de
cana, Jésus descendit à capharnaüm) ici,lieu renfermant des objects entassés con-
fusément (le bordel) (le musée comme bordel). action capharnaüm: (jeu) ici, lejoker (la
joconde) dont l'image est au centre de la nappe est souillée, polluée, épidémiée par
les haricots (WET PAINT) alors je l'ouvre (ma guele) en hurlant : oh ! oh ! les beaux
haricots (faire la liaison) donc,jouissance de pouvoir hurler enfin dans le musée du
louvre dontle chuchotement est au pouvoir (paralysie - infirmité du public düü à la
sublimation ,au mythe ect) ici,j'accomplis un geste de déparalysie miracle, (noces de
cana — multiplication — épidémie. Alors je demande au public de répeter avec moi
(comme si nous étions aussi à la conce ... chansons de fin de repas de mariage) un-
deux- trois : oh! oh! les beux arts — ictos, ici regrain "culturel" (la disco au louvre,
donc comme un disque-jockey , dique — joconde plutôt) je "fête après la faim du repas

des noces ,ici, il s'agit en fait des aventures de "jim Cana" le disque — jockey bien connu dans les boites de nuit (conserve) donc, vroum ! vroum ! je termine la perform-ance en vrombissant dans le public (ici il s'agit d'un capharnaûm aprés noces ou;il etait une fois le louvre dans la bergerie...(entendez moutons de Panurge) donc ,je dévalle dans la foule comme sur une piste de karting, (it would e stupid to rush past those masterpieces) mais, apràs tout,c'est la vie ! vrom ! vroum ! sans renverser les quilles...Louvre—fermé. I should have asked them what they wanted; though! quad à la jarretelle de la mariée...c'est pas dit dans l'histoire ...de l'art.

(Louvre)

KEN JACOBS

Two kitchen chairs were positioned one above the other on separate floors, windows behind and doors to a stairwell before them. A length of twine ran along the outside of the building entering the windows and another traveled the staiwell to tie onto the middles of their wooden backs. Tilting one chair forward or back tilted the other and it was possible to leave the chairs standing in these unstable positions.

(About 405E. 13th St.; #3)

GERALD LINDAHL

— Extension of technology (with what intension)
— Microcosm of communication
— Grommet as clue
— feedback loop — reality — machine — reality
— All aspects of a feedback loop are affected simultaneously by any event in any part of the loop at any time
— Systemic organization (audio occlusion) delusion
— The electronic recreation of reality is easily altered — reality through the looking glass may or may not reflect
— The power of the middle man/machine.
— Grommet as clue — does anyone guess the significance of the grommet clue — is there any significance
— Behind the scenes (screens)
— Communication as obfuscation (the image of image)

(Grommets #3)

JAN BITTINGER and JOHN SAVAS

Tie to Order was a short play performed by Jan Bittinger and John Savas. It was enacted on and around a twenty foot tower constructed in the auditorium of P.S.1. The play consisted of simple everyday acts and movements such as sweeping with a broom, looking into a mirror, climbing, carrying and throwing. The tower provided a perfect set with it's three levels and ladders up two sides.

The only words spoken were:
Coming from
Brings to
Climbs up
From below
Reaches or takes off
Moves around
Climbs down
Picks up
Stands or leaves

These phrases were chosen randomly from a transcript of the events. Spotlights were set up on the tower and aimed directly into the audience. This was done to exaggerate the theatrical quality of the piece and to confront the audience with their own passivity. There was also a pulsating electronic drone throughout the performance which gave the play an overall aura of anxiety and nervousness.

(A Tower at P.S.1)

LARRY MILLER

Sleep America . . . Go to sleep.
I want you to sleep. I want you to sleep.

In Grommets, there are 2 holes for your eyes.
There you can sleep-deep-sleep-deep-sleep-deep-
sleep-deep-sleep-deep-sleep-deep-sleep-deep-
sleep-deep-sleep-deep-sleep-deep-sleep-

I want you to sleep. I want you to sleep.
Stay here and sleep.

The 3rd hole is my eye into your 3rd eye.
You-me-you-me-you-me-you-me-you-me-you-me-you-
me-you-me-you- stay here with me-stay here with
me-stay here with me-stay here with me-stay
here and sleep-stay here and sleep-I want to see
you-I want to see you-stay here with me-you-
stay-you-stay-you-stay-stay here with me-I want
to see you.

The earphones are live.
Only you can hear-only you can hear-only you can
hear-sleep-sound-sleep-sound-sleep-sound-sleep-
Listen to my voice-listen to my voice-listen to my voice-
sound-sleep-we're simpatico-we're simpatico-we're
simpatico-stay here with me-stay here with me-
I want to hear from you-I want to hear from you-
I want to hear from you.

The 3rd eye is live.
Look into my eye-look into my eye-look into my
eye-you-me-you-me-you-me-you-me-we're simpatico-
we're simpatico-we're simpatico-stay here with me
and sleep-deep-sleep-deep-sleep-deep-sleep

You-me-we're simpatico-stay here with me and sleep.
Go to sleep America. I want you to sleep.

(Grommets #3)

ILHAN MIMAROGLU

As the title may imply, *Sketches for Mao* are preliminary studies for a composition titled *Mao*, which, in turn, will be part of a trilogy —the two other parts being *Bach* and *Shah*. These sketches were developed especially for Jean Dupuy's show to meet for an hour's worth of music. The techniques employed are those of the "classical" studio, the sound sources electronic, and the voice reading fragments from Mao's texts belong to G8ung8or Bozkurt. Once they serve their purpose in Dupuy's show the sketches will not be heard elsewhere, but many of their elements will constitute the essential structural material for *Mao*, which is designed as a much shorter piece.

(Grommets #3)

CHARLIE MORROW

WAS FIRST EVENT ON TOWER—JEAN GAVE ME MY WISH
GOT THERE & IT WAS COLD AS HELL

226

DISTANCE OF TOWER FROM AUDIENCE CHAIRS IMMEDIATELY FELT BAD
SANG TWO SPRING SONGS WITH RATTLE: MOON OF THE BREAKUP OF ICE (ME)
EAGLE & BEAR (CREE)
CLIMBED TOWER & SANG A DREAMSONG (MIND FIXED ON VISUAL IMAGES IN-
SIDE & NOT ON VOICE BARELY HEARD)
SAW BOAT-ISLAND-AERIAL VIEW OF CITY
CAME OFF TOWER DISCONCERTED & SANG OTHER DREAMSONG IN AUDIENCE
JEAN ASKED ME TO DO REMAINING PERFORMANCES ON TOWER
"YOU LOOK GREAT"
"I FEEL TOO FAR"
SO THE REMAINING PERFORMANCES WERE LESS CEREMONIAL/MORE FRAMED
END DAY A MAGIC SHAPE FORMED FROM ELAINE HARTNETT, YOSHI WADA,
OLGA ADORNO & MY OWN WORK.
HAD BEGUN TO FEEL I WAS DEALING WITH A SPACE
IN END a blend of harmonies blessing it

(A Tower at P.S.1)

COME MOSTA-HEIRT

Devant un tableau Baugin,dans la grande galerie du musée du LOUVRE, ja'ai bu un verre de vin rouge.

J'étais habillé de blanc avec une chemise ample (du père) et une grande écharpe berbère qui me permettait del dissimuler au départ mon visage et de le laisser ap-paraître progressivement au cours de l'action.

Je m'inclinais lentement et portais à mes lèvres,le verre.Jè relevais la tête pro-gressivement laissant couler lentement entre me lèvres et sur la chemise blanche le breuvage rouge qui s'épanouit en un triangle rosâtre sur le blanc immaucleé.

Je buvais d'une manière rituelle.Dans ce lieu sacré,je dégustais la vin et randait un hommae papillaire à la peinture qui me plaisait. J'ajoutais au plaisir du regard le plaisir du verre. Le tout en une estrème concentraion.

(Louvre)

ANDREW MOSZYNSKI

Activity: watching a painting
        listening to pre-recorded music
Duration: one minute
The artist can't help it. He becomes a tourist for sixty seconds. The audience is watch-ing the tourist watching a painting. The music is a memory collected earlier during his trip; it surfaces. French museum, Italian painting, German music, American tourist.

(Louvre)

(with Variety Moszynski)

The cinema is seen through a hole in the screen, looking at two people watching the film, eating and making.out. The film is not seen, but the reflected light from the screen makes the scene visible or invisible at irregular intervals.

(Grommets #3)

ANTONI MUNTADAS

May 1 '73 I went through all area between 11th. and 14th. Streets and First and "A" Avenues. Four spots were considered as characteristic because of their particular smells. These four locations show an itinerary and describe the environment that sur-rounds 405 E. 13st. The proposal is to walk through the area and recognize its par-ticular smells. This is part of a projected map of smells of N.Y.C.

(About 405E. 13th St.)

ORLAN

—Je suis habillée d'un manteau trois-quart noir, et d'une jupe également noire.
—De dos ua public, face à la toile.
—A l'aide de ma main droite, je mets une palette de peintre en plastique blanc derrière ma tête, comme une auréole.
—Je décris un quart de cercle avec cet objet, du dessus de ma tête jusqu'à ce que mon bras s'arrête à l'brizontale.
—Je tourne lentement la tête, je tiens entre les dents un gros pinceau, la tête entraine les épaules, puis la poitrine, puis la taille et enfin les jambes.
—Je suis face au public.
—Mon bras droit se trouve à gauche.
—Je déplace le bras en faisant passer la palette sous ma tête.
—Je montre les dents, puis la palette et mon bras passent à droite à l'horizontale.
—Ma main gauche se saisit de la ceinture de mon manteau.
—Je suis revêture d'une toile photographique noir et blanc me représentatn nue.
—J'arrache le triangel de mon pubis, je montre cette représentation de mes poils.
—Sous ce triangle apparaissent mes vrais poils que j'ai au prélable rasés et recollés avec de la colle à postiche.
—Je prendes la palette dans la main gauche en montrant le côté que je n'ai pas encore montré ; ce côté collant à l'air.
—Avec ma main droite, j'arrache par touffes mes poils.
—Je les colle au centre de ces croix, comme des touffes de peinture.
—Lorsque mon pubis est imberbe, je présente la palette devant mon visage (j'ai toujours le pinceau entre les dents).
—Je prends avec tous les doigts le manche du pinceau.
—Avec un geste ample, je fais sembland de predre de la peinture sur la palette (en vérité, j'avais déjà mis de la peinture noire sur le pinceau).
—Avec le pinceau je repeins poils sur mon pubis, et sur toile photographique.
—Je remets la palette côté blanc comme une feuille de vigne devant mon pubis.
—J'enfonce le manche du pinceau dans le trou de la palette.
—Je pivote très lentement sur la gauche.
—Je marque un temps de profil.
—Je suis á nouveau de dos, face á la toile.

(Louvre)

CHARLES RICHARDSON

The quality of the colors in the painting is deep, rich, and intense. The vibrancy of midsummer greens and blues. Blue is in the sky, in the distant foliage and mixed in the shadowed recesses of the tree and grass. A range of greens is present in the tree, grass and shadows; pale whitened green reflecting light, muted yellow ochre green sunburnt and dying, primary green full of life, deep green of mature foliage and greens darkening towards blue and black. In contrast to this, the tree trunk is brown, red brown, and black with hints of moss green. Surrounding the crown of the tree is a halo of light blue against the sky and light green against the landscape.

(3 Mercer St.)

JEAN DUPUY

Tarts: 40 lbs flour, 600 apples MacIntosh, 10 lbs sugar, 20 lbs butter, 150 bottles of French red wine, 100 lbs of italian bread. We cooked the soup the day before. We were 3 persons and it took 9 hours. Soup: 35 gallons — 50 lbs potatoes, 10 bunches celery, 4 lbs mushrooms, 35 pieces leeks, 20 lbs. carrots, 15 lbs. onions, 10 lbs turnips, 25 tomatoes, 20 bunches parsley, salt, pepper, mint, oregano, curry, 1 gal. soy sauce. Whiskey, heavy cream (12 quarts). We used 6 blenders.

(Soup and Tart)

I based my piece on the Renaissance perspective system (the vanishing point) as illustrated in the Durer engraving. I reconstructed this arrangement by setting up a long and narrow table on which I placed Olga as model. I sat facing her, looking with my right eye through a grommmet which was the fixed point of view (my recreation of Durer's "Obelisk"). This grommet was suspended with thread from the ceiling to a drawing table on which a grid paper was placed. I transferred onto this paper the image I saw through a glass grid situated between Olga and me.

My view extended 180 feet beyond the suspended grommet to encompass a large window behind which framed a view of the courtyards that, in turn, revealed the neighbor's windows and a well lit loft. I, then, added two elements to this theatrical depiction of classical perspective—a mirror placed on the drawing table, in front of me and a video monitor located beside Olga's hands. The monitor was connected to an outside camera in the public room directed at the viewer's profile. As she/he looked through the grommet hole situated at 4 feet facing my back. Thus there resulted an interactive chain of perspectives through the two grommets:

I sat looking through the suspended grommet at Olga and the extended view behind the glass grid, making the drawing simultaneously I looked also at each viewer's profile as it appeared in the monitor. At the same time, the viewer saw Olga, the same fixed perspective image I was facing, the drawing I was making, the back of my head and also my face, reflected in the mirror (placed as I already said, on the drawing table), and, in addition his/her own profile on the monitor. Olga saw my face directly and surprisingly a reflection of the monitor on the glass grid; therefore she was able to see the viewer's profile as well.

Note: on the photography an unclear image of the still camera which took the place on the monitor, for the purpose, of Babette Mangolte's profile.

(Grommets #4)

OLGA ADORNO

For an object show **About 405** Jean asked me to be part of, I decided to make a piece which was to represent a slice of apple tart. Place two mirrors against the slice that would allow one to see a whole tart. With Jean's help I completed the object. I made the tart from water, salt and flour. Painted it realistically with acrylics and varnished it. The angle was figured out by Jean—60 degrees. Setting the slice between the two mirrors completed a circle of 360 degrees. Six slices of a tart so familiar to many people who visited Jean at 405 E. 13th. The object reflected—beyond sentiment—its nature again.

(About 405 E. 13th St.; 3)

Pooh Kaye visited Jean and me one evening and brought with her a pair of shoes she had found on the street along the way. They were two black shoes (different), found, brought, given, enjoyed, and laughed about. One male and one female, one left and one right, one tight and one loose. I began a drawing of a female/male to fit the shoes. Using the walls on each side of the gallery, on one wall I drew half of a male figure. Plus the male shoe, I set down on the floor. On the opposite wall I drew half a female figure. Plus a female shoe. Drawings were outlines of myself and John Savas.

(13 × 33)

Back and Front Drawing Show at the Fine Arts Building, I was working in books doing drawings of "What's on my Mind"—of a personal and introspective nature. I was also experimenting with baking sour dough bread. But one time the bread came out so hard that it was impossible to eat it and so I kept the loaves. One was round, one was oblong, and it struck Jean so funny that I kept them and after awhile added a photo of giant sea lions. Then I put it all in a large plastic bag and kept it hanging around....

(Front/Back)

ANDREW MOSZYNSKI

(Grommets #4)

NINA LUNDBORG

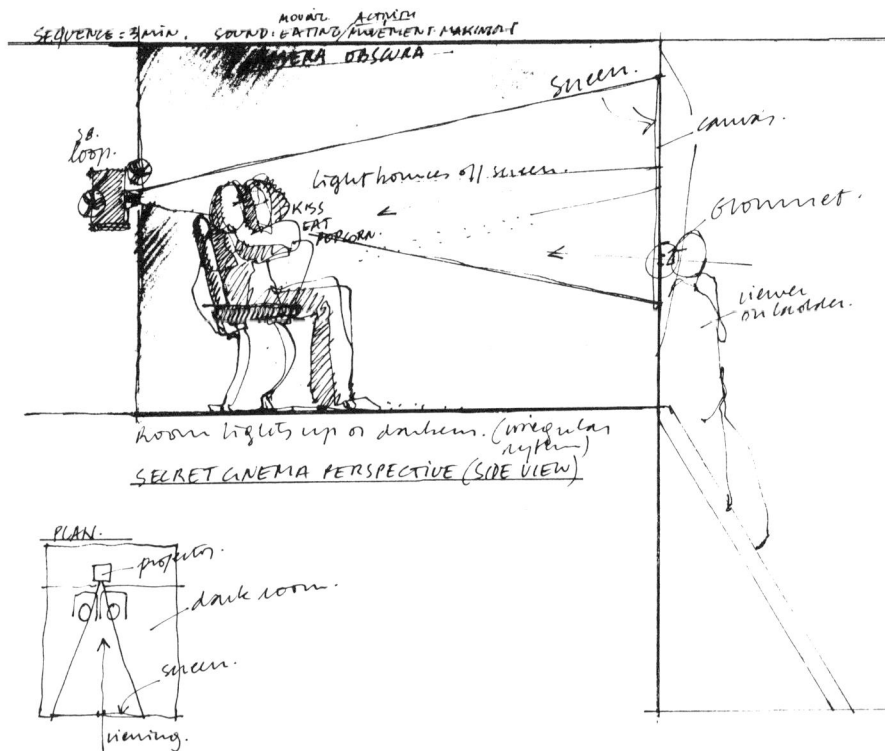

230

WHITE WALLS OF THE P.S.1. AUDITORIUM WITH A SET
OF SPONGES SOAKED IN ACRYLIC PAINT ATTACHED
TO MY BACK & ELBOWS. ——

THE DANCE ARISING FROM LISTENING TO THE INSIDE
RYTHMIC STRUCTURE OF MY SYSTEM AND LETTING
THE INSTRUMENT FOLLOW IT'S OWN PATTERN
AROUND THE BIG ROOM. ——
—— CLIMBING THE TOWER, LOOKING — RED, YELLOW, BLUE
—— MOVEMENT MATERIALIZE'D ——   PURPLE ,

(Tower at P.S. 1)

RICHARD HAYMAN

Chant A Cappella   Song for living   Rip Hayman '78

for wandering chorus — sing lines in any order —

is to lay   is to laze   is to rest   is to sleep   is to dream

is to sense   is to wander   is to feel   is to imagine   is to hear

is to see   is to believe   is to trust   is to exchange   is to share

is to live   is to play   is to find   is to look   is to enter

is to reach   is to touch   is to move   is to place   is to have

is to need   is to use   is to do   is to continue   is to grow

is to be   is to change   is to age   is to think   is to search

is to travel   is to discover   is to renew   is to learn   is to open

is to meet   is to desire   is to recognize   is to embrace   is to unite

is to relax   is to receive   is to behold   is to hope   is to free

is to ask   is to wish   is to follow   is to allow   is to reserve

is to begin   is to plan   is to achieve   is to end   is to return

(Chant a Cappella)

ALISON KNOWLES

Take a New Name

The Kwakiutl Indians inhabited lands in the Northern part of this country and Canada. Their culture was full of ritual, games and ceremonies of which *Take A New Name* is one. The reason for the ceremony and how they chose and awarded the new names I do not know. At the Inge Baecker Gallery in Germany some years ago, each guest that arrived at the performance could choose a new name from a bulletin board, and a girl pinned it on. The name was worn during the performance. At the Whitney the performer was seated on a revolving stage. As it turned she slowly spilled a bag of beans in a circle. The beans were the vehicle to carry the new name to the spectator. So, she would pick up a bean, locate a person to whom the bean (name) seemed appropriate and toss it to them while speaking out the new name. Some of the names used were:

One Having an Itch	Protector
One leaning forward	One Carrying Much Weight
High Cloud/Low Lake	A Mere Splash in the Pan
Mountains Underfoot	Prairee Cactus
Great Mother Thunder	Shoes Too Tight But Keeping up A Smile
One Hidden Under	Little But Effective
I Know its Friday	One Needing the Trees
Jimmy	Rose etc.

(One Afternoon on a Revolving Stage)

with Buczak, Tyche Hendriks, Bracken Hendricks, Jessie Higgins

The above group found themselves in Naples one spring, on a balcony overlooking some trees and a lot of noise. This group, the adults in it, were concerned with constructing a gift for a man named Peppe Morra. Some time later each appeared on the same balcony with an object from the street or beach to put together to make the gift. There was a certain time involved in the looking, and a certain time involved in the making since the group was moving out of Naples the following day. Their selections were: the sea-weathered lower sole of a shoe, a large wooden flat used in fishing (size of a baseball), a birdcage, and a musical wisdom clock. The float, the sole and the clock were placed inside the birdcage, the pieces accessible through the door of the cage. The whole thing was easily suspended by the hook on the cage. The object was presented and the group departed for elsewhere by jumping onto a moving trolley, Peppe Morra running behind laughing and crying and waving simultaneously. Departures from Naples are always like that.

The Musical Wisdom Clock Event was performed on the platforms of a tower with the same people and children who had made the visit to Naples. A chart was made of events that might take place. These events were simple and nonskill oriented; for example, releasing a paper snake or following a ping pong ball with a flashlight. The performers were each given a number from 1-6. A chuck-a-luck (dice throwing machine) was used to find the numbers and determine the event and the performer involved. Three dices were thrown at once. The first two numbers called out were the performers (say 2 and 4) who would be doing their own event. The last number called was the number of minutes that event would go on. Jessie planned to do cartwheels and backflips when she heard number four. The nasal buzz of a darkroom clock ended the activity, the chuck-a-luck was spun again and another series called out from the top of the tower by Geoff. Brian and Geoff were stationed at the top of the tower with numerous Chinatown noise and light devices such as smoke snakes and firepowder. Alison wore Japanese masks and shook beans in a gong. Tyche searched the floor for the missing ping-pong ball and Bracken sometimes read cards about fish and birds, sometimes climbed ladders to the top. If doubles were spun a solo was the event, triples meant ceasing activity and passing a single note up the platforms. There were usually two activities going on, sometimes two in one space but usually not. With the smoke dragons and firepowder, the masked bean-shaker and the cartwheels, the scene of the Musical Wisdom Clock Event was quite like a vertical three ring circus or perhaps the kind of conglomerate seen emerging from a German Coo-Coo clock exactly on the hour.

(A Tower at P.S. 1)

Recreation of THE BIRTH OF VENUS with Alison Knowles as Bottticelli; and Venus (Jessie Higgins) her twelve year old daughter.

In the painting, Venus is rising from a shell at the edge of the sea. Two male Angels blow pink flowers, and create the breezes that cause her tresses to fly curly and golden in the blue air carrying the shell to shore where a female angel awaits her (Venus) with a pink cloak. As Botticelli, Alison wore an artist's atelier coat, and each of the three evenings began her performance, her creation of the painting anew. The child Venus had her hair braided into wool strands that were hung with small street objects such as keys and shoe heels. These strands were then stapled to the ceiling of the performance area and an electric fan which was installed in the ceiling facing toward her hair, acted as a breeze from the ocean. The small objects moved in this breeze. The long hair of Venus was made from blonde wool and attached to the child's own hair and curled around to cover parts of her otherwise nude body. The artist stapled great swirls and billows of found papers and street stuff to build up replicas of the green trees and pink flowers surrounding Venus. The child's long hair was extended with wool to the ceiling and the entire overhead area of the small theatre. At the feet of Venus were concentric circles of shoe parts seeming like waves. The shell was represented by a bolster pillow. Often during the performance of building the painting, artist and model sang country songs together. A pale moon, part of an old painting by the artist, shone behind the head of Venus. The model did an excellent job with the challenge of holding the pose for three hours, only occasionally resting on a high three-legged stool. For this performance two grommets were used. The first hole gave a viewing of the environment of THE BIRTH OF VENUS with artist and model building the painting. The second grommet showed the finished painting by Botticelli on a post card.

(Grommets #4)

DICKY LANDRY

I came late and the audience seemed to be very serious and getting more and more serious. I didn't know what I was going to do. As my turn came up I just decided to do a happy hand clapping rock and roll riff, which I think caught everyone by surprise and especially since I came out of the wings instead of stage front, this had an element of surprise. The riff is a well known one and was especially used during the rock and roll days of the early fifties. Bill Haley, Fats Domino, etc. etc.

(Soup and Tart)

CHRISTIAN XATREC

In semi-darkness I walked down the center-aisle to the very front of the church, and without turning, just facing the wall, I sang:

In semi-darkness I walked down the center-aisle to the very front of the church, and without turning, just facing the
wall I sang:

"Quand nous chanterons le temps des cerises
et des rossignols les merles moqueurs
seront tous en fête
Les belles auront la folie en tête
et les amoureux du soleil au coeur.
Quand nous chanterons le temps des cerises
sifflera bien mieux le merle moqueur,

Mais il est bien court le temps des cerises
ou l'on s'en va deux cueillir en revant
des pendants d'oreilles.
Cerises d'amour au robes pareilles
tombant sous la feuille en gouttes de sang.
Mais il est bien court le temps des cerises
en dents de corail qu'on cueille en revant.

Quand vous en serez au temps des cerises
si vous avez peur des chagrins d'amour
evitez les belles.
Moi qui ne craint pas les peines cruelles
Je ne vivrais pas sans souffrir un jour.
Quand vous en serez au temps des cerises
vous aurez aussi des peines d'amour.

J'aimerai toujours le temps des cerises
c'est de ce temps la que je garde au coeur
une plaie ouverte.
Et Dame Fortune en m'etant offerte
ne pourra jamais fermer ma douleur.
J'aimerai toujours le temps des cerises
et le souvenir que je garde au coeur.",

C.X.

(Chant a Cappella)

MARTIAL THOMAS

- je suis, ici, dans ce passage communiquant entre la salle des états et la grande galerie
- je suis, ici, et je me déplace.
- vous pouvez me voir à tout instant, dans ce passage et je vous y invite pour faire une promenade.
- je vous parlerai de la promenade autour du lac, l'Alster à Hambourg.
- je suis martial thomas, dans ce passage communiquant entre la salle des états et la grande galerie.
- je suis, ici, et je me déplace.
- vous pouvez me voir à tout instant, dans ce passage et je vous y invite pour faire une promenade.

(Louvre)

UNTEL

EN AVANT PREMIERE, UNTEL PRESENTE AUJOURD'HUI, DANS LA GRANDE GALERIE DU MUSEE DU LOUVRE SA COLLECTION TRES COLOREE: "TOURISTE," JEAN PAUL, NO. 1, VESTE BLANCHE, PANTALON AJUSTE BLANC AU MOTIF REPETITIF AU GRAPHISME ETUDIE. MAILLOT DE CORPS CERISE, ENCOLURE RAS DU COU, HARMONISE AU COSTUME. NO. 2, PHILIPPE PORTE UN ENSEMBLE NEIGE, TRES CONFORTABLE, IMPRIME DE COULEURS VIVES ET DYNAMIQUES,

VESTE DECONTRACTE BOUTONNE SUR LE DEVANT, PANTALON DROIT. TEE-SHIRT COLORIS ABRICOT. LE 3, WILFRID, A REVETU UN COMPLET WHITE TOUT SIMPLE, VESTE AUX POCHES SURPRIQUEES PANTALON SPORT. POLO 100% COTON, MANCHES COURTES, IMPRESSION POLYCHROME. LE TOUT RESTE TRES ORIGINAL ET JEUNE. A LA VILLE COMME EN WEEK END CES TENUES TRES LEGERES A PORTER EN TOUTES CIRCONSTANCES, RESTENT NEANMOINS TRES CLASSIQUES. LES BADGES ET ACCESSOIRES SONT AUSSI UNE CREATION: UNTEL.

(Louvre)

VILLARD DE HONNECOURT

LIX

"Here is the elevation of the chapels of Reims Cathedral and the way in which they are mounted one above the other *in the interior*."
"Here are the interior corridors and the surrounding arches."
"Vesci le droite montee des capeles de le glise de Rains et toute le maniere ensi com eles sunt par dedens droites en los estage."
"Voici l'élévation des chapekles de l'église de Reims et la facon dont elles sont étagées à l'intérieur."
"Vesci les voies dedens et les orbes arkes."
"Voici les couloirs intérieurs et les arches du pourtour."
The inscription placed at the top of document no LIX refers to the document no LX. (Villard could find no room for it where it actually belonged.)

LX

"In this document (no LX) you can see *the exterior* elevations of the chapels of the Reims Cathedral, as they are from the base to the summit. In this way they must be those of Cambrai if one constructs them. The last entablature must form the crenelles."
It is almost exactly the same now as it was in the middle of the 13th century when Villard drew it.
"Et en cele autre pagene poes vus veir les montees des capieles de le glise de Rains par de hors, tres le comencement desci en le fin ensi com eles sunt. dautretel maniere doivent estre celes de Canbrai son lor fait droit. li daerrains entaulemens doit faire cretiaus."
En cette autre page vous pouvez voir les élévations extérieures des chapelles de l'église de Reims, ainsi qu'elles sont depuis la base jusqu'au sommet. De cette manière doivent être celles de Cambrai si on les construit. Le dernier entablement doit former des créteaux."
While the angels above the buttresses, as you may see now, are clothed and have very short wings, Villard draws them nude with giant wings.
The crenelles don't exist anymore—they have been covered in such a way by a balustrade that just enough room for some intermittent horizontal foot supports has been provided in case the roof needs repair.

(13 × 33)

JULIA HEYWARD

This piece isolated a body-part, an arm, and gave its history by describing its function and its eventual doom. Its function was shaking hands as part of a man who was a public servant (minister). Eventually the arm gets a nervous disease and shakes on its own. Voluntary to Involuntary. "Love is an object." The text was read as jargon with gestures, singing and sound effects from a revolving stage. There was a film of the man with the arm shaking hands throughout the duration of the piece. "Love's an object, and I'm going to distribute it differently than Daddy. That's one revolution."

I felt deep reservations about performing this piece. It seemed obvious that I should do it because all the parts were handed to me by other people, and they fit together. Jean Dupuy chose a Church sanctuary for the performance space, the film was sent to me by chance in the mail (and it was exactly the right length of time), and my father had given me a tape of a sermon concerning his arms Time, Place, Sound and Picture. What more could make it real? Exploitation, and in sheep's clothing. I still wonder who I was working for in that piece.

TEXT

This is the story about a public servant who gave it out a little at a time every day of the year. He made his living 'giving to the living' shaking hands and we used to stand behind him and sing, SHAKE DADDY SHAKE! SHAKE DADDY SHAKE! SHAKE DADDY SHAKE! And I used to say you're gonna' wear your arm out shaking shaking. And I used to say you're gonna' wear your arm out giving it away a little at a time. GIVE ME FIVE. LOVE IS AN OBJECT!
And sure enough he wore his arm out. Hand me over. He got a nervous disease and his right arm is the only part of his body that is overtly affected.

> DADDY'S ARM SHAKES ALL DAY LONG
> DADDY'S ARM SHAKES ALL NIGHT LONG
> DADDY'S ARM SHAKES SHAKE DADDY SHAKE
> DADDY oh DADDY! HE'S GOT YOU ON AUTO-MATTY
> ALARM! ALARM! HE TOOK YOUR RIGHT ARM!
> ARE YOU MAD DAD?

(audio tape; Father speaking)
"I did actually ask God: 'God, what possible good and glory can you bring to me as preacher, or to the Kingdom of God, with a shakey hand?' God said to me: 'What one thing do you want above all else in your life?' I didn't want to flub that answer and I thought for a long time, and I said: 'God the one thing I need most is the ability to carry the awareness of your presence with me always.' And do you know what he said to me? He said: 'Every time I pull on your arm you remember that I am right there beside you."
(end of audio tape)
Daddy oh Daddy! HE'S GOT YOU ON AUTO-MATTY . . . . giving it out
don't give out
giving it out
a little at a time
giving out love
wearing himself out
don't give out daddy
don't give out
don't give out
don't die

Love's an object
A slave to physical laws
Love's an object
Love's an object

Displacement
Displacement
Displacement
Displacement

SSlave to physical laws

Love's an object
If you give it away,
If someone takes your heart,
you don't have it anymore.
Love's an object   Possession slave

Love's an object
          take   heart
it's gone. Blood kiss me.

PHYSICAL LAWS   PHYSICAL SLAVE
Love's an object
I object

Love's an object
A slave to physical laws
Science Devines Itself (Wilhelm Reich)
CHRISTIAN MATHEMATICS

"Give love and it will multiply."

$$|x| = 1$$

AFTERMATH SUBTRACTION
NOT X ✗ ✗ NOT X
NOT MULTIPLIES
BUT SUBTRACTS

$$|-| = 0$$

Someone takes your heart
AFTERMATH SUBTRACTION
Love's an object
Heart beats me
Love's an object
Heart beats me
Heart beat beat beat
Heart beat beat beat
Shake Daddy Shake
Gotta' a good beat
Shake Daddy Shake
Gotta' a good beat
Shake Daddy Shake
Heart beat beat beat
Shake Daddy Shake
To the beat of life
In the dance of death

Love's an object
That's one revolution (performer revolves slowly on revolving
            stage, miming the shape of a 'love object',
            holding it in her hands, displaying it to
            the audience, hoisting it to her shoulders,
            and then throwing it out towards one of the
            church windows! A pre-recorded CRASH! And
            a spot light hits the window but it is all
            an illusion, the window remains in tact.)

   * THE GIRL COLLECTS HERSELF AND LEARNS TO GIVE WITH CAPITAL RETURNS.

(3 Evenings on a Revolving Stage)

It was somewhat different with each new viewer but for instance, I would wait until the viewer leaned into the curtain and his/her gravity was vulnerable. I would start to talk. "If I was perfect I'd measure my weight in gold and then I'd sit and watch the stock market rise and fall." (Gently swaying with the person up and back). "This is a live stock market. WATCH IT! Rise and fall. LIVE STOCK BROWN COW NOW rise and fall . . . rise and fall LIVE STOCK SHOE FLY rise and fall . . . BROWN COW NOW, SHOE FLY DON'T Bother ME . . . rise and SHOE FLY DOE RE ME . . . rise and Mama don't like my shoe anymore, shoe anymore, shoe anymore" (repeated, still swaying rocking). "My mama's milk's the BEST and she loves me better than all the rest . . . rest . . . rest, Rise and fall . . . rise and fall . . . Eva Braun does it, rise and fall . . . NOT ME NAZI."

Some people would resist my persuasions and rhythms. Sometimes I would refuse to move, sometimes I would listen to them instead sometimes I would fight . . . rise and fall.

(Grommets #3)

The singing posture for the 'bird flute sound' is lips tightly closed or slightly opened using the nasal cavity to project the sound. The sound produced is much like the sound of a flute but not quite as windy. It is a very very powerful sound both in volume and in beauty. I have been working with a yodelling singing posture where the sound is largely formed in the throat area; although it may be moved around the mouth cavity to produce different volumetric sound qualities. It is a very active sound in that several pitches are always in the air with the capacity to control the timing (beat) of the oscillation.

TEXT

'Bird flute sound' singing . . . . .

I just wanna' be a little birdie..I just wanna' be a little birdie birdie birdie in a tree..behind the bush..in a tree..a little birdie birdie birdie birdie in a tree behind the bush I just wanna' be. But I can't just be cause the bush is burning. It's burning! It's burning! It's the BURNING BUSH and that's of course what it does it burns.....(bird calls)....

Well I heard that the seagulls and the homing pigeons and the love birds and the doves are all in revolt..IT'S A BIG COUP..they all on strike...IT'S A BIG COUP. The bush is burning, it's changing forms; that's one revolution...it's a big coup.

 The love birds are saying that love is so fascist.
 It's love! It's love! It's like money in the bank$
 GO-DOUGH..WAITING FOR IT
 And the doves are saying NOT ME NAZI
        NOT ME NAZI
 And the seagulls are saying 'down by the ocean, down by the
 ole' mill stream things ain't the way they seem. The NILE
 is not rising. The SON is rising. The NILE is not rising.
 The SON is rising and HE'S gonna' beat down on you. The SON'S
 gonna' beat down on you. The NILE is not rising..no more
 water to put out the fire of the burning bush. THE FEVER MOVES
 BRUSH FIRE RUSH FIRE THE FEVER MOVES.
 LIAR LIAR PANTS ON FIRE..DON'T FOLLOW DESIRE
 ZIPPA DEE-DOO-DA ZIPPA DEE-DAY
 MY OH MY THERE'S GOTTA' BE ANOTHER WAY
 MY OH MY THERE'S ONLY ONE WAY
POLLY WANTS IT FASTER.......WOODY WOODY PECKER
POLLY WANTS IT FASTER.......WOODY WOODY PECKER...(Woody Wood-
              pecker's call)

And the seagulls are saying, "Down by the ocean, down by the ole' mill stream things ain't the way they seem."
 1 2 3
EYE EYE EYE...rapid eye movement
 I HAD A DREAM...I HAD A DREAM
 JUST LIKE THAT OF MARTIN LUTHER KING
 I HAD A DREAM...I HAD A DREAM
 JUST LIKE THAT OF BILLY JEAN KING
 I dreamed I put mind over matter
 giving much time and money to the latter
 unto Caesar what is Caesar's
 and all that jive ain't it great
 oh yeah ain't it great to be a live
      wire
      shocks
      most
      definitely

              (Chant a Cappella)

CLAES OLDENBURG

Saturday, Jan. 29, 1966—no vibrations
Sunday, Jan. 30, 1966—no vibrations
Monday, Jan. 31, 1966—14 or possibly fifteen periods of vibration,
     each lasting approximately 4 minutes.

The night before Jan., 31, we slept in the front room due to heavy winds, where vibrations are least felt. We arose at 9:06 am, Jan. 31st. They are most felt in the center of the building and towards the rear, which may account for a report that the beauty par-

CHART FOR JAN. 31, 1966

	INTENSITY	DURATION		TIME EXPERIENCED	INTERVAL MINUTE
1	WEAK	TWO	MINUTES (?)	9:43 - 9:45 AM	47
2	STRONG	FOUR	MINUTES	10:32 - 10:36	24
3	STRONG	FOUR	MINUTES	11:10 - 11:14	23
4	WEAK	FIVE	MINUTES	11:37 - 11:42	27
5	WEAK	FOUR	MIN.	12:09 - 12:13 PM	1
6	STRONG	THREE	MIN	12:14 - 12:17	32"
7	MEDIUM	THREE	MIN. (?)	12:49 - 12:52	7
8	STRONG	FOUR	MIN.	12:59 - 1:03	11
9	STRONG	FOUR	MIN.	1:14 - 1:18	34
10	STRONG	FIVE	MIN.	1:52 - 1:57	10
11	WEAK	TWO	MIN.	2:07 - 2:0?	31
12	STRONG	FIVE	MIN.	2:46 - 2:51	12
13	MEDIUM	?		3:03 - ?--	
14	STRONG	FOUR	MIN.	4:12 - 4:16	

AVERAGE 3 5/13 MIN.

lor on front second floor does not hear them. Consider else that as a building rises the walls away more, the lever effect. Since putting in a new floor in the kitchen the vibrations seem more pronounced, perhaps the new floor has made the floor less elastic and less able to sway with vibrations. Note that this time is recorded from the kitchen clock on the stove, which is four minutes faster than the clock on the tower of the Con Ed Bldg. 23th recorded vibration: record interrupted by a phone call. This may have prevented also recording of an additional vibration between 13th and 14th as phone call forced absence of half hour. The vibrations sometimes follow a slow swelling rhythm.

(About 405 E. 13th St., #2)

PHILIPPE DEMONTAUT

L'action Le Nain.
En raison de l'exposition des freres Le Nain au Grand Palais, la toile de Le Nain ne se trouvait pas au Louvre le 16 octobre 1978. Mon action Le Nain s'est deroulée devant les Noces de Cana.
C'est comme si l'on avait reconstitué les Noces de Cana devant une toile de Le Nain

(Louvre)

TONY MASCATELLO

(Grommets #3)

GIANFRANCO MANTEGNA

PHOTOGRAPHIC DETERMINATION OF DISTANCE

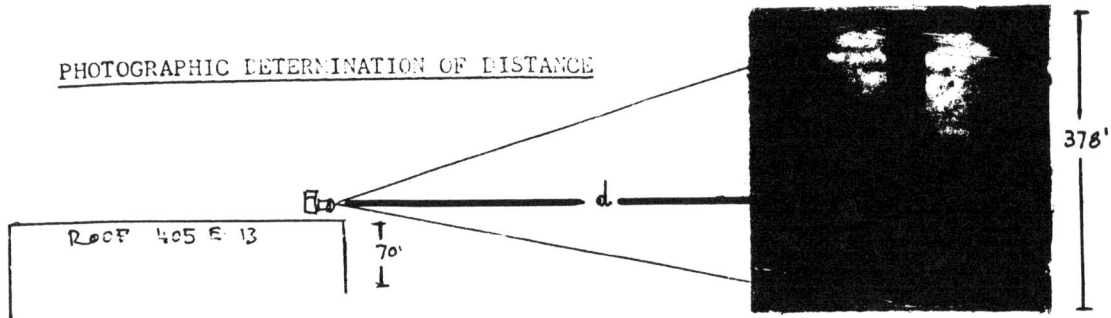

Using a 200 mm lens, whose angle of view is by
specification 12°30', and knowing the height of any structure or
landmark which can fit the whole lenght of the frame,
the distance between the observer and the reference site is given by:

$$\tan C = \frac{378-70}{d} = \frac{308}{d}$$

$$\tan D = \frac{70}{d} \qquad \text{or}$$

$$\tan C = 4.2 \tan D$$

$$C+D = 12°30' \qquad \text{substitututing}$$

(1) $\tan C = 4.2 \left[\tan (12°30'-C) \right]$ expanding double angle

$$\tan (12°30'-C) = \frac{\tan 12°30' - \tan C}{1+\tan 12°30' \tan C} \quad \text{substituting into 1}$$

$$5.2 \tan C + \tan 12°30' \tan C - 4.2 \tan 12°30'$$

$$\tan C = .177711$$

$$d = \frac{308}{.177711} = \underline{\mathbf{1733\ ft}}$$

(About 405E. 13th St.; #1)

240

Index

Martine Aballea, 89/153
Vito Acconci, 153
Olga Adorno, 23, 36, 42, 50, 59, 66, 75, 89, 131, 132, 135, 142/156, 157, 229, 230/48, 140
Arthur Aeschbacher, 90/154
Joanne Akalaitis, 23/191/20
Joseph Alessi, 106/111
Laurie Anderson, 23, 50, 100-103, 154-156/20, 48, 115
Mel Andringa, 59/156
David Appel, 59, 75, 157-159
Brendan Atkinson, 23, 106, 118, 135, 137/159, 160/100, 114
Charles Atlas, 24/160, 161
Claudio Badal, 106
Robb Baker, 32
Sally Banes, 48
Nancy Barber, 142/161/140
James Barth, 42, 50/162, 163
Carmen Beuchat, 50, 75/163/48
Kathryn Bigelow, 118/163/115
Jan Bittinger, 225,226
Jayne Bliss, 163,164
Robert Breer, 24/20
Cara Brownell, 75/164, 165
Brian Buczak, 165/183
Norvie Bullock, 106
Don Cherry, 66
Mocky Cherry, 66
Paul Cinelli, 107/100
Jim Cobb, 166/116
Cesar Cofone, 90/165,166
Maureen Connor, 51/167/48
Mitch Corber, 75/167
Diego Cortez, 24, 42/167,168/20
Jay Craven, 168, 169
Stephen Crawford, 107, 118/169
Jacqueline Crawford, 90/170
Jaime Davidovitch, 51/170, 171
Edit deAk, 20
Andy De Groat, 36/33
Phillipe Demontaut, 90, 144/171, 239/ 140
Frazier Dougherty, 120/171, 172/115
Lea Douglas, 91/172

Juan Downey, 107, 118, 128/102, 172
Charles Dreyfus, 91, 128/172, 173
Jean Dupuy, 24, 33, 36, 42, 47, 59, 67, 76/5, 10, 15, 74, 84-88, 134, 214, 228, 229/100-102, 140
Dana Egan, 162
Karen Edwards, 100
Ralston Farina, 24/175
Robert Filliou, 66, 92/173, 174
Bob Fiore, 110, 120, 128/102
Jared Fitzgerald, 60, 145/174/140
Kit Fitzgerald, 174
Simone Forti, 37/174, 175/32
Peter Frank, 10, 20, 41
Angela Frascone, 43/175
Jon Gibson, 26, 28/20
Philip Glass, 25, 36, 120/177/20, 33
Tina Girouard, 25/176/20
Heloise Gold, 77/175
Gollobin, 100
Wendy Greenberg, 60, 67/175, 176
P.I. Greene, 114
Jana Haimsohn, 26, 37, 51, 60, 66, 128, 146/177-180/32, 48, 140
Jacques Halbert, 92/181
Andrea Halpern, 43/180, 181/103
Deedee Halleck, 117, 129/32
Nancy Harris, 110/100
Suzanne Harris, 51, 137/181/48
Julie Harrison, 164, 165
Elaine Hartnett, 52, 68, 76/182/48
Jon Hassel, 76/182, 183
Richard Hayman, 68, 76/183, 231
Geoff Hendricks, 60/165/183
Timothy Hennessy, 92
Julia Heyward, 37, 52, 69, 129/235-238/32, 48
Dick Higgins, 43, 69/183-185
Gene Highstein, 136
Hisachika, 38/33
Nancy Holt, 120/114
Villard de Honnecourt, 143/235/140
Jerry Hovagimyan, 77, 137/185
John Howell, 5
Joel Hubaut, 92/224, 225
David Hykes, 68/185-187
Ken Jacobs, 225
Phil James, 74, 77, 80/187
Paul Jay, 109, 122/187/103
Poppy Johnson, 115
Scott Johnson, 77/188
Tom Johnson, 69/187, 188
Joan Jonas, 26/188/20
Philip Kaplan, 121/116

Pooh Kaye, 53/189/48
Alison Knowles, 43, 61, 77/232, 233
Fred Krughoff, 109/100
Irene Krugman, 111/102
Michael Krugman, 38/189, 223/32
Shigeko Kubota, 109, 121/189
Dicky Landry, 27/233/20
Kwan Lau, 38/189, 190
Emile Laugier, 121/190
Lefevre, 190
Jeffrey Lew, 121, 137/114
Nancy Lewis, 36/190, 191/33
Gerald Lindahl. 52/225
Nina Lundborg, 78/230, 231
Mabou Mines, 38/191/32
Anthony McCall, 28, 196/20
George Maciunas, 44, 70, 146/193/140
Gianfranco Mantegna, 26, 109, 123/191, 192, 240/102, 115
Lizbeth Marano, 109, 122, 135/101, 116
Walter de Maria, 144/140
Marshalore, 192
Tony Mascatello, 27, 44, 53, 70/193, 194, 239/20
Gordon Matta Clark, 26, 108, 122, 135/194/100, 103, 114/20
Tim Maul, 15, 53, 78, 93, 140, 147/194-196
Dick Miller, 45, 130/196-199
Larry Miller, 54, 78/193, 226/48
Stephen Paul Miller, 15
Ilhan Mimaroglu, 226
Antoni Miralda, 111/199
Richard Mock, 129
Gregory Molnar, 93
Jacques Monory, 93/199
Alan Moore, 103
Charlotte Moorman, 111
Charlie Morrow, 79/226, 227
Come Mosta-Heirt, 93/227
Andrew Moszynski, 61, 94/200-202, 227, 230
Charles Moulton, 77/188
Donald Munroe, 27, 53, 123/199, 200/20
Antoni Muntadas, 111/227/101
Chris Murphy, 111, 123, 137/100
Jacques Ohayon, 94/202
Claes Oldenburg, 124/238, 239/114
Patty Oldenburg, 123/169
Orlan, 94/202, 203, 228
Nam June Paik, 39, 54, 70, 124, 130/204, 205/20, 32, 100
Charlemagne Palestine, 52, 54, 70/182/205-208/20, 33, 48
Richard Peck, 39/203/33
Wendy Perron, 64
Lucio Pozzi, 61/203, 204
Richard Prince, 55/208, 209

Yvonne Rainer, 25, 28/209
Marc Rattner, 100
Charles Richardson, 228
Peter Van Riper, 39, 78/209, 210/32
Larry Rivers, 110, 130/101
Walter Robinson, 20, 21
Tonie Roos, 130/210, 211
Jean Roualdes, 95
Arthur Russell, 29/211/20
John Sanborn, 79/174, 211
John Savas, 80/225, 226
Carolee Schneemann, 28/212, 213
Joan Schwartz, 27, 122, 212/20
Dale Scott, 42, 44/213
Richard Serra, 28/213-215/20, 32
Stuart Sherman, 79/215, 216
Alison Sky, 124
Terry Slotkin, 216
Kiki Smith, 147/140
Michael Smith, 58/216, 217
Tony Smith, 125/115
Richard Squires, 105/101
Ellen Sragow, 134
Fred Stern, 105/217, 218
Bill Stone, 148/140
Anne Tardos, 105/218/101
Gail Teton, 59/157, 158
Martial Thomas, 95/218, 234
Nancy Topf, 28, 39/219/33
Turnbaugh, 219-220
Untel, 94/220, 234, 235
Yoshi Wada, 79/220
David Warrilow, 23/20
Sylvia Whitman Palacios, 29/221/20
Hannah Wilke, 29, 45, 125/221, 222/20, 115
Janelle Winston, 79/223
Wilson, 222
Irene Winter, 105/102, 116
Christian Xatrec, 69, 80, 84, 148/234/140
Daisy Youngblood, 222
Zadik Zadikian, 136/222
John Zorn, 222, 223